INSIDER OUTSIDER

INSIDER OUTSIDER

Belonging and Unbelonging in North-East India

Edited by
Preeti Gill & Samrat

AMARYLLIS

AMARYLLIS
An imprint of Manjul Publishing House Pvt. Ltd.
•7/32, Ansari Road, Daryaganj, New Delhi 110 002
Website: www.manjulindia.com
Registered Office:
•10, Nishat Colony, Bhopal 462 003 – India

This edition first published in 2018

ISBN 978-93-88241-35-9

This edition is authorised for sale in the Indian Subcontinent only.

Cover Design ©PealiDezine, peali.duttagupta@gmail.com

Printed and bound in India by Thomson Press (India) Ltd.

To the people of North-East India... all of them, Dkhars and Bongols, indigenous and migrants.

CONTENTS

PREFACE

Samrat

Among the stories from North-East India, a compelling and untold bunch revolves around the experiences of the 'outsiders' in the region. This is a fascinating case of role reversal; people from communities that are majorities in India or the countries around its North-East live in the region as oft-persecuted minorities. Theirs is a story that begins, typically, with the partition of India in 1947. It is a story of those who suddenly, with the drawing of new international borders, found themselves as nowhere people in hostile lands. These people and their descendants are still, seventy-two years on, victims of Partition. Their experience of being and becoming refugees is, two or three generations later, still not over—the debate over the National Register of Citizens in Assam is proof.

The danger in any tale of victimhood is the obverse: victims on the one hand and villains on the other. This is a dangerous and, with rare exceptions, an untrue binary. In order to avoid such a false binary, we have looked at these powerful human stories in a wider context of insider/outsider. This experience of being both insiders and outsiders in post-Independence India is one that is, remarkably enough, shared across divides in India's North-East. We sought out accounts of the parallel experience of the North-Eastern peoples as minorities in 'mainland' India, and the tortuous process of their reconciliation to an Indian identity, to bring balance to the narrative.

The dividing lines between the insider and the outsider are often confusing and unclear, even for those who have grown up experiencing being 'othered'. In the hills of the region, in towns such as Shillong for instance, the clash was often seen as one between tribal insiders and non-tribal outsiders. However, the Chakma tribals, the Chin tribals, and the tea tribes of Assam have all faced the outsider tag in the North-East, and the discrimination that goes with it. In the plains of Assam, the Assamese Hindus and the Bengali Hindus, who share not just commonality of religion but also of aspects of identity including, in many cases, surnames, have been at loggerheads time and again over the decades. The outsider here is determined largely by linguistic identity, though it would be a rare Bengali from Assam's Brahmaputra Valley who does not speak fluent Assamese. Merely speaking, reading and writing the language, therefore, is not enough to be considered a real insider: in order for the Bengali Bhattacharjee, Goswami or Talukdar to become an insider in Assam, denial of a Bengali heritage is a necessary prerequisite.

The hostility towards the Bengali in Assam and more broadly in North-East India is because migration from East Bengal is and has long been an explosive political issue in the region. There are real fears among the local communities of being overwhelmed by migrants. However, panic is not conducive to rational analysis. There is a tendency among regional chauvinists to view the entire Bengali community in North-East India as Bangladeshis. This is unfair, since there were Bengali populations in these lands long before Bangladesh came into existence.

In Assam, the chauvinists would like to see only descendants of the original indigenous inhabitants of the land remain there. However, even if this xenophobic and unconstitutional idea were to be accepted, the question would remain: Who are the descendants of the original inhabitants of Assam, and who indeed were the original inhabitants? How are descendants of original inhabitants to be determined—by 'purity of blood,' as some would like, or by the simple expedient of looking at the surname and linguistic identity, as is done in everyday practice?

This question resurfaced strongly in recent times due to the efforts to draw up a National Register of Citizens and debates over the controversial draft Citizenship (Amendment) Bill. The Supreme Court has refused to clarify on this matter of original inhabitants, but the question has not gone away from the public imagination or political life.

Since experiences and worldviews differ between individuals and groups, we have tried in this anthology to bring on board voices from different communities to give a sense of several varied experiences and positions on being insiders and/or outsiders. We presented prospective writers with the topic and left it to them to interpret it in whatever way they wanted. What we have ended up with is a quite interesting mix of responses.

Some of our attempts to include voices from across the region met with failure or only partial success. We were eventually unable, for instance, to bring in a strong voice from Nagaland, despite repeated attempts, because two successive writers from there agreed to contribute to this anthology but subsequently could not do so for their own personal reasons, by which time we were past deadline. One writer from Meghalaya initially agreed but eventually backed out owing to paucity of time. Our hopes of an essay from Mizoram also did not bear fruit. These have left lacunae in this volume that we regret.

The only consolation is that completeness was never a possibility. Any anthology such as this was always doomed to be incomplete. The region itself is vastly diverse, with around 220 languages being spoken, and adherents of numerous and multiple faiths, and it would take an encyclopedia in several volumes to bring voices from all these varied groups on board. Such completeness was obviously well beyond the scope of a book like this. Perhaps, if there is a second volume in the future we can remedy some of the omissions of this volume.

What we have here is a mix of short non-fiction by writers and journalists, along with essays by academics, and a couple of poems, to bring to light some aspects of the complex story of insiders/outsiders—because each of us is often simultaneously both—in and from North-East India. Our hope was that this broad mix would allow for mood, emotion, and atmosphere, but also help in the diffusion of knowledge essential to mutual understanding. If this book can serve as the starting point of an informed dialogue on the topic between writers, artists and intellectuals from the region, it will have served its purpose.

BONGOLS, CH*NKIES AND ROLE REVERSALS: AN INTRODUCTION

Preeti Gill

The hills of the North-East are beautiful, and it never ceases to amaze me how green and rain-soaked they are. Growing up in Madhya Pradesh, in the very heartland of this country, I never saw anything quite like them. Travelling through lush forests, full of hanging creepers and dripping green ferns and tendrils hanging out from every rock and hillside was a sight so wondrous that I was entranced on my very first trip to Nagaland some twenty-five years ago. High mountains, green valleys, trees that seemed to reach for the skies, the clear lilting sound of birds... these were quiet places, far away from India's teeming cities and towns.

Meeting people across the states of the North-East has been a rewarding experience—the stories I heard over these twenty-five years of travel and work have exposed me to a world that is still largely unknown and somewhat misunderstood in the rest of the country. And this is despite the efforts of the government and concerned communities of citizens to reach out and bridge cultural gaps and distances. The fact that many young people are making their way to the Indian 'mainland' to study and work means that they are more visible now—their distinctive features and lifestyles are more familiar today than they were, say, twenty years ago. Having said that though, there are still 'miles to go.'

The seemingly quiet hills and plains have seen bloodshed, violence and simmering discontent for decades; some of it still seethes under the surface and breaks out every now and then in the most horrific ways. Jungle battles erupted across the Naga Hills and the Mizo Hills, later to spill onto the plains and hills of Tripura, Assam and then Manipur—names that roll off the tongue easily, but with an exotic ring to them. There is nothing exotic, though, about the violence and bloodshed that scarred the area and its people—these remain, festering wounds which continue to plague many like an unending nightmare.

As someone who has worked in the area on issues of 'women and conflict in the North-Eastern states,' who has also worked closely with writers and activists there, I am constantly asked one question: 'What brings you to the North-East? You don't belong here.' My answer is always to say that I love the region, enjoy going there, and that I have a 'special' connect and many, many friends, and also that I like to scrabble around in order to understand peoples and cultures that are different from mine. It's the desire to look at the insider/outsider binary existing in the North-East and see what happens if we ask people to look at it from the prism of their personal lives and stories.

Thus, Samrat, my co-editor, and I dredged up a bunch of extremely interesting and unusual pieces that are intensely personal and ask some of the most crucial and complex questions of what makes us who we are. Who is an Indian really? Why are we made to wear our nationality, our identity, on our sleeve? Why are we required to constantly prove ourselves as Indian nationalists, as patriotic citizens? Can we not just be human, people who live together as neighbours, very different, very distinct, but still inhabiting the same space in a peaceable, gracious way?

In February 2013, an eighteen-year-old from Arunachal Pradesh entered a shop in busy Lajpat Nagar asking for help to locate a relative's home—a common enough occurrence. But what happened to him there was not so commonplace. He was abused, and his appearance, his blond streaked hair became an object of ridicule. When he objected, he was surrounded by armed men and beaten to death. I was in Mumbai attending the Kala Ghoda festival at the time, and this came up in the course of our discussion that very evening. Scores of angry, young Arunachali students studying in Mumbai asked why this should have happened in the country's capital. Why were they not safe? Was India not their country?

People from the North-Eastern states say that this is about racism, that Indians practice some of the worst forms of racism based on colour and difference in facial features, not to speak of caste, class and gender. This was not a solitary incident. Underlining the ethnic differences to ridicule and insult, name-calling to mark out the 'other,' beatings, molestations and sexual violations have all been part of the landscape of our cities. Perhaps what is changing slowly is an increasing awareness, especially among the youth from the North-East, that they cannot ignore this, that they need to affirm their rights as Indians. They are here to stay. They come for education and jobs and they have as much of a right to be here as anyone else.

The feeling of looking different and being from another ethnicity, religion, language group, of having different food habits and a distinctive way of life is not a new thing. It is, in fact, what has always made India inclusive and given Indians resilience and the ability to accept and adapt. It is imperative to address the issue of verbal abuse, racial incitement and physical harm based on such differentiation that we see rampant across the length and breadth of the country.

This anthology has been an attempt to look at the 'outsider', and the circumstances under which they also become an 'insider', and vice versa. What we often shortsightedly overlook is the fact that we, too, are outsiders and strangers elsewhere, in other spaces and neighbourhoods. Or that just the arbitrary drawing of a line can create a new border and we may be left outside of it, having to migrate, to relocate. To face xenophobic hatred and possibly get killed.

Seventy years after the Sylhet referendum and the consequent partition of India in 1947, a pall of nostalgia for a lost homeland continues to loom over the people of Sylheti origin. Anindita Dasgupta and Neeta Singh's essay, 'In Search of Lost Time', describe this in detail. 'Unexpectedly severed from their ancestral land, the Sylhetis looked with hope to the larger Assamese homeland for acceptance and the opportunity to build a new life. Their loss became even more poignant as the very existence of Sylhet was completely wiped off the map of India, when the territory was absorbed into the newly created East Pakistan, and then in 1971 more permanently, Bangladesh. Unlike the creation of "two" Punjabs and "two" Bengals—which were also dramatically partitioned at the same time—no "second" Sylhet was created on the Indian side of the border.' Although the anarchy, communal tension and bloodshed unleashed during the partition of Punjab was different, the despair and loss experienced by the uprooted Sylhetis is much the same. The Sylhetis had an easier 'dislocation' and more time to settle their properties before they left. Nevertheless, a lot of problems persist to this day. The Sylhetis who were consequently settled in the North-East region of India, and in particular Assam, never quite reconciled to being there. Like most displaced communities in the world, a part of their imagination still remained rooted to the folk history of the 'lost land.'

Anindita Dasgupta and Neeta Singh have recaptured some of this fragmented history primarily through personal family histories. 'While the partition of Sylhet was a momentous event for the Sylhetis, surprisingly it failed to capture the imagination of Partition historians until about fifty years later. Consequently, the history of Sylhet remained, to a large extent, in the realms of obscurity, though alive in the collective memory of the personal experiences of the Sylhetis themselves. Though some insightful research has come to light in recent years, many of the eyewitness accounts of the time have been forever lost with the passing of the Partition generation. Nonetheless, periodically, some of these personal experiences have been captured in the popular and literary works of Sylheti writers who have kept this story alive in poetry, essays, novels and other genres of creative writing.'

Why do we remember the past? Why does the collective folk history of a people tend to remember fateful and catastrophic events like the 1947 partition of India? Is it to find answers to questions of identity and belongingness? Or as eighty-year-old Parmesh Sen (who was living in Calcutta at the time) is quoted in Anindita and Neeta's essay as saying, 'Perhaps our sense of identity was sharpened by the fact that we were often considered outsiders in Assam, particularly in the few years right after Partition. During those tension-filled days, we would be starkly reminded of our past, though we wanted to move into the future.'

In the states of the North-East, widespread anxieties about being reduced to a minority in one's own 'homeland' are often fuelled by politicians and vested interests, and the simmering anger and suspicion is directed at the 'outsider'. The Bihari labourers, the Punjabi or Marwari traders and shopkeepers, the Bengali clerks or petty officials are easy targets. This is reflected in slogans like 'Outsiders Go Home' or derogatory names like 'vai' in Mizoram or 'dkhar' in Meghalaya. And intermarriage with an outsider, a plains person is seen as one of the worst social offences.

However, as Sanjoy Hazarika says in his new book *Strangers No More: New Narratives From India's North-East*: 'A fundamental principle of migration is that people usually, when given the choice, move to safer lands than their own where they feel secure, whether on one side of a border or a different part of the globe. Although they prefer to be closer to home, they are driven by need to lands with greater safety standards and history, where they can find livelihoods and decent incomes but also where they find similarities of culture, social traditions and religion.'

In the story titled 'Growing up with Mrs P', Anjum Hasan writes of a family in Shillong in 1979, forced to reckon with its foreignness, its being different, and the awkwardness of being hated. Several of the pieces in this anthology are either placed in Shillong or somehow manage to circle back to Shillong. Is this because so many young people studied in its various wonderful schools? Or is it because Shillong in the 'good old days' was cosmopolitan and accommodating, liberal and easy to live in? For Anjum, Mrs P typifies this cosmopolitanism: 'Mrs P represented that generation in the compressed history of Shillong who straddled different, even conflicting, worlds with dignified grace. The sense of tradition that she preserved was itself the result of many changes but it gave her the necessary anchor and the courage to regard Shillong's hybrid world with equanimity.' So what happened for it all to change so drastically?

Binayak Dutta's 'Collapse of a Colonial Cosmopolity: The Social History of Transforming Lives and the Space Called Shillong' points to this. He sees Shillong as a product of colonial reconfiguration of native spaces where the British government desired to encourage European settlers and invalids to set up offices and establishments to attract trade and more people. Shillong as a capital town and growing cosmopolitan centre was a popular attraction for the youth eager to make a mark for themselves in life beyond the immediate environs of their ancestral homes.

The peace and orderliness transformed with the partition and the transfer of Sylhet to East Pakistan. Suddenly, with the influx of Bengali migrants who 'infiltrated' the Khasi-Jaintia Hills, things changed dramatically in Shillong. It saw its first anti-dkhar demonstration as far back as 1952 when tribals protested the inclusion of non-tribals in the district council. Constitutional institutions set up to safeguard the interest of the tribes came to be popularly perceived as opportunities to convert these tribal areas into exclusive zones of tribal hegemony. Cosmopolitanism was the first casualty in the practice of constitutional protectionism in these hills.

Today, decades later, there is a complete transformation of

character in this hill town. Patricia Mukhim, the editor of the *Shillong Times* wrote in 2013: 'The politicization of ethnicity has been a vote-getting strategy for many since 1979. All the bloodshed and violence of that era can be traced to the desire of a few politicians to acquire political power by stressing on differences and by creating a fear psychosis that non-tribals would walk away with our land, our jobs and our women... It was a reign of terror... but few dared to speak up... So we all kept silent and obeyed the diktat of organizations that acted like social policemen.' Much of this is described in the intensely personal pieces by Paramjit Bakhshi and Samrat.

In 'How We Got Here: A Brief History of Being Dkhar in Shillong,' Samrat writes: 'By the time I was around seven years old, my world was already divided into groups.' Psychologists have a word that explains this tendency to form in-groups or out-groups—'belongingness,' and this is the crux of the 'problem.' In the 1980s, Shillong went through curfew after curfew following deadly assaults by Khasi groups on Nepalis, Bengalis, and later, other non-tribals. Many left their homes and businesses and moved to other towns. Samrat finds it odd that this issue hasn't received the coverage it deserves since 'this is a community from which many journalists, writers, academics and filmmakers have made a mark at the national and international levels. Perhaps the silence persists because this is the community that has suffered extreme violence for three successive generations. It is the silence of the repeatedly oppressed.'

Paramjit Bakhshi's 'I, Dkhar' is an honest, searing indictment of living in a place that has grown increasingly hostile to outsiders. When he says 'I do not trust lines,' he is referring to all the lines drawn across the lives of people whether it is the Radcliffe Line partitioning the subcontinent or the Inner Line Permit that 'allows' you to travel in your own country. The dkhar has no community to call his own. 'I am an outsider here and my wife (who is Khasi) will be an outsider in small town India elsewhere. Apart from large metros there is no real India of "unity in diversity" for people like us. And our children, if they continue to live here, will have to renounce half of their identity. And one wonders if our grandchildren will chant the slogan, "Khasi by blood and Indian by accident".'

Mahua Sen talks of the absence of belonging in her essay 'Chronicles of a Death Untold'. She says 'I have never felt at home anymore and I always feel that others own the ground more than I do', describing the terrible death of Gauri Dey who was walking home one day in 1987 when she was gang raped, and her pregnant belly ripped open. She was killed because she was Bengali, because she was different, because the local lumpens called her a Bangladeshi. The story is hidden away as a dark secret, one more ugly story among the many. When Mahua first came to Delhi after college in Shillong, she wanted to claim the space as an equal. She says she may even have tried to have 'consciously concealed the context of my identity, which was filled with the echoes of the melancholic, dejected ancestry and community of my origin,' just in case it hindered assimilation. But this does not happen for 'they are insiders on the outside and outsiders on the inside'. She has inherited this unbelonging and has tried to escape the ambiguous topic of home, for the most part of her adult life. 'The Bengali Hindu population of Shillong is the only community in India to have suffered double displacement on communal grounds, twice within a generation. We inherited the collective fate of the Punjabi Hindus of West Pakistan and the Kashmiri Pandits' and so it is that 'absence of belonging has always been ingrained in my wiring. This condition plagues most people of the community in my generation. We are the second generation of this lineage and it's probably too soon for us to construct an indestructible notion of homeland beyond the superficiality of the material.'

In contrast, 'Home' by fiction writer Jahnavi Barua talks about her family's origins and ancestry. The affection for Shillong, the home of her grandparents and, later, parents—a beloved space filled with family and friends—evokes the sunny memories of a gentle life among green hills and deep forests, the inconstant weather with colonial and Assam-type houses dotting the landscape, memories of a happy childhood, of laughter and warmth, of sharing stories over food and cups of steaming tea. Her family rarely spoke of loss after they left Shillong in 1972. But she is conscious that she is now, curiously 'an insider who was now an outsider'. As she says, 'By the time the states separated in 1972, our family had been residing in Shillong for nearly ninety years. Where else would we call home?' From Shillong to Guwahati, to Delhi, Manchester and then Bangalore, there have been many relocations, many adjustments and the taking on of new identities, but only that one home that still evokes nostalgia and longing.

Mitra Phukan, well-known writer and translator from Assam, tells the poignant tale of Ganor Mastor, the music teacher whose life is slowly destroyed by the same xenophobia and racism and resentment the outsider faces. The music teacher came from 'the land south to these green mountains known as the Khasi Hills, and had settled here a generation or two ago, after Partition. They had come up from what was then East Bengal, which became East Pakistan.' A few years later, this name, too, would change, and the land would become Bangladesh. Once he arrived here with his family he needed to find work, the old parents died unable to reconcile to the new land, his sisters were married off. And all he had was musical training from Shantiniketan and his beloved esraj and sitar, and so he would play even in the midst of all the turmoil. In this strange land, it was 'only through his music that he felt a connect to his past life.' He settles in once he starts to teach music to young people, but all too soon Meghalaya is a new state and the Khasi students union unleashes terror on all dkhars. Once again his life is full of fear, and now that he is old and frail, he moves away to Calcutta to his son's poky flat, becoming an old man belonging nowhere.

Ankush Saikia talks about the protagonist of his fictional thrillers, describing him as the 'Man in the Middle,' the outsider who can view things objectively. 'The outsider has always been an attractive figure for storytellers... By virtue of being an outsider, he observes and notices things that may escape the attention of those who belong. It can also help him avoid taking sides, thus having an objective view of things. At the other end of the spectrum is the insider, another interesting figure—for those who can conjure him up, as the specifics of belonging are harder to create than the details of being an outsider.' People and events could always be viewed from different angles depending on where one stands. For him, the outsider (who may also have once been an insider) is a complex being for he falls between the cracks, exists in layers and displays multiple realities. Even in school, he saw the layers of 'difference'—the outsiders were not one large indistinguishable bunch, some of them were more outsider than the others. The outsiders, that is to say the non-Khasis and non-tribals, were always conscious of their status, but within this group the Assamese boys occupied a somewhat different position, being mostly non-tribals but at the same time from a neighbouring state, and from the North-East.

Sanjoy Hazarika, veteran chronicler of the North-East among many other things, writes about 'Insiders, Outsiders and Those In Between' for 'after all there is much in a name'. He, too, begins with an ode to Shillong (where most of his treasured memories belong), going on to give us a definition of who constitutes the outsider and brings in Nagaland, Manipur, Meghalaya and Assam and the shadowy figure of the much reviled and hated Bangladeshi migrant. Elsewhere, he writes about his mother who resisted all suggestions that she should leave after the new state of Meghalaya was created in 1971. Shillong was her marital home and she had a greater sense of belonging here than anywhere else. Her life was full of friends, gardening, her work at the Mahila Samity, and she valued it. Being Indian, he says, is no easy task these days and what the young people of the North-East are doing is a courageous thing for they are engaging with the idea of India.

In another essay, 'Phenomenon of Impunity: Terror Regime, Human Rights and Victims of Political Injustice in Manipur', Thounoujam Brinda talks of political injustice perpetrated by the state on the people of Manipur. For decades, Manipur has been a violent theatre of militancy and counter insurgency by state actors and the civil administration with extra-judicial killings, disappearances, rape, illegal detentions, etc. Manipur was declared a disturbed area and the draconian Armed Forces Special Powers Act (AFSPA) was enforced in 1980. The brutal killing of Thangjam Manorama set the stage for an unprecedented protest in front of the historic Kangla Fort in Manipur's capital, Imphal. The naked protest staged by activists of the Meira Paibis stunned the nation. The images flashed across India and the world, shaking people both outside and inside the 'Indian mainland' out of their complacency. As Manorama and the Meira Paibis became symbols of state oppression under AFSPA, another frail young Manipuri took centre stage—Irom Sharmila, who was already on a fast to death protesting another incident where twelve civilians lost their lives to army firing in a small village called Malom.

Shalim Hussain's 'Growing Up Miyah' is set in 1993, when he was just five, and talks of how one day, he along with a friend, decided to run away from boarding school. They walked some twelve kilometres in pelting rain and storm, when they were caught (thankfully) by an elderly gentleman who took them home, fed the Miyah boys a hot meal and gave them shelter for the night, despite the prudent advice of fearful neighbours. The fear and distrust caused by the demolition of the Babri Masjid and the Bombay riots had travelled to Assam. That same year in October, hundreds were killed and their houses burnt, because they were Muslims. Shalim did not understand the extent of the violence or its brutality then, but in 2016, he became part of a fierce bunch of poets writing intensely political poems on their lived experience of poverty, exclusion and disillusionment. The reason is that Muslims of Bengali origin lived under the constant ignominy of being called illegal migrants in their own country. Calling them outsiders when they speak and write in Assamese and record it as their language in census after census amounts to socially normalised bigotry.

The personal story narrated by Sonal Jain through the diary of her grandfather Mehar Chand—which she discovered just as she was writing 'Chronicle of Forgetting'—connects the wildly disparate worlds of Lahore, Meerut and

Shillong. 'So with history as a constant companion (and mostly not a welcome one), Mehar Chand traversed different geographies, sometimes hopeful, and sometimes hopeless. The Partition once again tore apart the life he had created in Calcutta. The soap factory was looted, and the family barely escaped with their lives and dignity. The factory was in a Muslim-dominated area and there was no going back to that area given the post-riots divide between the Hindus and the Muslims.' Suddenly, though, Shillong mirrors that other land left behind, when in the 1980s, the agitation against foreigners breaks out: 'We were now suddenly dkhars in this land Mehar Chand Jain had come to decades ago. The violence of history catches up once again. Suddenly, fear punctuated the everyday and all experiences.'

This anthology has two poets—Mona Zote, one of the strongest, most powerful voices in Indian poetry today, and she comes from Mizoram; and R.G. Lyngdoh from Meghalaya. Mona Zote's 'Boat-Building' embodies fear, hope, and everything in between when she writes:

I think he's building a boat
He needs to go away
He wants to make sure everyone is safe
Because the water's rising.

And she ends the poem with:

Boat-building is a child's endeavour.

Is it a note of futility here or the hope that only a child can have?

R.G. Lyngdoh's poems 'The Migrant Labourer,' 'Justice' and 'Equal Citizens' are much more descriptive. For example, he talks of the migrant labourer as a resilient being who struggles, who is often knocked down but continues to rise despite all that life has thrown at him:

Fate may have dealt you a cruel hand, yet
You never fail to hope and your faith never dies,
Humbled, I can only stand to salute your resilience.

In 'Justice,' he paints a fearful scene at night when the outsider is attacked and beaten to death. However, there is justice in the world, although it is a terrible, vengeful kind where an innocent child has to pay for the sins of the father.

In conclusion, let us turn to Sanjoy Hazarika when he says, 'Attitudes are formed by experiences and narrated in stories; these stories become texts, are embedded in books and taught to generations who pass on the word. The volume of words becomes a torrent of cement and brick, building high walls of division. Those inside the wall are privy to special information, or so they believe. Those outside are the *bahirormanuh*, the outsiders.' However, let us not build these walls, for the only thing that will work is dialogue and acceptance of the 'other' as an equal.

IN SEARCH OF LOST TIME[1]

Nostalgia for the Sylheti Homeland

Anindita Dasgupta
and
Neeta Singh

Aamar mon kande-re Padma-r chorerlaigya
Aamarobhagya-r ontorkande-re poradesherlaigya

(My heart cries for the islands on the river Padma
My unlucky soul cries out for my poor country)[2]

– HEMANGA BISWAS
Singer, composer, author and
political activist (1912–1987)

Leaving Sylhet

Seventy-one years after the Sylhet referendum and partition of India in 1947, a pall of nostalgia for a lost land continues

[1]Inspired by the title of Marcel Proust's novel in French of the same name.
[2]From 'O Srihatt-e Gananatya Andolan'. Debray, S. (Ed.). *Sribhumi Srihatta: Sreehatter Samskriti Bishayak Prabandha Samkalan,* Durgapur. Durgapur Srihatta Sammilani, 1995. Translation from Bengali ours.

to loom over the people of Sylhet origin, who resettled in different parts of North-East India, and in particular Assam. In 1874, the British conjoined the Bengali-speaking Muslim majority district of Sylhet with its under-populated Assamese-speaking Hindu majority neighbour ostensibly to make the new province 'financially viable'. Thus, Sylhet remained a part of colonial Assam from 1874 until 15 August 1947, when it was ceded to East Pakistan, following a hurriedly organised referendum in July that year. Almost immediately after the British Viceroy Lord Mountbatten's radio announcement of the referendum in June of 1947, many Hindu Sylheti families, uncertain of their future in a Muslim-majority district, began migrating to other parts of Assam. Subsequently, after the 1950 communal riots in parts of Bengal, there was a massive exodus of Hindu Sylhetis who, fearing for their lives in an atmosphere of uncertainty, fled their beloved Sylhet, little suspecting that they were destined never to return.

Unexpectedly severed from their ancestral land, the Sylhetis looked with hope to the larger Assamese homeland for the opportunity to build a new life. Their loss became even more poignant as the very existence of Sylhet was wiped off the map of India when the territory was absorbed into the newly created East Pakistan in 1947, and then in 1971, even more permanently when Bangladesh was created. Unlike the creation of 'two' Punjabs and 'two' Bengals—which were also dramatically partitioned at the same time—no 'second' Sylhet was created on the Indian side of the border. Only a mere sliver of its land—three *thanas*[3] with a total area of 709 square miles and a population of 23 million—was subsequently joined with Assam's Cachar district to form a

[3]Police station jurisdiction

new sub-division, Karimganj. With the passing of time, Indian Sylhetis increasingly began associating themselves politically and culturally with greater Assam in general, and with Cachar, in particular. But like most uprooted communities around the world, a part of their imagination still remained tied to the folk history of the lost ancestral land through deeply personal oral and written narratives about loss, displacement and nostalgia.

After Partition, the critical question for the Indian Sylhetis was how to come to terms with the emotional trauma of the permanent loss of ancestral land. More significantly, the immediate need at the time was for them to put down more permanent roots in the neighbourhood of Assam. Like other parts of East Bengal, with the mere flourish of a pen, Sylhet ceased to be '...a tangible geographical space any more for hundreds and thousands of people, and it became a part of the past—a space in memory'[4]. Tossed around like ships on a turbulent ocean, Sylhetis were forced to make life-changing decisions due to circumstances completely beyond their control.

While the partition of Sylhet was a momentous event for the Sylhetis, it failed to capture the imagination of Partition historians until about fifty years later. Consequently, Sylheti history remained, to a large extent, in the realms of obscurity, though very much alive in the collective memory of personal experiences of the people themselves expressed through language, culture, literature, music and way of life. Though some insightful research has come to light in recent years, many of the eye-witness accounts of the time have been forever

---

[4]Das, S.K. *History of Indian Literature: 1911-1956, Struggle for Freedom: Triumph and Tragedy.* New Delhi: Sahitya Academy. 1991.

lost with the passing of the Partition generation. Nonetheless, periodically, some of these personal experiences have been captured in the popular and literary works of Sylheti writers who have kept this story alive through poetry, essays, novels, and other genres of creative writing.

'But I have seen that land'[5]: The history of Sylhetis in Assam

To understand the complexities of the partition of Sylhet, it is essential to take a peek into the history of the Sylhetis in Assam. Historically and culturally a part of Bengal, Sylhet was incorporated into the neighbouring Chief Commissionership of Assam in 1874, where it remained in an uneasy, even hostile, partnership until the referendum. Together, they formed the two valleys of Assam—the Assamese-speaking Brahmaputra Valley and the Bengali-speaking Surma Valley, which was later elevated to the status of a province after the amalgamation. According to the East India Company's official correspondence, this was done not only for administrative convenience but also for economic benefit, as Assam did not produce enough revenue to sustain itself. Neither the Sylhetis nor the Assamese were happy with this union and for the next few years, both unsuccessfully demanded that Sylhet be returned to Bengal.

The Sylhetis settled down eventually in the hills and plains of Assam as their English education and experience of working for the British in Bengal provided them with job opportunities. They became a quintessential presence in Assam's emerging urban centres, particularly in professional

[5]Biswas, H. (n.d.) *Aami je dekhechhisheidesh.* Retrieved on 10 April 2017 from http://preyrona.blogspot.my/2008/02/list-of-mass-songs-ganasangeet.html

positions, government jobs, trading and other emerging sectors of the colonial economy. In fact, their economic activities were spread over both valleys of Assam between which they enjoyed ease of movement almost on a regular basis. This gave rise to both a grudging admiration and growing hostility towards them among the local Assamese population.

While the English-educated Sylhetis lived and worked in the urban areas of both valleys, their ancestral home in Sylhet would often be taken care of by a relative who had chosen to stay back. Joint families and extended kinship networks were used to maintain the landed property 'back home', while on holidays and festive occasions, the city-folk would return to their *desherbaari* (village home). At the same time, the younger generation in Sylhet would be encouraged to move from *desherbaari* to the *town-erbaari* (town home) to pursue English education in the cities. Consequently, many of them took up jobs in the cities, and hardly ever returned home permanently. Sylhet thus became the distant desherbaari for the young English-educated generation[6].

In his memoirs, Professor Digindra Chandra Datta reveals that his father decided to stay back in the desherbaari in Sylhet to take care of the ancestral property and to ensure the preservation of important religious ceremonies and rituals while his three other English-educated brothers held important positions in the distant towns. In return the three brothers had always ensured that he had sufficient means to live a comfortable life 'back home' as he had been

---

[6]This paragraph is based on Dasgupta, A. 'Denial and Resistance: Sylheti Partition "Refugees" in Assam', *Contemporary South Asia*, 10 (3), 2001. Note that not all Sylhetis were English educated, though this section focuses more on such groups.

deprived of an English education and other benefits of city life[7]. Similarly, Surama Ghatak, in her autobiography *Surma Nadir Deshe* (In the Land of the River Surma), describes her childhood journeys from Shillong to Sylhet during the annual festival of Durga Puja: 'As soon as the puja vacations began, we left for the [Sylhet] plains,' she wrote. 'I can never forget my *desherbaari*... When the *puja*s and all the fun ended, we returned from the [Sylhet] plains to the [Shillong] hills[8].' It is not surprising therefore, that by the turn of the twentieth century, the destinies of the people of both valleys had become intrinsically intertwined, both economically and socially.

It must be remembered, however, that the economic domination and social position of the Sylhetis was not always unchallenged by the emerging Assamese middle class who viewed the former as an obstacle to their own economic opportunities and upward social mobility. Increasingly, the political rhetoric of the Assamese leadership focussed on the danger of the native Assamese being swamped by the Hindu Sylhetis in the urban areas. Their fears were further stoked by the ongoing migration of Bengali Muslims from the Mymensingh district of East Bengal. Since the early twentieth century they had been migrating to Assam in search of land in the rural areas, adding a new dimension to the stresses on economic resources and the ruling government. Thus, the two rallying cries of the Assamese nationalists in the early twentieth century were to '...separate Bengali speaking districts of Sylhet and Cachar from the administrative unit

[7]Datta, D. 'Aamar Atmakatha' and Mukherjee, K.B. (2000), 'A Great Betrayal' in Nihar Ranjan Datta and Mihir Kanti Datta (Eds), *Adhyapak Digindra Chandra Datta-r Janma Satabarshiki Swarani*, Calcutta: No publisher.

[8]Ghatak, S. *Surma Nadir Deshe*. Kolkata: Anustup. 2001. Translation from Bengali by Anindita Dasgupta.

of Assam in order to free government offices from the clutches of the Bengali Hindu employees'[9], and for more stringent regulation of the continuing Muslim migration from Mymensingh. Repeated efforts to separate Sylhet, however, were unsuccessful. The situation remained unchanged until the rise of communal politics in the subcontinent, which led to Mohammad Ali Jinnah, the president of the Muslim League, in 1946, demanding that Assam be included in his six-province vision of a separate Muslim state, Pakistan. The resultant outcry and protests by the Indian National Congress in Hindu-majority Assam was perhaps the catalyst for the viceroy's decision to let the people of Sylhet decide their own fate through a referendum. Interestingly, it was this referendum, which provided the Assamese an opportunity to finally fulfil their long-standing demands.

Against the backdrop of such a complex scenario preceding Independence, the fate of the ordinary man hung in the balance as the political big-wigs proceeded to execute their hastily drawn plan for the partition of India. At the same time, in the North-East, unsuspecting Hindus and Muslims of Sylhet cast their votes, braving the monsoon rains and floods, and communal tensions. The result of the referendum was announced on 14 July on the radio. A total of 2,39,619 votes had been cast in favour of joining East Pakistan, and 1,84,041 votes for remaining in Assam, India. The decision was clear, as a majority of 56.6 percent of Sylhet's Muslim majority population had voted to join Pakistan. The dice had been cast, propelling the Hindu Sylheti community towards their new destiny in Assam.

---

[9]Chaudhuri, S. 'A God-sent Opportunity.' (2014) Retrieved on 12 April 2017 from www.india-seminar.com/2002/510/510%20sujit%20chaudhuri.htm

'Unsettled' in Assam

'The Government of Assam at the time played a very active role in settling the uprooted Sylhetis in Assam, though the major burden fell mainly on Cachar,' writes Monirul Hussain[10]. The Bengali-speaking district of Cachar, to which the vestiges of Sylhet had been joined, seemed like a natural destination for many of the displaced, allowing them to assimilate into a familiar environment. It also helped that Karimganj—historically a part of Sylhet—already had a considerable Sylheti-speaking population of its own. Hussain goes on to observe that many of the refugees who settled down in the Assamese-speaking Brahmaputra Valley gradually assimilated into the surrounding Assamese culture, though Bengali remained widely spoken all over the valley[11].

At the same time, there was a resurgence of the age-old Assamese apprehension of the return of pre-Partition Bengali presence in Assam. The conflict between the two valleys over the adoption of Assamese as the official language of the state in 1960 further complicated inter-community relationships. Moreover, during the six-year-long Assam Movement (1979-1985)—organised to deport undocumented Bangladeshis from Assam—this relationship had become even more tense. The issue of foreign nationals largely overlapped with Bengalis because, historically, most of the latter came from the same cultural region of Bengal. The blurring of boundaries between the post-1971 Bangladeshi immigrants in the Brahmaputra Valley and the original Bengali population in Assam, led to further tensions within Assamese society. This was exacerbated

[10]Hussain, M. *The Assam Movement: Class, Ideology, Identity,* New Delhi: Manak Publications. 1993.
[11]Ibid.

by concerns over the impact that the 1971 migrant presence might have, not only on the economic resources, but more importantly, on the demographics of the region.

'Perhaps our sense of identity was sharpened by the fact that we were often considered outsiders in Assam, particularly in the few years immediately after Partition,' remembered Paramesh Sen, who was a young boy at the time of Partition. 'During those tension-filled days, we would be starkly reminded of our past, though we ourselves wanted to move into the future.' A young Sylheti scientist pursuing research in Europe revealed that '...there was a sense of grievance among the Sylhetis who felt that Partition had been unfair to them, and that the Assam government did not make a sincere effort to retain it within India.' He also related how his grandparents and relatives would reminisce about the 'good old days in Sylhet' at family gatherings, and sometimes get 'quite emotional.'

Nostalgia and Three Sylheti Writers

Much of what is known about Sylhet Partition today is drawn primarily from personal memories and family histories passed down to the younger generations, and from the literary works of a handful of writers who provide invaluable insights into the minds and hearts of the Sylheti diaspora. For instance, in the poetry of the Sylhet-born Hemanga Biswas, a political activist, poet and composer, nostalgia and heartrending sadness for the lost homeland is powerfully expressed in simple, straightforward, everyday Sylheti language. What strikes the reader is the poet's plaintive cry for recognition when he reiterates the question, *'Do you all know me? Do you all know me?'*

Hobiganj-er gang-cheelaamishonyedilamura
...Dana bhaingyaporlamaami Koilkata-r upor
Tomraaamay chino ni? Tomraaamay chino ni?

A seagull from Habigunj, I flew to the skies above
With broken wings, I fell on top of Calcutta
Do you all know me? Do you all know me?[12]

Several years later, the words of Shaktipada Brahmachari, an eminent poet from Assam's Cachar district, continue to resonate with the same lingering sense of nostalgia:

We had our house in Sylhet district
Yet we are refugees...
Yet we are refugees...
the words burst into the air
to release the bad breath of bitter experiences...[13]

In these poignant words, Brahmachari expresses his own sense of rootlessness as well as the suffering of the thousands of displaced Sylhetis who left their homes and sought refuge in different parts of Assam after Partition. The poet also perhaps laments the subsequent disappearance of Sylhet within the boundaries of a foreign country that was now beyond the reach of its scattered population.

In more recent times, the sentimental connection with Sylhet resurfaces in the works of the well-known novelist

---

[12]Biswas, H. (n.d.). *Hobiganjer Jalali Koitor*. Retrieved on 10 April 2017 from https://www.youtube.com/watch?v=N1VIA9YZg7s. Translation from Bengali ours.

[13]Chowdhury, S. 'The Partition fiction very few people read: The literature of displacement from Assam's Barak Valley.' (25 March 2017) Retrieved on 15 April 2017 from https://scroll.in/article/832762/the-partition-fiction-very-few-people-read-the-literature-of-displacement-from-assams-barak-valley

Amit Chaudhuri, whose mother had moved from Sylhet to Shillong after the referendum. It is not surprising, therefore, that the images of Sylhet and Shillong appear in almost all of Chaudhuri's novels. In his book *Odysseus Abroad,* he presents the protagonist, Ananda, as a person of Indian Sylheti ancestry just like himself. When Ananda encounters a waiter at a Tandoori restaurant in England who speaks with a Sylheti accent, Ananda feels that 'he was near home' (though his own parents did not speak with a similar accent). Chaudhuri writes: '...the notion of Sylhet imparted to him (Ananda) inadvertently by his parents and relations—as an emblem of the perennially recognizable...'[14] nostalgia or longing for the lost world. It is this 'perennially recognizable' nostalgia of the larger Sylheti community which was 'inadvertently' passed on by the Sylheti elders to the younger generation who had never seen or known the land of their ancestors.

The works of Biswas, Brahmachari, and Chaudhuri, though separated by a considerable expanse of time, are testament to the continuing wistfulness of a community that refuses to relinquish the memory of its past. The emotions expressed are startlingly similar though the writers belong to different generations. While Hemanga Biswas was born in the land he reminisced about, and Brahmachari in neighbouring Cachar, Amit Choudhuri appears to write himself back into the folk history of 'Sylhet' which had never 'existed' for Sylhetis of his generation.

[14]Wood, James. 'Circling the subject: Amit Chaudhuri's novel *Odysseus Abroad*', *The New Yorker.* (24 May 2015)

The Perennially Recognisable[15]

For the younger generations who have never seen the old ancestral land, the notion of Sylhet is an imagined space or world, which is brought to life through the narratives of older family members[16]. These stories eventually became symbols of the 'perennially recognizable' ancestors who inhabited that past. One of them was Choudhury Bharat Chandra Das. He was an adventurous and enterprising Sylheti who had moved out of Sylhet district to neighbouring Cachar in the 1880s. For the first few years, he worked in a tea estate, and eventually bought three tea estates for himself. His brother-in-law became one of the best-known lawyers of his time at the Dibrugarh High Court in northern Assam.

His son, Pranab, was born in 1900 in Shalchapra Tea Estate in Cachar. A small entrepreneur, Bharat Chandra had worked hard to give his children an English education, which enabled his older son to take up law, and younger son to secure a coveted job in the British Civil Services as a police officer in 1920. Many years later, Bharat Chandra would return to Sylhet to buy a house in Subid Bazar area, which was eventually sold off to a Muslim family at the time of Partition.

While in government service, Pranab was frequently transferred to different parts of Assam like Shillong[17], Sibsagar and Dibrugarh. His son, Pradeep, fondly recalled that he had to change schools '...thirteen times' and '...had many friends

[15]This phrase is taken from: Chaudhuri, A. *Odysseus Abroad*. London: Oneworld Publications. 2014.

[16]This section is based on interviews with Sylhetis in Assam and Shillong.

[17]Shillong remained the capital of undivided Assam until the creation of the new state of Meghalaya on 21 January 1972, when Shillong became the capital of Meghalaya, and Assam moved its capital to Dispur in Guwahati.

all over Assam.' He could also speak a smattering of some of the local languages like Khasi and Manipuri, a skill he would proudly demonstrate at family gatherings. Pradeep and his five brothers were born in different parts of Assam, depending on their father's job postings. Pradeep was born in the tea-growing town of Dibrugarh in Upper Assam in 1935.

Pranab was posted as the sub-divisional police officer in Habiganj, Sylhet, at the time of the referendum and placed in charge of maintaining law and order on those two fateful days—6 and 7 July 1947. Many years later, his grandchildren would hear stories of those two days from their grandmother, and they would tremble fearfully, wondering 'what could have happened to Grandfather' if he had been attacked in the course of carrying out his duties. Most significantly, his niece shared that Pranab had a certificate of domicile in which he had declared his permanent residence to be in Assam long before 1947.

Pranab was among the first to leave his official posting in Habiganj and return to his home in Shillong immediately after Partition was announced. All Assam government officials—Indians as well as Europeans—posted in Sylhet at the time of the referendum were given the option to 'select the government he wishes to serve,' and asked to 'furnish replies within one week in their own handwriting'[18]. Those who had chosen to accept the government's offer to relocate to Assam were required to handover their jobs to their East Pakistani counterparts latest by 14 August 1947 and return forthwith to the 'Indian' side. According to Digindra Chandra

[18]Mukherjee, K.B. 'A Great Betrayal' in Nihar Ranjan Datta and Mihir Kanti Datta (eds.) *Adhyapak Digindra Chandra Datta-r Janma Satabarshiki Swarani*, Calcutta: No publisher. 2000.

Datta's memoirs, this was the cut-off date for all employees to be reinstated in their jobs on the 'Indian' side of Assam. The Government of Assam had categorically stated that it would take no further responsibility for any employee who stayed back in Sylhet after 15 August[19]. Pranab was one of the luckier officers who made it back within that timeframe. But there were a large number of Sylheti officials who were not re-absorbed, and had to fight long drawn-out legal battles for reinstatement. Digindra Chandra Datta was one of them.

Little did Pranab know, on that fateful morning of 15 August, that he and his family were making their last journey out of Sylhet, and that neither they nor their children would ever return to live on the land of their ancestors again. 'It was a very difficult decision for him, but he believed that someday he would be able to come back,' his son, twelve years old then, recalled. But this was a decision that Pranab had taken consciously, as the land to which he was travelling was also his own. It was the land where he had been born, the land where he had married his wife Hemangini, the land where his six sons had been born, the land across which he had moved frequently in his capacity as a police officer. He had lived the better part of his life working in different parts of Assam's two valleys, rarely ever returning to his Sylhet home except to attend family functions. It was ironical that he found himself posted in Habiganj at the time of the referendum and had to opt to return to Assam which, in fact, had been his home for most of his life. His sons recounted that Pranab spoke Assamese and Manipuri with the same fluency as he did Sylheti and 'Calcutta Bengali,' and had many close friends all over Assam.

---

[19]Ibid.

During those uncertain times, many of the people caught in this conundrum did not clearly grasp the legal implications of the redrawing of boundaries between the newly formed states of India and Pakistan, while many others did not totally believe that the separation would be permanent. Most significantly, Pranab did not anticipate the future implications of this move—that his descendants would be viewed as 'outsiders' for the next half century in the very land where they had been born and raised.

Many other Sylhetis like Pranab would choose to relocate to the Indian side over the next few years. The fact that there were comparatively fewer communal clashes in Sylhet than Punjab or Bengal gave the people more time to make this important decision, sell their properties and move to new locations. However, there was a massive deluge of displaced people from Sylhet in 1950 following the communal riots in other parts of Bengal.

'Every day I would hear that refugees are coming to Shillong,' said Manjusha Datta, who was a little girl of about ten living in Shillong at that time. 'I had no idea who a "refugee" was!' She recalled that her grandfather, a philanthropist, explained to her: 'They have come away from their homes and it is our duty to help them.' Thus, said Manjusha, 'I went with my grandfather to the refugee camps to assist them in order to fulfil my duties.' She remembered that many old established families of Shillong helped the refugees and made arrangements for their children to attend school. Manjusha also revealed that her family had its historical roots in Assam for more than half a century before Partition. She had in her possession two gold medals dated 1878, won by her great grandfather as a young student in Assam. 'We are indeed, Assamese,' she said. 'We are Bengali-speaking Assamese.'

Remembrance of things past[20]

Written and oral narratives of the trauma of the Partition experience on both sides of the subcontinent, and in particular the Sylheti diaspora, have raised a plethora of questions, not least of which are: Why do we remember the past? More importantly, why does the collective folk history of a people tend to remember fateful events like the Jewish Holocaust and the partition of India? Why has the Partition experience become embedded in the collective memory of the generations that never experienced it first hand?

The answers to these questions perhaps lie in the fact that the hastily drawn lines in Punjab, Bengal, and Sylhet together unleashed an unprecedented movement of people across the newly drawn borders. The population movement itself is one of the largest in recorded human history and the echoes of Partition remain writ large on the psyche and character of all three nations (India, Pakistan and Bangladesh) that eventually emerged out of its ashes. It has become as one writer describes it, '...a topic of much myth-making, intense polemics and considerable serious historical research.'[21]

First- and second-generation survivors and displaced populations have never forgotten the trauma of Partition. Oral narratives, historical accounts, and the literature of the period provided fertile material to fire the imagination and longing for the lost homeland leaving an indelible mark on the collective memory of the Partition diaspora. This phenomenon

---

[20]Inspired by the title of Marcel Proust's English translation of the French novel *In Search of Lost Time.*

[21]Bose, P. 'Dilemmas of Diaspora: Partition, Refugees, and the Politics of "Home"'. (2006) Retrieved on 9 April 2017 from http://refuge.journals.yorku.ca/index.php/refuge/article/view/21344

is best explained in William Dalrymple's words: 'Partition is central to modern identity in the Indian subcontinent, as the Holocaust is to identity among Jews, branded painfully onto the regional consciousness by memories of unimaginable violence.'[22]Acclaimed Pakistani historian Ayesha Jalal has called Partition 'the central historical event in twentieth century South Asia... A defining moment that is neither beginning nor end, Partition continues to influence how the peoples and states of post-colonial South Asia envisage their past, present and future.'[23]

As a result, the most recurrent theme in post-Partition discourse is nostalgia and memories of the lost homeland. The literature of the period, replete with imagery and symbolism associated with Partition, adds a new dimension to the historical and oral narratives of the period. Closely linked to literature is the impact of the rhetoric of political leaders of the time, like the erudite first prime minister of independent India, Jawaharlal Nehru, who on the night of 14 August 1947 uttered the fateful words, 'Long years ago we made a tryst with destiny. At the stroke of the midnight hour when the world sleeps, India will awake to life and freedom.' These words not only struck at the collective hearts of Indians, but have continued to reverberate into the twenty-first century with undiminished force.

Partition stories of prominent writers of the period like Saadat Hasan Manto and others of his ilk have played a significant part in the transfer of memories into the

---

[22]Dalrymple, W. 'The Great Divide: The Violent Legacy of Indian Partition,' *The New Yorker*. London Review of Books. 29 June 2015 Issue. Retrieved on 13 April 2017 from

[23]Ayesha Jalal quoted in Dalrymple, W. (2015) http://newyorker.com/magazine/2015/06/29/the-great-divide-books-dalrymple

collective emotional conscience of a particular community. The powerful imagery of Manto's *Toba Tek Singh* in Punjab, Sunil Gangopadhyay's *Purba-Paschim* (East-West) in Bengal and Homen Borgohain's famous short story in Assamese, *Ismail Sheikhor Sondhanot* ('In Search of Ismail Sheikh'), are poignant reminders of the plight of the dispossessed, displaced and innocent victims of Partition in all the three theatres—Punjab, Bengal and Sylhet—where the drama of Partition was played out. These stories are symbolic of the madness of Partition as people who once belonged to the same land had now become separated by arbitrary lines hastily drawn on the ground, changing their lives forever.

In the case of the post-Partition generations of Sylhetis, collective memories of Partition are arguably shaped by their unique resettlement experiences in Assam. Historically, a part of the greater Assam since 1874, after Partition, 'the foreign national issue largely overlapped with the Bengalis' writes Hussain (1993), which ' added a new dimension to the existing relationship between the Asamiyas and Bengalis in Assam[24]. Consequently, the 'otherization' of the Sylhetis not only resulted in their becoming 'unsettled' in Assam even after 'settling' down permanently, but was sometimes a hindrance to their assimilation into wider Assamese society. This labelling as 'outsiders' kept them tied to the folk history of an imaginary homeland from which they had been severed, leading to the creation of nostalgia communities. Salman Rushdie, in his novel *Shame*, writes that the longing for the homeland is countered by the desire to belong to a

[24]Hussain, M. *The Assam Movement: Class, Ideology and Identity*. New Delhi: Manal Publications, 1993.

new home, so the migrant remains a creature of the edge, 'the peripheral man.' These are feelings and tensions all too familiar to those who left Sylhet after Partition.

'I can't forget, but I don't remember what'[25]

Why is there this nostalgia for a lost homeland which the younger generation have never seen or experienced? Perhaps it is due to the inherited historical memories of devastating events that their elders experienced. Perhaps growing up listening to the stories of family members who survived the tragedy of Partition, or perhaps growing up on Partition narratives which are so emotionally charged that they can shake the very soul of even the most hardened sceptic. Such exposure provides not only the terms of reference for later generations but also constructs a sense of history, which in turn provokes empathy for ancestors who experienced those traumatic events. In the same way, the stories narrated by Sylheti elders to their children and grandchildren, though not as violent or shocking as those of the Punjab, also became an integral part of the collective consciousness of the Sylhetis. Thus, a community's oral or folk history becomes so deeply embedded in their consciousness that it overshadows and subsumes any factual historical accounts of the same events. For those who lived through those times it is the oral history that legitimises those events.

Similarly, later generations of the Partition diaspora have had to negotiate their identities in the new nation-states

[25]Taken from Leonard Cohen's song of the same name. Retrieved on 5 May 2017 from http://www.azlyrics.com/lyrics/leonardcohen/icantforget.html

where they may still be regarded as 'outsiders.' As minorities, the collective memory of their past provides them with the tools to construct their own history or counter-history in order to give them a sense of their unique identity and legitimacy within the historical narrative of the dominant community in the adopted land. It is also reflective of the primal desire to affirm their own ethnicity, culture, traditions and religious beliefs while at the same time assimilating with the local culture.

A community's desire to affirm and protect its identity is evident in the fact that despite the lapse of seventy years since Partition, the overlapping of their Assamese and Bengali past still remained the basis of the identity of the Indian Sylhetis. Manjusha Datta, whose father also possessed a certificate of domicile in Assam, aptly expresses this identity in the following words: 'By nationality, we are Indians; by domicile, we are Assamese; by descent, we are Bengalis.'

The importance of collective historical memory of a people cannot be underestimated. Besides written historical records, oral narratives of a community play a significant role in providing the younger generations a sense of their past. However, with the paucity of historical and oral records of the period, the present generations who have not grown up listening to stories of Partition, the experiences of their ancestors may even question the relevance of remembering an event that is possibly beyond their imagination. Therefore, it becomes even more imperative for historians to chronicle the stories of the fast dwindling Partition survivors.

In the final analysis, it is through its historical past and its cultural heritage that a society propagates itself. Perhaps nostalgia and 'remembrance of things past' is also a community's way of protecting itself from repeating the mistakes of the past, for as in the famous words of George Santayana: 'Those who cannot remember their past are condemned to relive it.'

Note: The names of the interviewees in this essay have been changed to protect privacy.

GROWING UP WITH MRS P

Anjum Hasan

It is an autumn afternoon in Shillong and my entire family is huddled together on a large, cold bathroom floor. I have begun to weep and my five-year-old sister, so far merely solemn, receives the signal and joins in wholeheartedly. Dozens of men, brandishing sickles, knives, meat cleavers and other impromptu weapons, are swarming through the garden that runs around our house. Their checked woollen *tapmokhlieh* shawls flap behind them like angry wings.

The year is 1979 and we live in a house on a little ridge set back from the street, with grocery shops and a typing school on street level. The orange trees have glossy leaves and there is a single, stunted pomegranate tree that my grandmother says is haunted. At night the dusty skylights look opaque, coated with a bottle-green darkness the colour of the orange tree leaves. In my mind, these skylights at night somehow insert themselves into my grandfather's stories. They are the perch from which characters are observed by God or the Devil, as the case may be. I am seven years old, not as grave and inquisitive as my eight-year-old brother (who my grandfather has lately nicknamed 'Science'), nor as petulant as my little sister.

October means Durga Puja. At pandals in the neighbourhood, we have managed to just get a glimpse of

Durga's pasty face and bloody lips. She is largely hidden away from our two-feet-high eye-levels by the excited movement of adult bodies. This is our first year in the house above the busy street. Over time, we shall come to recognise these signs of a changing season—Durga, unfazed, her makeup still gleaming, will preside over men dancing on the beds of open trucks as she is taken on her last journey; quilts will smell of mothballs till months of use makes them smell of old cotton and sunshine again.

What happens today will also merge with these images and become part of what we associate with the end of autumn. Trouble. A procession in protest against 'outsiders' or dkhars is going on rampage. Just days earlier, newspapers had been describing Durga Puja festivities in a Shillong that is now hard to recognise. 'Cinema halls had arranged for midnight shows, and people were seen returning home at dawn after watching plays and a variety of other programmes at various Puja pandals. Only one case of attempted shoplifting was reported from Police Bazar where a group of respectable-looking ladies unsuccessfully tried to steal saris from a reputed clothes shop.'

But soon the spell is broken. The *Shillong Times* issues of early November will record statistics about the 'trouble': 'No. of arsons—9 houses gutted, attempts to set fire to 40, 1 taxi burnt'; a teacher's dead body will be recovered from a gorge; and on 17 November 1979, 'house owners apparently acting at the behest of a militant section' will be reported as 'pleading helplessness' at having to 'ask their non-tribal tenants to vacate their houses immediately—in some cases within a few hours.' Durga Puja will often in the coming years take place in an atmosphere of anxiety in the face of provocation, celebration tempered by mourning.

The rioting spreads to our neighbourhood. We draw our curtains and talk in whispers. My grandfather peers through a chink and motions us to come and look. Three men in *tapmohkhliehs* are setting fire to the shop across our house called Laboratory Aids, run by a large, genial Punjabi businessman. I have never quite figured out what this shop sells, and now I imagine those obscure objects of crystal and metal melting into each other, their mystery lost to me forever. What will become of A La Carté, the Chinese restaurant with dim red cabins where we have on occasion noticed couples flirting clandestinely?

Then hordes of men are in our garden and we are in the bathroom—children sobbing, grandparents panicky, parents tight-lipped. Our Khasi landlady, Mrs P, lives next door. She has asked us to come over to her house if we ever feel threatened in any way. The bathroom door is closest to the side gate that leads across a tarred compound to safety. Mrs P had perhaps been thinking of a bullying knock on the front door, a stone chucked onto our corrugated tin roof, an ominously large gathering in the football field near our house—anything that could make us feel ill at ease. But we are besieged. The men are running amok around us, banging on doors and shouting abuses. Opening the bathroom door to run to safety on the other side is out of the question.

We sit frozen there, a family forced to reckon with its foreignness. But not for long. The hooting and thumping sounds from the garden are beginning to melt away. We cannot see her, but Mrs P is suddenly out there, reasoning with the mob. Leave them alone, they aren't dkhars, she shouts. They're my people. Everybody knows it isn't the truth, and yet the rioters seem to succumb to the act of grace inherent in that lie. Or do they let us go because of who she is:

the widow of a Civil Service officer, an aristocratic matriarch with severe butterfly-shaped glasses who thinks nothing of ticking off an armed mob as if they were truant schoolboys?

ଓ

In the years to come, my parents will often suggest that those who consider us—long-time residents—outsiders deserve to be pitied more than feared. In the middle of our siege in the bathroom, my mother ventured out into the front room to cover up the record player so that no stone-throwers could spy it and target it through the window. I imagine her being this absurd largely through a sense of defiance and not just out of concern for the record player. My parents have lived other lives from the perspective of which the conflicts in this small hill town border on the quaint.

My father teaches English at the newly opened university with a sense of mission; my mother's memories of Partition, of being uprooted from Peshawar as a child because her family was Hindu, and starting all over again in another country, will always seem to her more immediate and terrible than anything that could happen to us here. The inheritance of us children consists of a handful of things—English literature, North Indian food, stories of Sufi mystics passed onto us in the language of our grandparents. These are fragile things in a town so distant from the plains, with a population as mixed as Shillong's. We are apparently always in danger of growing up uncultured.

Over time, as my parents lose connection with that other world, spending their long winter vacations in Shillong, not going back except in memory, their past will become chimerical. And for us, this is all there is. Even though we shall never again come as close to the 'trouble' as on that autumn evening in '79, its shadow will seep into the rest of our lives—the thrill of shut down schools; the fear of being hurt; the sad calm of curfew evenings; the awkwardness of being hated.

Our encounter with Mrs P will take us into the heart of a Khasi family and later, as adults, in contrast to our parents' evocation of the plains, give *us* that mirror in which to see our past. We hang out with Mrs P's grandchildren, insinuating ourselves into their lives with quiet persistence. Their many-limbed family is strangely organised—missing fathers and husbands, odd relations who potter around the garden or live in villages outside the city, brothers and sisters at perpetual war with each other. The house itself is full of alcoves and anterooms to hide children at play. The family cooks on a wood fire and coal-fed hearths burn throughout the winter. Somebody is always poking at a fire or warming her behind at one.

Mrs P's ancient father, a tall toothless man in a creamy dhoti, turban and the sleeveless tunic called *jymphong*, sits in the parlour that looks out onto lawns, flowerbeds and, further away, the low dark hills of Nongthymmai. He teaches us how to make paper boats by an open window. In the hall hangs a large black-and-white, blurry-at-the-edges portrait of the dead and handsome Mr P. The carpeted sitting room is where the older grandchildren have parties, at one of which I learn the expression 'too big for one's boots.'

Some of Mrs P's children bring a little more of the world into the big house. A visiting son-in-law, the Indian ambassador to a vagueness called Yemen, might take over the sitting room. He sets up an open-reel tape recorder; the silky black spools capture our shy, hesitant pop songs and his own pounding on the piano, singing what always seems to feature an image of ships coming back from sea.

Mrs P's son, an Indian Administrative Service officer, belongs to a cadre that has banished him to distant Maharashtra. When *he* returns, we will smuggle out LPs from our father's collection to impress him, in return for which he will let us thumb through his books on the English royal family or give us rides on his gleaming Enfield.

Mrs P, when she dresses up to go out, will wear a silk jainsem as lush as the gems at the tip of her dangling gold earrings. She might take us with her to a wedding, a posse of some scornful and some shy children all bundled into tartan shawls from her chest of drawers. Her grandchildren. My siblings and I. The church is packed. We don't sing the hymns from the Khasi hymnbooks with their delicate translucent pages edged with red ink, because we would be embarrassed or can never find the right page. The bride is always too far for us to be able to discern her face but the old women cry nevertheless, moved by something they witness all the time. We fidget and giggle while Mrs P scolds us in heated whispers and is immediately composed again, intently following the proceedings, her scolding no more than the mime of a scolding and we no more than miming obedience. Afterwards, 'taking' tea in the bride's house, I will begin on my early experiments with kwai. The twist of lime paste on the fresh leaf and the hard, potent nut will send its hot surge through me and make my head spin dangerously. Riding back home in the taxi, the kwai's glowing after-effect will fend off the knife-edged cold of the winter evening.

When my mother cooks for Mrs P, we feel that our presence in the big house acquires greater legitimacy. She sits propped up with pillows on her vast four-poster bed, recovering from yet another bout of illness, and we march in solemnly, each bearing a covered steel bowl of something. We hang around watching her devour the food. She loves this rich fare—keema matar swimming in golden mustard oil, aloo parathas, stuffed beef kababs, thick kadi, cloyingly sweet gajar halwa. Seeing her eat with silent concentration, her hold over things weakened by illness, is always vaguely disturbing. We are secretly pleased about her passion for our mother's cooking but also realise that Mrs P is not perfect, she can be bribed. She gives us butter biscuits in return. We sit at the edge of her bed, our laps full of crumbs, while she rounds up the meal with her favourite utterance: 'I haff no money.' This she says without any regard for context.

Nevertheless, she does behave like the inevitably rich. When she airs the handsome black Austin her husband has left her, it is always an impressive sight. The old lady—stern, friendly, distracted, greedy, kind—her face behind the butterfly glasses the colour of sunlight on snow, wearing her voluminous jainsem and her polished black pumps, driving the hunchbacked car in circles in the compound. Then there are her many different tenants—us, Bihari grocers, Assamese sweet shop owners, Nepali firemen. There is the big house, elegantly old. There are trips to see less affluent relatives in the rural outreaches of Shillong that we accompany her on, bundled into the same shawls. Somebody will always be lounging in a doorway as we come into hard mud compounds. Mrs P will gruffly produce warm bread from the folds of her cloak; a few tightly folded notes might change hands.

☙

She knew us as children and often treated us as interchangeable, so it would never be possible for us to have a real conversation with Mrs P. To us she seemed both distinguished and funny; we privately made her 'I haff no money' into a mantra that we could use to conjure her up. Yet, we liked her air of faded gentility, even if it meant that we would always see her as if from afar and take her actions to represent the actions of women like her—the kind who lived in old houses, had money worries and recalcitrant children. She loved the black Austin, stored butter in wooden cabinets with chicken-wire meshes, was wary of pressure cookers. We knew such things about her.

She evokes for me what Philip Larkin calls 'local lives'—that ineffable cosiness of '... gates and lamps/ In high stone one-street villages, empty at dusk,/ And side roads of small towns...' But we who lived next door punctured that picture with our very presence. We were both spectators and participants in their everyday tableaus—family quarrels, drunkenness, obsessive gardening, exotic relatives. We derived much of our imaginative resources from this world but also had to contend with, what in Shillong was known as, being 'Hindi'. To be a Hindi who happened to have no Hindi hometown to visit during the winter break, who spoke Hindi haltingly, who didn't quite fit in with the other more resolutely Hindi Hindis, was an awkward sort of Hindi to be.

On our right, across the compound was Mrs P and her intriguing family; on our left, across the road, was another, contrasting universe. The family that owned the slightly disreputable A La Carté, which the arsonists had eventually left alone in 1979, commended itself to us largely because of their TV set. There, on Sunday mornings, we would watch *Star Trek* or *Chitrahaar* in silent awe. Our love for television, our weakness for its fantasies, seems of a piece to me now with our fascination for Mrs P. The two families couldn't have been more dissimilar—one with its old-worldy airs, where people dressed their best for church, stoked the kitchen fire all evening, tended geraniums and begonias, and observed the slow-moving world through creamy lace curtains. The other was the world of the immigrant trying, despite his mere toehold, to put down his roots. The TV-owning family lived in a haphazardly built concrete house behind A La Carté, and eagerly absorbed the new Hindi-speaking images that television first brought into Shillong in the early '80s.

We became dedicated watchers of these disparate worlds. *Watching*. People walked in and out of A La Carté on Sunday afternoons, laughing, confident. Mrs P's saddest daughter played the piano. Her wild grandson rode their pet Alsatian like a horse till it died. Science walked purposefully around the garden, stuffing leaves into bottles and shaking them with water, trying to get them to reveal their natures.

How did things seem to those being watched? Mrs P saved our lives with a certain nonchalance. We were grateful to her, of course, and then grew to understand how she had not behaved out of character, that she was a confident cosmopolitan. Her existence combined within it all the influences that the Khasi community had been subject to in both recent and remote history. Her husband had been a senior officer in a bureaucracy fashioned by the colonisers. Her prized Austin was made in England. Her lace curtains and full-length mirrors, the sturdy contours of her 'Assam-type' bungalow, its polished wooden floors and stuffed sofas, evoked the English feel that the British had tried to recreate in Shillong. Her Christianity could be traced to missionary activity in the hills from a little more than a hundred years ago. She needed her broken Hindi to get by with her tenants, her tartan shawls were spun in Ludhiana, and many of her grandchildren would study, live and work elsewhere in India.

Mrs P represented that generation in the compressed history of Shillong who straddled different, even conflicting, worlds with dignified grace. The sense of tradition that she preserved was itself the result of many changes but it gave her the necessary anchor and the courage to regard Shillong's hybrid world with equanimity. Her orderly domestic universe, encircled by the equally reliable spheres of church, friends, relatives and tenants was her sustenance. Later generations would find this carefully built-up world constricting, and the larger world that was pressing upon them, alarming too. But for us, the dkhars, Mrs P was Mrs P because of the seeming invincibility of her roots. We would have to learn how not to be charmed by this if we wanted to acknowledge our own mixed-upness.

As we grew out of childhood, 'local lives' seemed to give way to something meaner. Mrs P's merely rhetorical, if persistent, 'I haff no money' would in another generation translate into cold-hearted avarice. By the time Mrs P died in the mid-1990s, we were ready to leave Shillong, even though the rest of the country was a blur and we suffered from the vertigo of not knowing exactly who we were.

A version of this piece first appeared in
The Little Magazine, Volume 5, Issue 2 & 3, 2004.

MAN IN THE MIDDLE

Ankush Saikia

The outsider has always been an attractive figure for storytellers—many of us will instinctively recall the figure of the lone gunslinger in Westerns riding into town and entering the saloon. By virtue of being an outsider, he observes and notices things which may escape the attention of those who aren't outsiders, i.e., those who belong. It can also help him avoid taking sides, thus retaining an objective view of things. At the other end of the spectrum is the insider, another interesting figure—for those who can conjure him up, as the specifics of belonging are harder to create than the details of being an outsider. R.K. Narayan's Swami comes to mind as one such character, a boy living deep within a very specific world, that of a small town in South India, and for whom the outside world is distant and far-off. The very specificity of his existence, the ordinariness mixed with the small dramas that constitute a boy's life, is exactly what raises it to the level of the universal.

I had for many years, while working in Delhi, a vague idea of writing a dark book about the city, a sort of noir thriller. It was only when I returned to the North-East that the book actually started taking shape in my mind. The character of the detective came about for the sole reason that he would be someone who, by virtue of his profession, would have to travel around the city, thereby allowing him to access different layers of society. In fact, I hadn't even read much crime fiction till then. And along with the complexities and extremes of that sprawling city, I suppose I unconsciously attempted to make the detective as much of a complex figure as I could (that realisation comes to me only now). This meant he had to be an outsider in Delhi, someone who never felt at home there. Of course, Delhi is a city of immigrants and refugees in the first place, so his background and upbringing would have to contribute to his sense of alienation.

I made Arjun Arora the product of a mixed marriage; his father is Punjabi while his mother is Nepali. He is born on a cold and rainy day in January in the year 1971 at the civil hospital in Shillong. Those who've lived in Shillong will know that January is usually a grey and gloomy month when, after the festivities and sunshine of December, the streets get deserted (the college students and tourists have gone home by then) and the town retreats into itself. I saw this couple all by themselves in the chilly government hospital, welcoming a boy into the world. His mother had previously lost a son at birth, so that makes Arjun's own survival something of a matter of luck. Arjun's father is a Partition refugee, someone who arrived in Calcutta from newly divided Punjab as a child with his parents, and then later ended up working as a construction company supervisor in the North-East. The woman whom he meets in Guwahati and ultimately marries, Arjun's mother, is someone whose forebears were migrants to North-East India from Nepal to serve in the armed police under the British.

So, there is the dislocation of a mixed heritage right from the beginning, especially with a 'combination,' Punjabi and Nepali, that isn't too common in India in terms of mixed marriages. It is hinted in the first book featuring the detective, *Dead Meat*, that Arora's mother's relatives have all but forsaken her on account of her choice of husband, while Arora isn't very close to any of his relatives from his father's side. It is almost as if this is presaged by that lonely birth in a cold hospital in a town that will treat him, when the time comes, as an outsider.

Who could I have been thinking about when I gave Arjun that particular set of parents? No one specific couple, of that I am certain, but at the back of my head would have been people I had come across, from what is easily termed as 'mainland' India, ordinary people who had landed up across the North-East to work in various trades or occupations: a Bihari shopkeeper in a small town in Arunachal Pradesh, a Malayali teacher in an 'English medium' school in Nagaland, a Punjabi supervisor of a Bengali Muslim construction crew in Assam. These are people who usually fall between the cracks, who are neither here nor there, eking out lives of unseen heroism as they earn a living and raise a family. I suppose somewhere, in some corner of my mind, would have been the question—what would it have been like for an only child to grow up with a father like that? Some of the inspiration for Arjun's father would have come from there. As for Arjun's mother, her community, the Nepali or Nepalese, is one which has, over the decades, spread across the North-East (and beyond), while still being viewed as outsiders in many places (just like Bengali Muslims from what is now Bangladesh), especially when seen in the context of elections.

Arjun Arora grows up in towns across the North-East on account of his father's work (as a construction supervisor). When he is in his teens, his father is shot in the kneecap by insurgents in Manipur, and the family relocates to Delhi. Later, while serving in the Army (which he ultimately has to leave due to his insubordination), Arora returns to the North-East for a couple of years. He is an outsider there, but has also become an insider of sorts, and yet is destined to remain an outsider. The nostalgia for his lost years in the North-East means that he always has one foot in the past, even as he struggles to stay afloat in Delhi.

After having written two books with Arjun Arora (the second was *Remember Death*), and now writing the third one in the series, I suppose I have the familiarity with, and enough distance from, Arora's character to recognise certain aspects of him better. While writing a novel, decisions are taken, so to speak, on the fly. The name of a character, the hairstyle they sport, the car they drive, the parents they have, the trials and tribulations they face, to name a few things—these I have usually found myself coming up with pretty quickly. It is only later that their deeper significance, if at all any, becomes evident.

I grew up in Shillong in the 1980s. We had landed up there when my father decided to return from America, and chose the place where he had taken up his first job (St Anthony's College, which he had joined after doing his BSc. and MSc. from Ramjas College in Delhi). Tezpur and Biswanath Chariali in Assam, my parents' places, were, back then, a day's journey away by bus. I went there during the long winter holidays, and spent time at my grandparents' places. So, right at the start there was this dislocation between two places, Shillong and Assam, leading to two lives that had nothing much in common, and then there was also, till a certain age, a vague nostalgia for an America I didn't remember too well. I suppose what this led to, in an unconscious way, was a realisation that people and events could always be viewed from different angles, depending on where you stood. In a large and diverse country such as India, most people will have a sense of this, but I think it is not something that is likely to be explored or thought about, but rather to be simply taken as a given.

About a decade ago, I had gone to Ladakh during the summer, from Delhi, where I was then working. At dinner one night in the common dining room of a guesthouse on the outskirts of Leh, a young Belgian man told me, in halting English, that I seemed 'Westernised.' I suppose this was because of my jeans and the fact that I spoke English decently. I didn't know what to say to him then; only later did it occur to me that I should have told him that I, like many people in India, existed in *layers*: I spoke in English with tourists, or my colleagues or friends; I spoke in Hindi as I went around Delhi; and I spoke in Assamese with my parents and relatives back in Assam (and even there, I was conscious of urban and rural speech patterns, and tried to change my speech so as not to stand out). I think I saw my detective as someone who existed in layers as well, but what defined him was his solitary existence, in his flat in a large and impersonal city. He is someone who is adrift, without roots, and in that he is also a representative of a new type of Indian, one free for the most part from regional or neighbourhood ties.

At school in Shillong, I occupied a somewhat strange middle ground. There were only a handful of Assamese students, as most Assamese people had slowly left over the years after Meghalaya became a separate state in 1972 (and Shillong ceased to be Assam's capital). The outsiders, that is to say the non-Khasis and non-tribals, were always conscious of their status, but within this group the Assamese boys occupied a somewhat different position, mostly non-tribals but at the same time from a neighbouring state, and from the North-East. We were, to put it in concrete terms, for the Khasi boys, somewhere in-between the Naga and Mizo boys on one side and the Bengali and North Indian boys on the other. So that was another form of layering, of status, and again it was something which I think none of the boys questioned even though they were aware of it; things were what they were.

Larger events from the outside world occasionally broke through the cocoon of childhood. There was the anti-foreigner agitation, which started in 1983 in Assam, and then the anti-outsiders stir in Shillong a couple of years later. I heard stories of killings and violence taking place in different places in Assam, but with the child's scale of reference, so that they seemed like events from far-off places. During the troubled state elections that year, a cousin brother of my mother's and his friend were assaulted with rods by people from the students' groups, because they were working for the Congress candidate, my uncle. A white bulge of bandage on the friend's broken nose, above his moustache, was what stayed in my memory. Later, during the troubles in Shillong, events had the similar sense of far-off happenings. We played football and cricket in the nearby field whenever there wasn't curfew, and went to school once in a while to collect or handover assignments—classes had been suspended, and that was a great thrill for us. Once in a while, we saw curfew breakers being chased by the CRPF men. Over time, this developed into something of a game between the curfew breakers and the bored CRPF men. It was only many years later that the happenings of those times became clear to me. But even back then, I knew that people who were different were being targeted (mainly Bengali Muslims in Assam, and Bengalis and Nepalis in Shillong). They were what academics and journalists nowadays like to refer to as the 'Other'.

While in Assam I was an insider, and while in Shillong I was an outsider, but even there overlaps occurred, as I might be an outsider in certain contexts in Assam, and an insider in certain contexts in Shillong. The anti-outsider sentiments in Shillong I could at times almost identify with—when I viewed it in terms of my experience in Assam. I think the end result of this was that, again maybe unconsciously, I found it very difficult to choose sides. In fact, I never *wanted* to choose sides as, in every situation, I could somehow see things from another point of view, or even several points of view. Something of that impartial gaze must have made it into the character of my detective.

Even as I was writing the detective books, I was doing a bit of travelling around the North-East. Growing up, Shillong and parts of Assam had been familiar to me, but there were many other places I hadn't visited, and so I started moving about after pitching a couple of long-form articles to national newspapers and magazines. A story on hydropower projects in Arunachal Pradesh took me, among other places, to Pasighat, and from there to a village some way up the Siang, which is one of the main tributaries of the Brahmaputra. Pongging was a village inhabited by the Adi tribe on the slope of a hill by the river (a light brown then just after the rains), and about half-an-hour away from the crumbling main road—over a suspension bridge, through a forest, and along cliff sides. The village had a patch of land down by the river where rice and other crops were grown. I do not intend to go into the politics of dams here; suffice it to say that there were voices both for and against the proposed Lower Siang project just downstream from the village (the reservoir's water level would come to just below the village, submerging the cropland—there were some who didn't want this to happen, and others who were willing to take the compensation money and move to Pasighat town). Talking to one of the villagers, what I found interesting was the fact that their forefathers had come down to the present location from another, higher-up village many decades ago. He said there had been some fighting, and a related factor would have been the scarce cropland on the hillsides, which hadn't been able to support a growing population. So, a group of families must have come down and settled here in Pongging where they found some cultivable land. It was the simple imperative to survive that had led them to move. For someone passing by that main road in a car, the sight of this village on the green slopes high above the river, with the drooping *toko pat* or palm-leaf roofs of the large huts, would probably conjure up visions of unchanged traditions and a deep connection to the earth. It would be more difficult to picture the earlier migration of the villagers and the hardscrabble fight for existence they faced.

On the way back, after crossing the suspension bridge over a smaller tributary river and climbing up to the main road, I met a young couple from the village with their two small children, waiting for a passing Sumo taxi to go to a town higher up. One of the children was tied to the mother's back—I found it hard to imagine how she could have walked through that tough terrain. But she had no complaints. Rather, she seemed embarrassed before me, maybe on behalf of the villagers, that there wasn't even a motorcycle track to their village. The old migration of the villagers, and now the divide between the present folk over the dam—there were shades of the insider/outsider theme there as well.

In fact, the tribe known as the Mising in Assam (mostly found towards the eastern end of the state, on both banks of the Brahmaputra), known for their stilt houses and riverine existence, were said to be Adis who had come down to the plains ages ago, and had then become partly Hinduized. The British supposedly stopped the flow of the Adi tribe (or the larger Tani group) down into the plains, thus permanently dividing the two groups. Even today, the language of the Adis and the Misings point to a common origin. So there comes the idea of flux, of people always on the move, in groups large or small, and seen from that perspective, no one can really be said to belong, or be an insider, in the truest sense. We are all travellers. It's just that some of us have a keener sense of this than others.

A few months before going to Pasighat, I had undertaken a bone-jarring twelve-hour-plus ride in a Sumo taxi from Shillong to Aizawl via Silchar. I had gone to Mizoram to do a story on the lifting of prohibition in that small Christian state, and had to endure another long, ten-hour Sumo taxi ride from Aizawl to Champhai and the Myanmar border, from where drugs in the form of heroin and methamphetamines were being smuggled in from the other side. In Aizawl, I stayed with a friend of mine from school in Shillong. He took me around to meet some Young Mizo Association (YMA) members who were helping the excise and narcotics people in nabbing drug smugglers. One evening, an MLA from the opposition Mizo National Front (MNF) came over (he was, in fact, one of my friends' brothers-in-law). Upon being told that I was an Assamese, he somehow managed to veer the conversation (I think we had been talking about the Myanmar border then) around to the fact that Mizo villages had once been self-sufficient and had no need for outside assistance.

What he had managed to string together was the neglect of the famine situation in the erstwhile Lushai Hills district by the Assam government in the late 1950s, which had led to the rise of the MNF, and subsequently the practice of forced village regrouping by the Indian Army to tackle the MNF fighters. This had then led to old villages being abandoned and later a growing urban population in Aizawl, paving the way to the state's dependence for food grains and other necessities on the mainland.

I think what the MLA with his nationalist or sub-nationalist vision was trying to tell me (and which his party no doubt told the masses) was that this dependence was the result of outside interference, by the Assam government, and then by the Indian Army. There was another viewpoint too: a professor from Mizoram University told me that the population increase in the hilly state had meant that the state's food production—still dependent to a large extent on *jhum* or shifting cultivation—wasn't sufficient. And the rural areas, as I had seen on my way to Champhai, still looked poor and neglected. The MLA would have slotted me as someone linked to the Assam government by virtue of my community alone, giving me allegiances I had never felt. I tried to lighten the mood by pointing out that even the spirit (generally referred to as 'B.E.') used in the mixing of illicit liquor came from outside, from Myanmar. I think this angered him, and he abruptly stood up and walked out of the room. I felt embarrassed, and could make out that my friend felt the same, but then we dealt with it in a way that I think had something to do with our school and our friendship—we just didn't discuss it, and we forgot about it. It was almost as if the MLA himself had been the outsider for the time he sat with us. Later, however, he did send over a golden jubilee souvenir of the MNF for me.

What is called the North-East is not a homogenous entity. It is rather a diverse grouping of communities—this is mentioned time and again, and is correct, but how it works out on the ground has to be studied as well. Towards the end of 2016, I went to Manipur by road from Dimapur in Nagaland; there was a magazine story I had to do, as well as some research for the third Detective Arjun Arora book. With reference to the magazine story, Manipur as a setting for strife and misery was something that had been explored by writers and journalists coming in from outside. But I felt there were certain angles that had been left out. One was the impact of Brahminism, especially a corrupted form of neo-Brahminism on Manipuri society, creating an elite class that gradually appropriated available benefits to themselves. Viewed against this background, the insurgent groups with their leftist ideology could be seen as an expression of class as much as an opposition to the Indian state. In any case, these groups with their bases just across the border in Myanmar's loosely governed northern areas had over time morphed into something quite different.

A friend who had been asked for 'contributions' from his family business by one of the groups now drove around with a licensed pistol. People like him, and his family and friends, lived in a separate world, sending their children out to study and frequently flying out to the Indian metros. On the other side were people like the lady I knew from the Extra-Judicial Execution Victim Families Association, Manipur (EEVFAM), whose husband had been picked up as a suspected insurgent by the police commandos and shot dead. Now she was raising two sons on her own. Those who could, got out of Manipur. There were girls from the hill tribes—Zou, Tangkhul, Hmar, Paite—I had met previously in Delhi's Hauz Khas Village, working in the small designer shops, an air of sadness about them. All of them had the same thing to say—there was nothing to do back home, except maybe work in the fields, which they didn't want to do. A retired DG of police who had survived ambushes of both Naga and Meetei insurgents told me that the non-tribal category (the Meetei) in Manipur had been an 'artificial creation,' and that the Brahmins had introduced untouchability as well—you had to have a bath if you touched a tribal. So many layers, and the economic currents and cross-currents running through them, could fill a book by themselves. Was it any wonder that most stories turned it into a simple A versus B or India versus Manipur story? Each state, each community, had its own lines drawn, and increasingly in the North-East, in once egalitarian tribal societies, you now had to have money to be a true insider.

The third Arjun Arora book will see him journeying to Manipur and Nagaland in connection with a case involving the murder of a young girl in Delhi. It seemed to me that there was a good opportunity to treat through fiction, to dramatise the North-Eastern experience in Delhi (and also the outsider's experience in the North-East), especially in the context of those vexed words one hears nowadays—'racism' and 'discrimination.'

I spent fourteen years in Delhi, and had a deeply lived experience as someone from, and with people from, the North-East. Travelling ticketless on buses, being penniless halfway through the month, bailing out friends from police stations—there were a lot of experiences, some good, some bad, but always interesting. I suppose I became something of a Delhiite myself after a couple of years, learning to give it back as good as I got it. It is a tough city, and the weather—from freezing cold to boiling hot—seems to lend an extra edge to the aggression of its inhabitants. I saw the hostility of the city as something to be tackled head on, and by the time I became a salaried worker, I had made my peace with the city. Something from my father's experience might have influenced my attitude. He had been a student at Ramjas College in Delhi University's North Campus in the late '60s and early '70s. And as a hostelite at that college, he was part of a small group of boys from Assam who were stuck between the two large traditional lobbies, the Jats and the Biharis. He survived that experience, and even made a few friends among the Jats.

After I left Delhi in 2011, there seemed to be an increase in the number of news reports about cases of assault on people from the North-East in Delhi and other metros. This problem had always existed, even when I had been in Delhi, and was partly the result of cultural differences. But it had never been this widespread. While student groups and NGOs blamed racism and a discriminatory attitude, there were attempts by the government to address matters, including the recruitment of a large number of men and women from the North-East by the Delhi Police. With reference to Delhi, looking at the places where these incidents were happening, and to whom (students, workers, or professionals), I saw that a large number of cases involved workers in low-paid jobs who had to live in areas that were often no better than urban slums.

What used to happen earlier was that the people from the North-East who landed up in Delhi were mostly students or working professionals, who left after a couple of years, or stayed back, but usually in colonies or areas where they weren't bothered much. Indra Vihar in North Delhi, where I first stayed after reaching Delhi, has turned into a North-

Eastern colony of sorts, with the locals living off rent and shops catering mostly to students. I never heard of any problems there. However, there did seem to be a significant increase in people from the rural areas of the North-East, with little or no qualifications, coming to Delhi just to scrape out a living—working in malls, restaurants, and factories. Their level of pay, as I have said, led them to stay in crowded areas no better than urban slums. It is mostly in areas such as these that problems occur.

But why had there been an increase in people coming from the North-East in search of low-paid jobs in Delhi and other metros? The answer was the increase in the numbers of the unemployed in the North-East, the heavy dependence of the hill states on Central government funds, where a limited number of government jobs (many of them up for sale) were the main form of employment. Many young people came even from Assam, where population growth had surpassed the ability of the state economy to provide employment. There were a large number of youths from the impoverished North Bank region of Assam (north of the Brahmaputra) working as security guards in the south Indian states. With the activities of active and surrendered insurgent groups creating a negative atmosphere for outside investment, and a lack of focus by state governments on revenue generation (indeed, politics had largely turned into a matter of getting one's hands on Central funds), it was no wonder the sons of the soil had to leave for cities in the mainland, sometimes getting cheated in the process. A few of them might come back and try and strike out on their own, but those cases are few and far in between.

The Bezbaruah Committee, which was set up by the Ministry of Home Affairs to examine the issue (after a nineteen-year-old student from Arunachal Pradesh was beaten to death in Delhi in 2014), also pointed out that one of the main problems was an exodus of people from the North-East to take up low-paid jobs in the metros (jobs which should have been available in their home states). Its report focuses mainly on Delhi (as that is where most of the people coming from the North-East land up), and notes the 'changing socio-economic and educational background' of the migrants post the year 2000 (it says earlier, they were mostly Central government employees and students coming for higher studies), and their difficulties adjusting in areas with low rent where the local population was usually conservative. Significantly, the report says that the trend of migration will continue 'till such time that similar (job) opportunities emerge in the North-East itself'.

India is a large country with many diverse cultures and ethnicities, and if you look for differences, you will find them. It is harder to look for things that link us, no matter where we are in the country: Kishore Kumar playing on the radio in a haircutting saloon, a steaming bowl of Maggi somewhere in the hills, the conversation between strangers in a train compartment, a cup of tea at a roadside shack. India goes on (to paraphrase R.K. Narayan), and hopefully my detective uncovers more of the true nature of the country even as he solves his cases.

COLLAPSE OF A COLONIAL COSMOPOLITY

The Social History of Transforming Lives and a Space Called Shillong

Binayak Dutta

The idea of a place as a space is not without its share of imagination of the people that live in it. It is the people that give a place its character and colour. The above philosophy fits perfectly with Shillong, which was a product of colonial re-configuration of native spaces. The birth of Shillong was a product of a complex engagement amongst the colonisers themselves and between the colonisers and the native elite, reflected in protracted negotiations. This negotiation was at the root of the cosmopolitan character of the space, which became a place. This cartographic transformation affected all shades of its inhabitants—both the outsiders and the natives, who gave the place its name. Therefore, in early 1866, when the headquarters of the Sylhet Light Infantry Regiment and the office of the deputy commissioner were transferred to Shillong and Iewduh, unlike most of the other colonial hill stations, Shillong was conceived by its European creators as a site that was to facilitate not only the ends of European colonial commercial interests of 'drawing out the commercial resources,' but also as a site for interaction between European officers and the Indian people. Till the establishment of the military and administrative headquarters in 1864, there were only a few scattered villages in this area known as Laban, Mawkhar, Laitumkhrah, etc. The civil station was located between the then existing Khasi villages. The desire of the colonial state, in the language of Brigadier General GD Showers, who for a short while was the Commissioner of Khasi and Jaintia Hills, was to encourage the settlement of residents in Shillong, beyond the ends of a mere 'weather retreat.' The government desired to 'encourage European settlers and invalids' to set up offices and establishments which 'would attract trade and population and call out more rapidly the resources of the district....'

With the constitution of Assam as a province of colonial India, under a chief commissioner in 1874, Shillong was made the capital of the new province. This administrative reorganisation along with the decision of the colonial state to make Cachar and Sylhet, predominantly Bengali districts, a part of the new colonial province only contributed to consolidating the capital's cosmopolitan character as people from the Assam valley and these districts came to join government service and relocate to the capital town. The seeds of Shillong's cosmopolitanism were embedded in its colonial heritage. Thus, besides the Khasis, to whom this land belonged, the first settlers in this station were the European officers who negotiated with the local Khasi chiefs to acquire lands, construct, and expand the colonial cosmopolitan station of Shillong.

Historian and the former chairman of the Union Public Service Commission of India, David Reid Syiemlieh, points out that, 'the government took [on] perpetual lease from

Syiem of Mylliem [chieftain] the portions now known as European Ward, Police Bazar, Jail Road and the cantonment. Laban and Mawkhar were added to the station in November 1878 and Lachumere Hill in 1895.' By 1913, the four villages of Malki, Laitumkhrah, Jhalupara and Mawprem were made a part of the town where a municipality had been established in 1910. The European officers settled on the Secretariat Hill overlooking the Wards Lake in bungalows, in what was called the 'European Quarters', an area encircled by the Bivar Road. The initial step towards expansion of the 'Station' was the establishment of a small market near the police station. The Thana Road came to form the core of Police Bazar, as the area came to be known.

Following the European administrators came the Bengali-speaking people from the different districts of Bengal who served as the clerical staff in the colonial administration offices. The Bengali settlement in Shillong was coterminous with the shifting of the administrative headquarters of the District from Cherrapunjee to Shillong in 1864. K.D. Saha, a researcher in the Anthropological Survey of India in Shillong observes in his study that 'reportedly at the time of construction of the District Headquarters in Shillong, 14 Bengali employees were brought from Cherrapunjee to the site for clerical work and were allotted land on Jail Road for settlement. [A] Majority of them were Hindus and from Sylhet, particularly northern Sylhet, and a few from other districts, namely from Nadia, Santipur, Jessore, Commilla (Tipperah) and Dacca.' Bengali Muslims came from Hooghly District and 'started their career as enterprising businessmen.' A major part of commerce including the business of transport was in their hands. Till about 1897, the Bengalis dominated as the 'native employees of the government'. While the Bengali clerks established their habitation in the areas of Jail Road, Thana Road and Laban, the Bengali businessmen came to concentrate their holdings around Police Bazar and Laban. In 1905, the Shillong Muslim Union came to be established with its office at Laban. By the 1920s, the Bengalis also came to establish their houses in other localities of Shillong such as Jaiaw, Mawkhar, Laitumkhrah and Nongthymmai as these localities were integrated into the colonial town.

But the Bengalis were not the sole contributors to the evolution of the multi-ethnic space of Shillong. The Assamese community also developed substantial holdings in Shillong since the last decade of the nineteenth century. Prafulla Misra, an influential Assamese intellectual settled in Shillong, observed that 'in the initial years, there were not more than 30 to 35 Assamese residents in Shillong; almost all were government servants...' The Assamese people engaged in government service hailed from Upper Assam as they were the hardest hit by the colonial rule and abolition of the *paik* system (a type of corvée labor system), which disturbed the traditional social organisation of Assamese society. It was only in the twentieth century that people from Lower Assam came to join their counterparts from Upper Assam and join government service. The Assamese settlement in Shillong was initially located in Laban and its adjoining localities. Therefore, Bishnupur and Malki were areas that witnessed a proliferation of Assamese houses. Subsequent holdings were acquired in Lachumiere, Oakland and Laitumkhrah. In 1896, the Assam Club was formed and started functioning from a rented house in Laban. The cultural and social life of the Assamese community in Shillong centred around this club. Migration of the Assamese to Shillong accelerated with the creation of the composite state of Assam after 1947, when 'Assamese representation in the bureaucracy was enhanced.'

The Nepalis were perhaps the earliest settlers in Shillong—their arrival in the colonial district headquarters could be traced back to the movements of the colonial army. Therefore, the history of the movement of the Sylhet Light Infantry and the 8 Gorkha Rifles is also the story of Nepalese migration into Shillong. Closely associated with the colonial military establishment, Nepalese settlements have been close to the European cantonments in Shillong. The Gorkha Pathshala School established in 1876 was one of the oldest schools in this region to cater to the children of Army personnel, the helpers and attendants of the British officers who were given elementary education through 'the medium of Nepali language.' The Marwaris engaged primarily in business, and the Biharis were a significant part of various dimensions of the service industry; milk-vending, hair-cutting, cobbling, butchery, laundering and loaf-selling were some of the major components of this cosmopolity.

Even in religious terms, the town had a fair share of religious diversity. Christians, Hindus, Buddhists, Muslims and followers of traditional religions coexisted to form the diverse social spectrum of the town. By the turn of the twentieth century, Shillong became, as historian David Reid Syiemlieh was to observe, 'a cosmopolitan town with a mixed population of locals, Europeans (administrators, tea planters and others who settled here on retirement), an increasing element of Bengalis who staffed the offices, Nepali crofters, enterprising Marwari traders and a small segment of other communities.' Territorial and administrative readjustments following the partition of Bengal and its annulment, expansion of Western education and Christianity and the tide of the anti-colonial movement had a major impact on Shillong. While population composition was reshuffled by a migration of both the tribal and non-tribal people in this provincial capital from time to time, nothing could change the cosmopolitan character of the town. Each community grew more deep-rooted and acquired cultural efflorescence with the passage of time. A major expression of this rooted life was in the flowering of community-sponsored vernacular schools, native clubs, community-specific literary societies, organisation of theatre competitions and annual religious festivals such as Durga Puja.

Apparently, the colonial period was a catalyst for the emergence of Shillong as a cultural melting pot where people from the plains of Assam in particular, and the neighbouring provinces of Bengal, Bihar and the distant land of Punjab, Rajasthan and Nepal, came to reside along with the indigenous population as government servants, army personnel, teachers, doctors, small traders, washermen and transporters. Most of these immigrant people settled permanently in their adopted land in what appeared to be perfect harmony and peace with their hosts. They contributed to the agricultural, cultural, economic and educational development of the region as a whole, and to the capital town in particular. As the capital town, Shillong emerged as a growing cosmopolitan centre, and was a popular attraction for the youth who aspired to make a mark for themselves in life beyond the immediate environs of their ancestral homes.

But over time, the space began to transform itself. The partition of India and the transfer of Sylhet to East Pakistan led to the migration and settlement of lakhs of East Bengali migrants in Assam. Thousands among them migrated to the Khasi-Jaintia hills. The birth of the Indian Constitution and the formation of mechanisms of constitutional protectionism reignited the tension between the tribes and the non-tribes in the hills. Constitutional institutions set up to safeguard the interest of the tribes came to be popularly perceived as opportunities to convert these tribal areas into exclusive zones of tribal hegemony. Cosmopolitanism was the first casualty in the practice of constitutional protectionism in these hills. As the headquarters of the post-colonial state of Assam, Shillong became the focal point of this new brand of politics. Therefore, when the District Council for United Khasi and Jaintia Hills was inaugurated on 27 June 1952, a black flag demonstration was held in protest of the inclusion of some 'dkhars' ('foreigners' in Khasi language) in the Council. One of the reports on the incident points out that when the Government of Assam nominated three non-tribal members to the Council, 'it created the condition of dissent against the government, which sparked into a protest black flag demonstration organised by an informal group of college-going Khasi students with the support of a crowd of five thousand. The student leaders were arrested and this further precipitated the conflict. On the following day, a crowd of 10,000 gathered at the Khasi National Dorbar Hall demanding the release of the student leaders. The student leaders were released and the issue of nomination of non-tribal members to the council was later handed over to the political leaders to resolve.'

Non-tribals who traced their origin in the hills to the early days of colonial rule found their position challenged as anti-dkhar agitations came out in public for the first time. Partition of the country and the Constitution's coming into force unconsciously perhaps introduced a new dimension in inter-community conflicts. It contributed to the new classification of a rival community of 'foreigners' who were perceived as impediments in the Khasi quest for self-rule. For the first time, the question of nationality coloured the construction of a political discourse based on homogenous geo-political spaces and exclusivity. Hill areas came to be marked on ethnic lines as exclusive zones and multi-ethnicity was viewed as transgression of community spaces. Violence was viewed as a legitimate means to homogenise geo-political and social spaces, in the name of protection of community interests. In the hill areas, tribal interests have been recognised as paramount, to the detriment of the other communities that had shared these spaces with the tribals for centuries. But this distrust was short-lived as the decision of the Government of Assam to introduce Assamese as the official state language put the non-Assamese people of the composite state against the Assam government. The tribal leaders from both the hills and the plains of Assam came forward and launched a movement to carve out a hill state away from Assam.

The birth of the hill state movement made the situation amicable between the tribal and the non-tribal communities other than Assamese. Linguistic chauvinism gave a boost to a political movement, which had its violent and non-violent forms. Gradually there emerged the demand for a hill state, initially within Assam and subsequently, outside it. When protest meetings came to be organised against the police firing on unarmed anti-language bill demonstrators at Silchar—the protests being a result of the anti-language bill agitations in Shillong—there was a newfound bonhomie between the local tribal leadership and the prominent non-tribal leaders. In a meeting at the Fire Brigade ground at Laitumkhrah, both tribal and non-tribal leaders voiced their grievances against the Assam government, led by Bimola Prasad Chaliha. Prof G.G. Swell shared the platform with non-tribal leaders like Prof Kapila Chatterjee and Bimal Sen Gupta who denounced the imposition of Assamese on the non-Assamese people in Assam. While persistently demanding a separate hill state, the All Party Hill Leaders Conference (APHLC) in their sessions adopted resolutions assuring 'non-tribal residents in the autonomous hill districts that their legitimate interests will be fully safeguarded in the proposed state.' The same assurance was also repeated in the APHLC election manifesto of 1972.

But the birth of the hill state transformed the attitude of the political leadership of the dominant community. Different measures were taken by the government that steadily eroded the cosmopolitan character of the capital town and the civil and political rights of the non-tribal minority communities. The first step to contract cosmopolitan space was the introduction of Meghalaya Transfer of Land Regulation Act, 1971, which prohibited the purchase of land by a non-tribal in the state of Meghalaya or the transfer of land from one non-tribal to another. This was followed by the introduction of rules that reserved government jobs and public employment for the local tribal population. The reservation policy of the government on public employment, which was introduced in early 1972, gradually stifled the scope for public interaction and sharing of space between communities, which was imperative for the sustenance of a cosmopolitan society. Gradually, a large number of non-tribal eligible voters were disenfranchised on the eve of the elections of 1977 and a fresh electoral roll was prepared for the assembly elections of 1978. The issue of permanent residence certificate was institutionalised by government orders and issue and renewal of trading license to non-tribals became more stringent. While all these steps constricted the life and liberty of the non-tribal minority communities in the state as a whole and the capital town in particular, it paved the way for creating insular oppositional identities between communities and pitted them against one another. The hill state was perceived as a haven for the protection of the tribes, who constituted more than 80 percent of the population. The achievement of the hill state did not end the tense negotiations between the people of this area. Shillong, as the capital of the post-colonial state of Assam, was at the core of these complex negotiations. As negotiations became intense, diatribe led to violence, culminating in major conflagrations.

At the turn of the new century, the colonial cosmopolity was replaced by ghettoes with their own narratives that justified their existence. It is important to gradually shift from causal to experiential history where memory plays an important role in the reconstruction of historical narratives. It would be worthwhile to close this piece with a narrative that could become proverbial.

This is the story of a man who sought to seek his fortunes in educational service far away from his ancestral home. Babu Rukshini Ranjan Sengupta, hailing from the erstwhile Sylhet district of colonial Assam, shifted base from his ancestral home of Baro Hal village, Maulvi Bazar, in the early 1920s. While he was put up in varying temporary accommodation in the early years of his stay in Shillong, he finally found his calling as a teacher in one of the schools there. The non-tribal migrant population had established a number of educational institutions in Shillong; they were a part of the process of establishment of many of the government schools that came to proliferate in this town as well. Among the many schools that dotted the landscape, the prominent ones were the Jail Road Boys, the Laban Bengalee Boys' and the Laban Bengalee Girls' schools, the Assamese High School, the Gorkha Pathshala, the New Colony Girls' School and the Lady Keane Girls' School, apart from the Government Boys' and the Government Girls' School.

Babu Rukshini Ranjan Sengupta began to reside in Laban, a predominantly Bengali locality, and teach at the Laban Bengalee Boys' School. Over time, his engagement with the place grew and his children also decided to settle down in Shillong in various government service positions. In time, the family also acquired a small holding at Moti Nagar, much before the Land Transfer Act came into effect. There was hardly any change in the dress or demeanour of Babu Sengupta. A strong, upright man walking about in a sparkling white dhoti, he was a familiar sight to many in town. When the agitations grew in Shillong in the spring of 1979, and the atmosphere was surcharged, it hardly ruffled him. The situation was the outcome of a bandh called by the local youth organisations in protest against the assault on Khasi border villages by the Assam police. The protest turned violent and became the source of continuous turmoil in the town. Since that episode of violence, assaults on the non-tribal population in public spaces became a regular occurrence. The disturbances in town and the skirmishes between the tribal youth trying to enter and disturb non-tribal localities only aggravated over time.

While tension festered, the situation reached a new low over an incident on 22 October 1979. It began when, after Diwali, the image of the Goddess Kali was damaged while it was being taken for the customary immersion. While the matter appeared to have been resolved within the locality with the guilty tendering an apology, things aggravated when the locality meeting at the Dorbar the next day demanded the closure of non-tribal shops for seven days, collective fine on the resident Bengali community and stoppage of performance of community puja celebrations in public places. A Shillong Bandh was declared the next day. As violence increased, the government clamped a curfew in town. When the curfew was relaxed for a short while, Babu Sengupta decided to move out of his house. While locality elders, both tribal and non-tribal, cautioned him against going outdoors and that too in a dhoti which made him stand out, he was hardly one to pay any heed. He walked out, never to return home alive. As the curfew was re-imposed, Babu's family members became anxious. His sons first ventured to the local police station, registered a missing persons report, and then visited various local hospitals to search for him. Their worst fears came true, as one of his family members was to later recount. Babu was found taking his last breath at the civil hospital, having suffered multiple stab wounds. He died some time later on the same day, finally succumbing to his wounds. This death had a lasting impression on the locality and an irreparable effect on the family. While the family lost their father, the locality was never the same. People who earlier went about in a similar sartorial manner as the late Sengupta immediately shifted to western outfits and the atmosphere of trust and bonhomie between members in the locality was surely dented for some time to come.

Late Rukshini Ranjan Sengupta was probably one of the early casualties of this collapsed cosmopolitan culture. But surely he was not the only one. The others who died within the first week of this conflict along with him were Ratish Chandra Ghosh of Sunny Hill and Prof S. Goswami who, initially, like Sengupta, went missing and whose body was later recovered from Lumubah. The wave of looting, arson and intimidation that was let loose consumed many more lives. In the wave of violence, forcible evictions resulted in the swelling of refugees in makeshift refugee camps. Eventually, the situation seemed to be under police control as relaxation of curfew orders was gradually increased till it was completely withdrawn before Christmas on 11 December. While stabbing incidents became regular and non-tribal residents became insecure, prohibitory orders under Section 144 of the Code of Criminal Procedure (CrPC) continued. Rumour-mongering led to local insularity as group meetings and ghettoisation became the order of the day. Violence and intimidation continued for months. On 22 December, renewed assault and arson erupted in different localities in Shillong. Though curfew was re-imposed, it was not before eleven more lives were lost. Jail Road, a Bengali-populated area, was attacked as were the localities of Pynthorumkhrah and Lumparing. Many shops belonging to the non-tribals were attacked and gutted. Although the situation was brought under control with the Army taking over the law-and-order duties, the town was never the same again.

Although the situation became apparently normal with the passage of time, these incidents had their aftermaths. Community relations in general became polluted with an air of suspicion and hatred. Rumour and rhetoric combined to poison common minds. Violence and forcible eviction from homes created panic, leaving people with no choice but to relocate to localities predominantly inhabited by their own community members. The town became completely transformed from a cosmopolity to a collection of ghettoes. Non-tribal settlers who had descended to Shillong in the nineteenth century and early twentieth century sold their properties and relocated outside the new state. Small business holdings shut shop. Despite the uncertain future that stared them in the face, they were certain that security of life took greater precedence than livelihood issues. Out-migration of non-tribals, especially the middle class, however, did not contribute to the recession of movements against the non-tribals—these continued in the name of 'anti-foreigner' agitations.

In the last four decades and a half, the character of the town has undergone a complete transformation, something that can primarily be ascribed to the violence that has become institutionalised as a result of three major communal conflagrations and a number of minor ones since 1979. One is often reminded of what Meghna Guha Thakurta had written in a different context: '...violence should not be always measured by external acts of murder, loot or abduction. ...it was the fear of being persecuted, the fear of being dispossessed, the fear of not belonging that caused many to flee rather than actual incidents of violence.' If the Census is any indicator, then there is no doubt that between 1971 and 1991, the tribal population of Shillong increased from 41.47 percent to 53.13 percent while in the same period, the non-tribal population has declined from 58.53 percent to 46.87 percent. Mistrust gave way to diatribe and diatribe to violence, reflected in major conflagrations.

The first violent engagement came about in 1979, where the Bengalis were identified as the principal adversaries. This was followed by the conflict with the Nepalis, who were viewed as the new adversaries in 1987, and then came the clash with the Biharis in 1992. While the cause for these riots could be contested, there could be little disagreement that these three major conflagrations and many minor ethnic clashes ensured the collapse of cosmopolitan Shillong. The magnitude of violence had a decisive impact on non-tribal minds. If the B.N. Sharma Commission Report on the 1992 riots was to be followed, then in 1979 alone, 34 persons of the non-tribal communities lost their lives. According to the reported cases, the number of wounded was as many as 145; the number of shops and establishments looted were about 225; as many as 9 houses were gutted and 50 partially damaged by arson; the number of families evicted were 143; and the number of displaced were 1500 scattered in 6 camps. The riots of 1979 started the anti-foreigners agitation in Meghalaya, when the local member of Parliament opposed the demand of some of the non-tribal civil society organisations for rehabilitation of the riot-displaced. For the first time, the slogan 'REFUGEES ARE FOREIGN NATIONALS' resonated in Shillong after the formation of Meghalaya. The anti-foreigners' agitations have been the core of any anti non-tribal movement in Shillong ever since. According to the Sharma Commission Report, the conflict between the local tribals and the non-tribals had became a regular feature since 1979, and in the decade 1981–1991, as many as 100 non-tribals lost their lives in sporadic ethnic conflicts. Casualties were recorded on the side of the tribals as well. But these were comparatively fewer in number. Violence gave way to more violence and became a cause to justify further ethnic polarisations and conflicts. In 1992, the number of tribals who lost their lives were 3, whereas as many as 27 non-tribals were killed as a result of this riot.

Hill areas came to be marked along ethnic lines as exclusive zones and multi-ethnicity was viewed as transgression of community spaces. Violence was viewed as a legitimate means to homogenise geo-political and social spaces, in the name of protection of community interests. In the hill areas, tribal interests have been recognised as paramount, to the detriment of the other communities that had shared these spaces with the tribals for centuries. Though homogenisations of spaces have militated against cosmopolitanism, both in philosophy and practice, Shillong as the capital of the Khasi Hills District could not escape this trend and remain an insular island. This was not just any ordinary town, but the core of the Khasi imagination of their configured modern polity. This paper is only an attempt at writing the story of the social history of the transformation of this colonial place, from its emergence as a colonial hill station to its becoming a colonial and post-colonial capital, and its subsequent impact on the space and its people.

References

Sinha, A.C. Sinha, Chacko, P.M. and Aier, I.L. *Hill Cities of Eastern Himalayas.* New Delhi: Indus Publishing Company. 1993. pp. 63-97.

Baruah, A.K. 'Ethnic Conflicts and Traditional Self-Governing Institutions: A Study of Laitumkhrah Dorbar.' Crisis States Programme, London School Of Economics, London: Working Paper no. 39. 2004.

Goswami, B.B. *Cultural Profile of Shillong.* Calcutta: Anthropological Survey of India, 1979. pp. 4–31.

Lyngdoh, C. Reuben and Gassah, L.S. 'Meghalaya Decades of Inter-Ethnic Tension.' *Economic and Political Weekly.* 29 November 2003.

Syiemlieh, D.R. *British Administration in Meghalaya: Policy and Pattern.* New Delhi: Heritage Publishers. 1989. pp 138–139.

Karna, M.N. *Social Movements in North-East India.* New Delhi: Indus Publishing Company. 1998. pp. 119-120.

Report of Justice B.N. Sarma Commission of Enquiry of the Disturbances at Shillong, 1992.

PHENOMENON OF IMPUNITY

Terror Regime, Human Rights and Political Injustice in Manipur

Thounoujam Brinda

Is there a possibility of a better society without 'forced nationalism'? The discriminative and destructive policies coloured by the deep-seated racism with which India treats the people of the North-East and its role in alienating these people further from India is undeniable. The militarism, gross human rights violations, rampant destruction and plundering of human and natural resources is facilitated by obnoxious corruption and bad governance, which work harmoniously to keep the people backward, ignorant and suppressed. There is a price to be paid for not subscribing to Indian nationhood. The wergeld for taking a human life is on an average ₹1,50,000 in Manipur. It can go up to ₹5,00,000 depending on the nature and background of the death and victim. For decades, Manipur has been a violent theatre of state military and civil administration under India. Thousands of extra-judicial executions, forced disappearances, mass public executions, rape, sodomy, sexual harassment, illegal detentions, forced evictions and displacements, torture, chemical war, looting and plundering and destruction of our natural resources and life are some of the phenomena that have been taking place in Manipur, in direct relation to the military or through their collaboration with the civil administration of the state with absolute impunity provided by legislations that violate India's Constitution and the Universal Declaration of Human Rights, primarily, to begin with.

A Brief Recapitulation of the History of Who Waged War on Democracy of Manipur

Manipur became a constitutional democracy in 1947. It adopted its written Constitution on 26 July 1947, under which a democratic election was held in 1948 through Universal Adult Franchise. Thus, the people of Manipur had a popular responsible government in the Manipur State Legislative Assembly (MSLA) by 1948. The king of Manipur became a constitutional hereditary monarch. Amidst the backdrop of several collusive plans to annex Manipur, in September 1949, the Indian government invited the king of Manipur to Shillong on the false pretext of discussing certain issues. Immediately upon reaching Red Lands, the royal residence in Shillong, the state police responsible for the king's security was dispensed with and the king was put under siege by the Indian military (Jat Regiment) under the 'full knowledge' and command of the civil authorities present there. In fact, the following facts classify it as a characteristic military coup. There was liberal use of confinement, coercion and blackmailing from 18–21 September 1949 on the king to pressurise him into putting his seal and signature on the pre-drafted Instrument of Accession prepared by India. The king was given no opportunity to consult and obtain the consent of the MSLA and the people. Under duress, the king was forced to sign the Instrument of

Accession on 21 September 1949. Officially, Manipur was merged into the Union of India on 15 October 1949. The MSLA was dissolved.

Manipur, from being a sovereign state, was reduced to a Part C state under the Indian rule. The sovereign state of Manipur was transferred to the charge of a nominated major general by India. India claims its legitimacy over Manipur through the instrument they choose to call the Merger Agreement Treaty between Manipur and India. With no accepted legal ratification, the legitimacy of the treaty has been a bone of contention between Manipur and India that India has refused to acknowledge. The dissent and resistance towards this forceful annexation have been dealt with state repression under the partnership of military and civil administration by suspension of fundamental rights of the people of Manipur. The stage was set for resistance.

Freedom of speech was curtailed and heavy militarisation followed. For want of space, only a few cases are cited here to illustrate how the Indian state has used undemocratic means and brutal military force to suppress the resistance and democratic demands of the people of Manipur. The Manipur Communist Party, led by Hijam Irabot, and the Manipur Socialist Party opposed the forced annexation of Manipur by India. They wanted the people to decide whether to merge with India or not and the document has not been discussed in public freely. Hijam Irabot started an armed Communist movement in 1948. The movement was crushed militarily and it came to an end with the death of Irabot in 1951. Mao agitation against the merger in 1948 was brutally suppressed by the police, killing one and injuring several. The demand for statehood from 1949 to 1972 was dealt with a heavy hand. When statehood finally came in

1972, it was considered too late by the Manipuri youths.

The 1960s saw the rise of armed resistance movements again. In the name of national security, fighting insurgency and maintenance of law and order, the state is systematically empowered by its legislations to repress any dissent violently, using military, paramilitary, state police and civil administration. So far, in all the discourses that have been made on killings during law and order situations, any discussion on civil accountability is left out altogether. From national issues, multiple communal and ethnic tensions sprung up under the rule of India. The military approach adopted by India to suppress the armed insurgency and democratic dissents in the region have yielded widespread massive human rights violations. On 15 October 1949, Manipur had five police stations and seven outposts with a total strength of 310 civil police and 13 Manipur Rifles personnel. Reportedly, Manipur today is manned by over 30,000 Manipur Police personnel and several unclassified strategic locations are occupied by Central forces. We do not have concrete information of the strength of Central forces stationed in Manipur. These state forces aid the civil administration in repressing any resistance that comes up while pushing through India's neo-liberal, destructive developmental projects that are devastating to the people and the environment.

At present, over thirty armed insurgent groups operate in Manipur. The state has been ruled successively by centrally appointed nominees and governments who are puppets of India. The state ruling class (members of the Legislative Assembly, politicians, contractors, bureaucrats, powerful police, military, landlords, underground groups and black market barons) is 'permitted' to loot the funds and grants (that India pays to the people of Manipur), make commissions out of development projects, facilitate the plunder and destruction. Thus, right after the forced annexation, ruthless and intensive state repression followed, marked by violent state actions, exterminations using fake encounters, forced disappearances, militarisation, widespread plundering of human and natural resources, and destruction of environment and traditional economy through corrupt governments in the state that are elected through vexed elections. These alienating policies and acts have caused more hatred, mistrust and anti-India sentiment, and have provided more justification for the self-determination struggle.

Legislations for Repression and Legitimacy of State Terrorism

Manipur was declared a disturbed area under the Assam Disturbed Areas Act, 1955. And the Armed Forces (Special) Powers Act, 1958 (AFSPA) was imposed in September 1980. These draconian laws have harmoniously worked with several repressive ordinances and laws that deal with crime and criminality as defined and approved by the state, such as: the Maintenance of Internal Security Act, 1971 (repealed) gave unbridled powers to law-enforcing agencies for indefinite detention of individuals, search and seizure of property without warrant and wiretapping. Then there was the Land Acquisition Act, 1894, that empowered the state to acquire land or in fact 'illegally displace people' in the name of *public purposes* and for *private companies*; the Prevention of Seditious Meetings Act, 1911; the Unlawful Activities Prevention Act, 1967 (the latest anti-terrorism law) with two amendments in 2008 and 2012, has increasingly empowered the state to arbitrarily brand anyone as a terrorist with more stifling and regressive but no safeguarding provisions. After several amendments, this act reincorporated the provisions of the notorious Prevention of Terrorism Act (POTA) for dealing with activities that are considered a threat to the integrity and sovereignty of India. Some of the disturbing provisions include the power of police to search, make seizure and arrest *without warrant or court order, detain accused up to 180 days without filing charge*; the National Security Act, 1980; the Terrorist and Disruptive Activities (Prevention) Act (TADA), 1985-1995 (now repealed); the Prevention of Terrorism Act, which gave too broad a definition to terrorist acts and powers to the state to criminalise people on arbitrary assumptions, the Criminal Procedure Code, the Indian Penal Code (Sections 120-B and 124-A, seditious activities and sedition, respectively); according to the Army Act, Sec 3(X), a person carrying weapons in violation of prohibitory orders in the disturbed area of Manipur is ipso facto an 'enemy.' Then there are the Assam Police Manual 'gallantry medals'; the Defence of India Act, etc. These laws have been enforced and implemented in Manipur in order to subdue and subjugate the people from determining their socio-political rights and destiny. Thus, empowered under these legislations, the state forces are provided impunity from accountability for acts that violate the basic democratic rights of the people whom India considers its enemy.

The AFSPA, Section 3, empowers the government (Centre or state) to declare any area as disturbed after which the Centre has the constitutional authority to send in armed forces to the area. Section 4 permits any commissioned, warrant or non-commissioned officer or any person of the equivalent rank in the armed forces in a disturbed area to kill, search and destroy any property, and arrest without warrant on 'suspicion'. Section 6 provides legal immunity for persons who exercise the powers conferred by the Act from the *purview of judiciary* except with the previous sanction of the Central government.

Thus, the course of justice rests in the hands of the Central government who would interfere in the matter only on the basis of political exigency suitable for Indian nationhood and its interests. The normal legal course of action, under the circumstances, becomes a political question. Therefore, the willingness or unwillingness on the part of the Central government to proceed with justice delivery is a matter of political justice or injustice. The Supreme Court of India has upheld the law as constitutional in 1997.

In the name of fighting insurgency, it has become the norm for law-enforcing agencies to kill people extra judicially in fake encounters and inflict torture with the objective to suppress the people of Manipur. There are wide allegations of fake encounter killings by the state security forces conducted in the name of fighting insurgency in the state. A fake encounter is the phenomenon of 'extra-judicial administrative liquidations' of persons, under custody or unarmed, by the Indian security forces.

While granting enormous powers and impunity to the law-enforcing agencies (military, paramilitary and state police), simultaneously, these legislations also reward them for their acts that kill, torture and oppress people on arbitrary grounds. They also provide immunity to the state forces from judicial reviews of their acts without safeguarding the civil rights and freedom of the concerned affected people.

To name some exemplary massacres: The Heirangoithong massacre, 1984—CRPF firing killed thirteen people and injured thirty-one civilians. Operation Bluebird, 10 July 1987—Assam

Rifles (AR) unleashed a reign of terror on the thirty villages in and around Oinam Village. People were rounded up in the camps, starved, tortured and humiliated. Men and women were segregated and were made to witness the torture of their family members. A woman was forced to deliver her baby in an open field in full public view while the troops jeered. Fourteen defenceless civilians were shot dead by the AR. The Tera Bazar massacre of 1993—the CRPF killed five civilians and injured several others by indiscriminate firing in retaliation to an attack on them. The RMC massacre of 1995—nine innocent civilians were shot dead by the CRPF. The Malom massacre—the troops retaliated to an attack on them and shot the civilians who were present at a nearby bus stop. Ten civilians, including a sixty-year-old woman were killed. The Ukhrul massacre of 1995, and the Churachandpur massacre of 1999 are some of the many untold massacres that are etched in the blood of Manipuris.

On the night of 10 July 2004, a strong, armed troop of 17 Assam Rifles picked up Miss Thangjam Manorama, a former member of the cadre of the proscribed Peoples' Liberation Army, from her home in Imphal East. She was tortured third degree in front of her family before being taken away from her house without issuing an arrest warrant. In the wee hours of the following morning, her naked deadbody was found with multiple bullet injuries in her private parts and thigh at Ngariyan Chingol, barely two kilometres away from a police station. Huge protests erupted against AFSPA. The historic nude protest of Meira Paibi (female torch bearers) at Kangla Fort remains testimony to how the collective sentiment of the people responded to the hurt heaped upon the dignity and plight of the victim who was raped and murdered by the Indian armed forces. The mothers stripped in front of the western Kangla Gate and dared Assam Rifles to come and rape Manorama's mothers. The state rose in flames. The AFSPA was removed from Greater Imphal Municipality area. After this incident, killings by the armed forces took a back seat. The Manipur State Police took over the primary role of liquidating people in massive fake encounters under the unified command of the oppressive regime of Chief Minister Okram Ibobi of the Congress party. The Ibobi regime from 2002 to 2017 saw the worst phase in standards of democracy in Manipur under India's rule.

Thousands have been massacred and countless disappeared, notwithstanding the untold sufferings to the innocent surviving victims. These acts are arbitrary and patronised by the Indian state for the mere end of suppressing a group of people whom they consider an enemy. These heinous acts are warnings to those who choose not to conform to the idea of Indian nationhood. Legitimate democratic dissent is thus 'legally' crushed using military might under the garb of false ideas of national security, law and order, peace, etc. These massacres, rapes and tortures stand testimony to the genocide and violent state repression the Indian state has been committing upon the indigenous people of Manipur. The defence of the Government of India (GoI) is that there is no armed conflict in Manipur and that it is an internal law-and-order problem. Paradoxically, Indian democracy has prescribed a different standard of democracy for the people of Manipur.

Crimes of the Indian Agencies in Manipur

It is common knowledge how these war crimes are committed upon the people of Manipur who are entwined in this armed conflict. The perpetrators of these crimes are openly empowered and protected by the municipal laws of India. Hence, people are governed by military laws.

The law-enforcing agents (Central and state), aided by civil administration, are empowered, encouraged by the state and are at liberty to tamper with evidence of crimes or matters related to crimes committed by them in the name of counter insurgency. Thus, 'counter-insurgency operation' is the means that justifies all acts of the law-enforcing agencies in Manipur. In all the reports lodged by the police in matters related to the rapes and killings involving the state forces, the victims are reported as militants who attacked them or tried to abscond, taking advantage of the darkness and vegetation. The gist of the story is similar everywhere. India's Constitution, thus, has a different applicability for the people of Manipur.

This is a well-acknowledged fact that gross human rights violations have been meted out to the native people of Manipur, which have resulted in an untold number of unnatural deaths, especially from fake encounter killings, forced disappearances, and chemical war. Human lives are considered to be mere commodities that can be destroyed at will by the state. The most evident proof is the collective petition of a trust, the Extra-Judicial Execution Victim Families Association of Manipur (EEVFAM) in the Supreme Court of India into 1,528 alleged fake encounters. Amusingly, the defence statement of India represented by its Attorney General, Mukul Rohatgi, while opposing any investigation or enquiry into the alleged fake encounter killing cases was that these happened during a 'war-like' situation and hence, do not fall within the ambit of CrPC. With this they also openly endorsed extra-judicial executions of the people of Manipur by the state security forces of India. And the Supreme Court has struck down this proposition with the contention that it is an 'internal disturbance' within the Constitution.

The Fundamental Rights in Part III of the Indian Constitution are guaranteed to citizens and non-citizens. The proclaimed essence of all fundamental rights—the right to life and personal liberty guaranteed by Article 21 of the Constitution to the citizens and non-citizens of India—has a different application for the people of Manipur, which is amply clear from the quality of life we are being made to live under. So, a legitimate inference that can be conclusively drawn here is that Article 21 of the Indian Constitution is not meant for the people whom India considers its 'enemy'. The state infringes upon this inalienable right of the people by treating us as the enemy of the state who must be exterminated and slaughtered using all war crafts that violate its own Constitution. For example, the Universal Declaration of Human Rights, 1948; Common Article 3 of the Geneva Convention, 1949, for Armed Conflicts not of International Character; International Covenant on Civil and Political Rights (ICCPR), 1966; International Covenant on Economy, Socio and Cultural Rights (ICESCR), 1966; Convention on the Elimination of all forms of Discrimination Against Women (CEDAW), 1979; Convention Against Torture and other Cruel, Inhuman or Degrading Treatment or Punishment Treaty (CAT), 1984, etc.

India signed the CAT, 1984, on 14 October 1997, but has not ratified it nor taken steps to bring domestic laws in conformity with the convention till date. An effort on a stand-alone Torture Bill was made in 2010. The Indian state is yet to give reasons for not ratifying the CAT till date. What happened to the 'Torture Bill' in 2010 must be declassified.

The BT Road Killing, 23 July 2009: An Administrative Liquidation Live on Camera

The Manipur Police Commandos overpowered and shot dead an unarmed twenty-seven-year-old Chungkham Sanjit, killed a pregnant woman, Th Rabina, earlier, and injured five others in the heart of Imphal City that day in 2009. The incidents took place at the height of fake encounter killings in Manipur. The crimes were committed by the Manipur Police Commandos in full public view.

Chief Minister Okram Ibobi applauded this in the State Assembly: 'Haatpa nattana upai leite!' (There is no alternative to killing!) He blamed the victims for state terrorism.

Massive widespread violent protests against the brazen crime seized Imphal Valley.

In August that year, *Tehelka* magazine exposed the crime through a series of photos that show an unarmed Sanjit being accosted inside Maimu pharmacy and later, his dead body is seen being dragged out. The then Director General of Police (DGP), Yumnam Joykumar, took shelter behind the defense that nowadays such photographs can easily be fabricated in a counter affidavit submitted in court to a case filed by Rabina's family.

Based upon this revelation, Chungkham Taratombi (mother of deceased Sanjit) lodged written information with the officer-in-charge, City Police Station (PS), who refused to register an FIR based on the information without assigning any reason. Taratombi further filed a writ petition before the then Guwahati High Court, Imphal Bench, praying for direction to register the FIR based on the information she lodged. In the case, Advocate Nongmeikapam Kotiswar represented the respondents as the learned advocate general of the state.

Accordingly, Guwahati High Court passed an order directing the registration of the FIR in the last week of August 2009. Thus, the police was forced to register a criminal case.

In the counter affidavits filed to the Public Interest Litigation (PIL), the DGP denied almost all the allegations the writ petitioner made and took the stand that the official version was the correct one.

The Central Forensic Science Laboratory, New Delhi, opined that none of the photographs were edited or morphed. It also declared that the sequence of seven photographs was shot from one camera within a span of five minutes.

In the video clippings that are available in the public domain and from those broadcast on the local TV channel, the then City PS Officer-in-Charge, Y. Munal, is seen showing a 9mm Mauser Werke pistol wrapped in pink paper to the media and the public is seen claiming that the gun was recovered from the encounter site.

However, the seizure memo shows a Tanfoglio pistol.

There is no report of any inquest being conducted on the spot. No forensic expert, photographer or videographer were called to the crime scene by the police.

The case has been trapped in the judiciary. In the charge sheet submitted by the CBI, nine police personnel of Manipur Police ranging from 'constable to inspector' in rank are the accused in the case.

Thounaojam Herojit, the State Liquidator Who Turned Prime Witness

Imphal Free Press, a local daily, published the extra-judicial confession of Thounaojam Herojit, head constable of Manipur Police, on 26 January 2016. The floodgate of the dark reality of extra-judicial administrative liquidation was opened and exposed through the oral testimony of the state executioner himself, which is easily substantiated with all the available material evidences in the public domain by now.

Thounaojam Herojit made the confession that he shot an unarmed Chungkham Sanjit in the 23 July BT Road incident on the order of the then Addl SP, A.K. Jhalajit, who also told him that the order had come from the DGP and chief minister. He confessed that it was a staged encounter and that a Mauser Werke was implanted at the crime scene later.

Apart from all the material evidence available to corroborate and substantiate the confession, there was no change in the status of the case under trial. Unable to have his judicial confession recorded, Herojit swore on affidavit about the killing before an Oath Commissioner on 17 February 2016 in the presence of several witnesses and submitted the same to the Sessions Court that had been trying the Sanjit killing case.

Meanwhile, Chungkham Taratombi filed a writ petition in the Manipur High Court praying to have the case reinvestigated afresh. This writ was sent down to the Sessions Court. And Herojit was suddenly left with no lawyer. The court appointed an amicus curiea. The court totally rejected the petition of Taratombi on 30 March 2016. In spite of several new evidences that came out in the form of exhibits and witness, the truth behind the Sanjit fake encounter killing case was suppressed again for the second time. The case dragged on and the court has till date refused to accept Herojit's judicial confession, neither on prayer nor suo moto.

His confession was treated and crushed as a lie. Herojit met with a near-fatal vehicular accident near his quarters on 30 April 2016. The car he was driving was crushed beyond recognition by a pickup truck that had no license plate nor headlights on. His scalp was torn and needed 31 stitches; his right leg and arms were broken.

Herojit, being a serial killer for Manipur Police, knows his organisation in and out. The state exhausted his use after the exposure of the Sanjit killing. He became a liability to the government. He became extremely vulnerable and time was running out. He would be called to the police station and locked up for hours on end. His house would be randomly ransacked without any formal procedure.

Purportedly, the state CBI team raided Herojit's house and seized three diaries without following any legal procedure. Herojit was not given a seizure memo of the seized/stolen diaries. Till today, no one knows what happened to those diaries or what is their current status.

On the brink of starvation and complete betrayal, Herojit decided to come out with the truth, implicating himself in this infamous case.

In February 2017, a team from the CBI, Delhi reopened the BT Road Fake Encounter Killing case after duly informing the Sessions Court, Imphal West. For the first time in the history of this case, A.K. Jhalajit was summoned by the CBI team in relation to the case. Before a third interrogation, Jhalajit reported sick. He obtained anticipatory bail from the Sessions Court which was challenged by the CBI in the State High Court. The case was again referred back to the Sessions Court. A single bench of Justice Nongmeikapam Kotiswar stayed the order given by the Sessions Court for the reopening of the case and ordered the CBI not to make any coercive move on Jhalajit, including his arrest. It may be recalled here that Mr N. Kotiswar, Justice of the Manipur High Court, in whose court Jhalajit had filed the case, represented the state as the advocate general on the same matter in an earlier petition. This openly violates the core principle of jurisprudence for the right of the litigants to be tried by an impartial judge/court. The judicial bias or impropriety, conflict of interest and gross professional misconduct are stark.

Herojit has made multiple confessions on how he became a 'serial killer' for Manipur Police. He was the prized asset of Manipur police during the height of the fake encounter phenomenon in Manipur. The 23 July incident is the killing that got exposed at different levels. But, as we have seen, in spite of having the public confession and a sworn affidavit on the killing of Sanjit by the killer himself, the government has continuously tried to silence him and prevent him from telling the truth. The government has instead protected and patronised the higher officials who have played criminal roles in this state terrorism. The decline in the standard of democracy and justice under the terror regime was plainly evident. The regime was encouraged to continue for three consecutive terms with absolute majority. Firstly, the regime represented India's interests and hence is patronised by New Delhi. The government and law-enforcing agencies work symbiotically to provide protection (from accountability) to the regime head and his associates for the massive war crimes they have committed in Manipur. Over 80 percent of the total number of 1528 cases of registered fake encounter deaths in Manipur have taken place during the tenure of one regime. In spite of ample primary material evidence available on the perpetuation of state terrorism on the people, the Indian state has failed to look into or take up the issue suo moto. Instead of an honest confession to the crime, the Indian state is busy defending and justifying its state terrorism in its own judiciary as well as on international platforms.

These are the facts that briefly depict how a free kingdom was conquered and turned into a war zone. The war was waged upon the people of Manipur in 1949. Manipur had been under the rule of a centrally nominated chief commissioner. Later, Manipur's status was promoted to that of a union territory and statehood in 1972. Successive regimes have ruled the people and they are the centrally approved local elites whom New Delhi trusts. They safeguard India's interests and are the direct beneficiaries of the funds, projects and grants that are paid to the people of Manipur. The Manipuri ruling class consists of bureaucrats, big landlords, contractors, black marketers and members of the Legislative Assembly who are often elected using military, muscle and money power upon the poor, illiterate and ignorant people who do not know what a free and fair election is and what their rights are towards deciding their life and destiny.

The regime imposed a reign of terror upon the people with absolute impunity and fearlessness. Human rights violations are de rigueur, and the surviving and liquidated victims of various political crimes are being denied justice deliberately. Outrage against the government has been high. But instead of fighting together to get justice, the state-ruling elites are actively covering up these crimes they have made into an industry. Thus, these core issues of the peoples' right to decide their life and destiny are politicised and thereby sidelined. Human rights and justice have consequently become political issues, which are often misused in the name of security by self-centred political barons who become black spots that destroy the democratic ethos and the core value of justice in India.

HOME

Jahnavi Barua

Memory is a curious creature. It beguiles and bewitches and it seduces you into recasting life's events until an altered reality, with little difficulty, replaces the original. There is no deliberate dishonesty in this, it is simply that the segments of life invested with the most emotion are thrown up in relief against the paler, less significant background.

The idea of home, for instance. Home. The word provokes an almost visceral response. It stirs up a hornet's nest of feelings ranging from love, longing and joy to sorrow, grief, anger and even bereavement. Wars have been fought, riots incited and nations divided by the emotion this idea inflames. In my own life, the thought of home has been a compelling one, a constant companion that I have carried around with me every day in some distant corner of my awareness. And not just the notion of home but the other thoughts that it ineluctably, but invisibly, brings in tow: belonging and unbelonging, homelessness, margins, centres, mainstream and other such uncomfortable constructs.

Against a natural inclination, I have led an itinerant life: my father was in the civil service, my husband a banker and in the wake of their frequent postings I have packed up and unpacked a home often enough for the word to evoke strong emotion. Too often I have entered a new class in a new school at mid-term or have walked into a clutch of unfamiliar women at a bank dinner. At these instances, one of the first questions I have invariably had to field is the one about where I was from. Not an unusual question in itself, the discomfort lay in how frequently I had to face it. This repeated examination of home made me feel shiftless. I would have liked to have led a less wandering life, one which allowed me a longer run in any town or city thus permitting connections to people and places to mature and solidify. Anyway, when questioned, without thinking I would reply, Assam, and then after a pause, Shillong.

Home was always Shillong. Home was the wooden house in Laban, built by my great-grandfather, Kamala Kanta Barua. Sometime in the late 1890s, my great-grandfather moved from Dergaon in the Golaghat district of Assam to Shillong. It was inevitable that he come here, since he worked for the Government of Assam and under British rule Shillong was the capital of the state of Assam and the centre of all administrative and political affairs. This was the first significant migration in our family in hundreds of years and the one that shaped the arc of my life. In the first few years after my great-grandfather arrived in Shillong he lived in various rented houses, all in the neighbourhood of Laban, a place where many Assamese who had moved to Shillong from the plains of the Brahmaputra converged in. It was here that my grandfather, Bhabani Kanta Barua, was born in 1911. He was one of seven children. After renting places for many years, in 1916, my great-grandfather bought a small cottage on a large plot of land from a local Khasi gentleman in the now familiar locality of Laban. There was now a permanent home in Shillong, something that meant a great deal to the family who had so far only a temporary place in it. This pine house was named Kamala Kareng, after my great-grandfather. Kamala's Palace, albeit a modest one. In the years to come, Kamala Kareng was to become the nerve centre of a rambling, extended clan and for many—and quite emphatically for me—it would represent home in every sense of the multidimensional word.

The family continued to live on in Shillong, although in an interrupted fashion, for the next fifty-six years. The nature of my great-grandfather's work and after him, my grandfather's and father's (they were all civil servants) took them to other places. But not for long and it was with a sigh of relief and joy they would drive up the narrow, winding road back to Shillong. When I was born in the winter of 1967, three generations of the family—my great-grandmother, my grandparents and my parents—were all living together in Kamala Kareng. With my arrival, the fourth generation made its way into the old family home.

A lot of life had been lived by the time I was born. My great-grandfather had died fairly young, and although he had distinguished himself at work and been awarded the title of Rai Bahadur for his efforts, he left behind a widow with a young family—the oldest boy still in college—and very little money for them. Hard times were in store for the bereft family. In addition to financial difficulties, in the succeeding years, two of my grandfather's brothers died—the older mysteriously drowned in the Brahmaputra, his body never recovered; another of a sudden, fatal bout of fever leaving my grandfather to take on the responsibility of the family. He met these challenges with his characteristic determination and discipline. To cut a long story short, after a period of some difficulty, he qualified for the Indian Police Service and that brought some of the family's worries to an end. In 1956, my grandfather returned to Shillong—and Kamala Kareng—for the last time, eventually retiring from there as Inspector General of Police in 1969. Towards the end of this stint in 1967, my father joined my grandfather in Shillong with his own small family. He had, after a circuitous childhood in the lee of his father's postings, graduated from St. Stephen's College in Delhi and thereafter, having cleared the civil service examination, opted to join the Indian Administrative Service in his home cadre of Assam and Meghalaya.

In 1967, Kamala Kareng was once again, happily, filling up to the rafters. The old house had changed somewhat in the meantime. As the family grew, there was need for a bigger house and from pine trees felled from a plot of land the family had in Upper Shillong, more rooms had been added to the old cottage. The result of this endeavour was a charming but not a very organised assortment of rooms which nevertheless served well the purpose of housing the large family. It was into this honeysuckle festooned house with a magnificent magnolia in the front garden and the famously abundant pear tree in the back that I arrived. This is where memory intervenes with its charming confabulations, playing its innocent tricks on the mind. I always say I was born in Shillong, and in a sense I was, but the fact was that my mother had come down to Gauhati—as it was known then—to her mother's house for the actual birth and I was, in the end, born in Gauhati in the Satribari Mission Hospital. Of course, after my birth we both returned immediately to Shillong and into the heart of the family. And a large bustling family it was, for in addition to my great-grandmother, my grandparents, my parents and I, there were always members of the extended family living temporarily within Kamala Kareng's warm walls.

And I loved it. I loved the warmth generated by this

confluence of people. On long cold evenings, the family along with the odd visitor from the neighbourhood gathered around the blazing fireplace and the air was thick with talk and laughter and the delicious smells of food being passed around the gathering. The kitchen was always bubbling and sizzling with never ending pots of tea being filled and snacks being fried. There was a constant coming and going and for a child there was always a friendly pair of arms to run to, a warm lap to lay one's tired head down in.

Kamala Kareng was only the nucleus of a wider family network in Shillong. In the Laban area lived children of my grandfather's only two surviving siblings, his two sisters, as did other family descended from the Dergaon branch. And there was more: my father's maternal grandfather too had his home in Shillong, in the lower reaches of Lachumiere, and more members of that branch lived in the neighbourhood. Just a little farther afield was my mother's family home. Although, by the time I was born, her family no longer lived there having moved down to Gauhati a few years after her father's early and unexpected death. My maternal grandfather had built an elegant double-storeyed wooden house on Nongrimba Road in Laitumkhrah, a gracious, vast house with its gables and sloping roof—my mother's home that I had never been inside but only admired from outside in later years. My mother's older sister and her family were still in Shillong and they lived at the summit of Upper Lachumiere, a spot with splendid views of Shillong spread out below. Much visiting took place between all these households and life was busy, powered by an energy that was unflagging.

Beyond the family there was Shillong itself to love. How could one not love this alluring town? Its elegant pine clad hills brushed the sky while murmuring brooks crisscrossed their flanks. The air was crisp, carrying with it the perennial scent of pine and of flowers in bloom: honeysuckle, magnolia and climbing rose. Quaint Assam type houses nestled in gardens bursting with colour: dahlias, camellias, hollyhocks, snapdragons, poppies, pansies, larkspurs, candytufts and roses that lay heavy on the tin rooftops. Ward Lake at the centre of town, a small jewel with its still green waters. And in the distance, the vast and mysterious Umiam Lake. There was something special about this place and its citizens mirrored this unique spirit with their tireless energy and good cheer. There was often laughter drifting out of the pretty cottages that lined the streets and most people seemed to smile as often as they breathed.

While it may seem remarkable that a child as young as two or three years old have any recollection of these very early times, I possess unusually clear memories of this period. Memories that cast a disproportionately long shadow. It is no coincidence that even today any perfume that catches my attention is one that builds around a core of magnolia, jasmine or honeysuckle. It does not need much investigation to fathom why I feel suffocated if I have to live in a house without a view. It is no surprise that if you were to offer me the choice of a vacation on a beach or of a holiday in the hills, it would be to the hills I would run.

Memory may seem to be a whimsical creature dancing to its own random rhythm, but that guise is just part of its trickery, a way to befuddle the helpless humans at its disposal. For memory is anything but arbitrary and the cues, the stimuli it sends out are anything but irrational. There is always a reason behind the shapes our memories finally assume and in the course of sifting through my own, I have managed to untie some formidably tangled knots. The intense warmth and comfort of familial life as was lived in Kamala Kareng in those years—and although we did not know it then, those would be the final years of the family's residence there or in Shillong after nearly eighty years of being there—imprinted itself indelibly on my young mind. In 1970, my father was posted to Haflong, another hill town, headquarter of the newly created North Cachar Hills district. My brother was born during the stint in this remote but beautiful town. There, in a cavernous colonial bungalow atop a steep hill I built upon my memories of hills and home and when we returned to Shillong in 1972, home was unassailably hills and mist billowing in through open windows and home was doors slamming as the wind raced mischievously through the house. Home was falling asleep to the patter of rain on corrugated tin roofs, clutching on to the warmth of the last embers in the fireplace. Home was peaches and pears and plums from the backyard, and home was the intoxicating scent of pine. Home was being in the heart of family, in the shelter of Kamala Kareng.

In 1972, the states of Assam and Meghalaya finally separated. The old Assam had already fragmented, many new states had been created in the preceding years—Nagaland, Mizoram and Manipur among others—but when Meghalaya was created the immediate consequence was the relocation of the capital of Assam from Shillong to Gauhati on the Brahmaputra River. This was not a smooth or easy transition. For all those making the move down to Gauhati, it meant an uprooting from their homes in Shillong. I was too young at that time to comprehend what was going on and fortunately, the turbulence in the city did not find its way to my family.

I know now that Shillong at that time had been aflame with strong local sentiment. Many of the local people, those ethnically of the place, had resented for years the waves of migration into their town and they now expressed their feelings openly and often, belligerently. I understand well how they must have felt. While people are willing to welcome a reasonable number of migrants into their homeland, they grow anxious when they sense they are being overwhelmed. There is a sharp escalation of collective anxiety and unease at losing an identity and ancestral lands, a combination of emotion that can only erupt in an explosion. I understand well these concerns but there is another perspective to consider.

The fate that befell Shillong is a fate common to many a capital city. By virtue of being the capital, a town or a city becomes the heart of that region: the administrative machinery is located here, the political institutions, too, and businesses take root in the shadow of these monoliths seeking sustenance from their proximity. People working in the government but naturally move to its epicentre. Business people follow; they all build homes and raise families. Schools are established to educate the children of these families, colleges follow, the arts and culture flourish and this is how life flows. My great-grandfather had little choice in leaving his home in the Brahmaputra valley and building another in Shillong, nor did many of the other thousands of Assamese who found their way there. Once the British had decreed Shillong the capital and set up base there, the rest was inevitable. Had they decided to establish a capital in Jorhat, that quiet, provincial town would have been overwhelmed too. All capital cities today are struggling with this same situation: one of waves of migration battering at their weary shores like waves against a crumbling cliff.

By the time the states separated in 1972, our family had been residing in Shillong for nearly eighty years. Where else would we call home? The paddy fields of Dergaon had slowly receded from the family's collective consciousness. Of course, they would always be remembered and Dergaon would always be home, but it was more of a home emeritus for those of us who had never lived there. More recent memories had replaced those older ones and they had deftly been woven into a tightly meshed tapestry that unequivocally read home.

I wonder sometimes what went through the minds of the family as they packed up a lifetime in preparation for the descent to Gauhati. It was in Shillong that my grandfather had been born. He had done his schooling in Laban and in that same school my father had received his education too. My mother had lived most of her childhood in Shillong, passing out from school here. Weddings, funerals, births and festivals had been celebrated in these narrow winding streets for nearly a century now. This was the only home they had known. Did they sense that this was no ordinary move, not simply another posting in the course of a civil service career? That in a few years, unlike the pattern in decades gone by, the family would not return and reunite in Kamala Kareng? That they would never again live in Shillong? I wonder if they realised that without any of the noise and fanfare that accompanied the more visible partitions they too were pulling out, once and for all, roots that had burrowed deep into the hills of Shillong.

Most of my family, while being friendly, sociable, reasonably good tellers of stories and thus interesting conversationalists, were never very expressive when it came to emotion. There was and is—like in many families in India, I suspect—a wariness of unseemly emotion and consequent intimacy. I was too young—five years old—when we left Shillong to even understand what was happening let alone pick up on emotion felt by the others in the family or feel any grief myself. A slow steady sense of bereavement was something that came to me later. And also the unsettling realisation that while for me Shillong was undisputedly home, others may have perceived me as an outsider there.

The family did not speak of loss in the years after it left Shillong and neither was there any resentment at the events or people who had precipitated this relocation. There could be many reasons for this, apart from a natural reticence. For a start, unlike the case with many other Assamese, Bengali and other non-tribals, events around our family's leaving had been largely peaceful. In fact, the direct reason for our departure was not any tension that the family felt directed at it but the fact that my father had been appointed Deputy Commissioner—also called Collector in other parts of India—of Gauhati, rather of Kamrup District of which Gauhati was the headquarter. Gauhati was also now the new capital of the new Assam.

Another reason for the turbulence-free move and thus the lack of conversation around it was that there were already a substantial number of relatives settled in Gauhati and in a sense, it was already half a home. My mother's family had moved down to Gauhati before 1972 and the separation of states. They had left when her father died, soon after he had retired. When we arrived in Gauhati, they were present to sweeten our settling in: her mother, my grandmother who was to play a pivotal role in all our lives; her brother and his family and a married older sister and her family. Lastly, but not insignificantly, the fact that my grandfather, sometime in the '50s, had built two houses side by side in the very central location of Uzan Bazaar helped alleviate any sense of uncertainty that the family could have felt. There was another home waiting for us when we needed it. In fact, although we did not know it then, in days to come these two houses would step in to fill in the void left by the loss of Kamala Kareng. The gracious neighbourhood of Uzan Bazaar—a locality although built around the famous Bazaar, not bazaar-like at all with its shady lanes and old Assam type houses set in rambling green compounds—that stretched from the south bank of the Brahmaputra to the Twin Ponds, the Jorpukhuri, was to eventually become another home.

However, it was not Uzan Bazaar that we came to from Shillong. It was the DC's bungalow we moved into. This magnificent colonial bungalow with its immense thatched roof stood on a rise, a small hillock that directly overlooked the Brahmaputra. I did not know it then but this river was to wend its way around my unsuspecting heart and become a sort of permanent home for me. At that time, the beauty of the house escaped me. What I was instantly grateful for was the fact that it stood on a sort of a hill and possessed a view—an unparalleled one, as it so happened, of the river as it flowed through the city—and for the fact that its size meant it could accommodate three generations of our family at once. Three because, we had lost my great-grandmother by the time we moved here. The bungalow was also conveniently located in the centre of town, and soon it became the extended family home Kamala Kareng had been: an assortment of relatives came to stay and hosts of others dropped in for lunch or to grab some rest on their travels across the city. I was reassured quickly that life as I knew it, so far, was safe and sound.

Except that it wasn't. While the structure of the family seemingly remained the same, the structure of life in Gauhati was different. Life in Shillong had possessed a certain intimacy.

Perhaps, it is in the nature of towns in the hills that houses and thus the people within them lean towards each other. People tend to walk everywhere: in the neighbourhood, and often beyond it within reasonable distance and sometimes, for unreasonable distances too. I remember wandering around Laban with my grandfather, early evening rambles after I was home from school. We must have been a curious sight, the pair of us: Kokadeuta, my grandfather, a big man, six feet tall and of robust build, and I, barely up to his knees, hanging on to his fingers. These walks were a treat I looked forward to with enthusiasm. Sociable to a fault and curious about all around me, I was suitably excited at the prospect of traversing the winding, up and down lanes. I loved the wind in my face, fragrant with pine and wood smoke, and the sight of the familiar wooden houses lit up warmly against the falling dusk. There was something to be discovered around every corner: a plum tree in fruit, a pear sometimes, blackberries growing wild in a hedge; an unfamiliar car parked at a cousin's meant visitors from out of town and if I was lucky, more playmates to play with. Part of the allure of these walks were the stories Kokadeuta told me as we wound our way around the narrow lanes: stories about the houses or trees or brooks we crossed along the way. Most of the history of our large family and most of what I know of Laban and Shillong I absorbed in this casual fashion. And the highlight of these excursions: the inevitable dropping in at a relative's or friend's house, something that gladdened immensely my friendly heart and fed my always willing stomach.

The walks ceased as soon as we came to Gauhati. In later years, especially after he moved to Uzan Bazaar, to the house he called 'Manikut,' Kokadeuta actively resumed his walking. But the DC's bungalow did not lend itself to walks as it was located in the middle of a busy commercial and institutional part of town. Thus, I found myself marooned, isolated, even if within a large and beautiful compound. The view from the wide back veranda of the house—it was actually the front as these bungalows were always built back to front to take advantage of the views—was undoubtedly spectacular: the Brahmaputra wending its way westward, straddled by the metal filigree of Saraighat Bridge. The sun setting behind the bridge, with the sky and river catching fire, could compare with any of the famous sunset point scenes we see advertised today. I had no disagreement with the house. It was the isolation I had an issue with. My only playmate was my brother and he was just three. There was only one other house within shouting distance—the SP's bungalow—and his children were much older, too old to play with us. Cousins arrived to spend time with us and they were a blessing but their trips had to be planned. Every trip involved a car. The smooth fluidity of life in Shillong where I had company in our own compound and within walking or climbing distance was lost. The wanderings with my grandfather and my time with him had come to a stop. Gauhati was a larger place than Shillong but paradoxically, to my young mind, it seemed more infinitely more limited. Life seemed to have shrunk, somehow.

Homesick, I missed all the little things one is wont to in this situation. I missed the weather in Shillong, it was too hot in Gauhati. I missed the seasonal fruits, the pears and plums and peaches, and I missed the scents and smells, the pine, the honeysuckle and wood smoke. I would grow accustomed to Gauhati in time, grow to love it and the sharp feelings of loss inside me would lose their edge, but at this time, I pined for home.

The adults, too, while never speaking of loss, spoke of longing. There was much talk of the trees left behind and whenever a relative who had stayed back in Shillong, sent down a sackful of pears from Kamala Kareng or another of squash from that famously fecund vine, it became an occasion to celebrate. The fruit was sent around to other family and friends. We ate the delicious fruit in every form—raw and stewed and baked into puddings. Tales of longtime neighbours and friends, stories of school—both my parents had studied there—and of school friends regularly made the rounds. There was shaking of heads over the inimitable taste of singaras from Delhi Mistan Bhandar and the excellent quality of fabric from Uncle's Shop in Police Bazaar. And any news from Shillong was eagerly looked forward to. Some happenings roused particular anticipation, such as news of Durga Puja in the Laban Naamghor. In 1922, the first Assamese Durga Puja had been celebrated in Kamala Kareng, with a handsome donation of fifty rupees from my great-grandmother. Subsequently, the Puja moved to the nearby naamghor, but the special bond it shared with the family endured and it was and would always be missed. The mood in the family was wistful, life had changed, they sensed that and they would have to move on.

Life changed unalterably in a couple of years when we moved to a new house in the Capital Complex in Dispur. This smaller house could not accommodate all of us—we had grown, too, since my younger sister was born in the winter of '74—and my grandparents left to stay in Manikut, in Uzan Bazaar. Except for a few temporary short spells, we did not live together again. And we soon became caught up with our new lives, as is the way of the world. I settled into a new school, made new friends, some of whom would remain by my side for years to come, but I missed Shillong still. The largest loss was the rupture of the way the family had lived. I missed my grandfather more than I could have conceived, and I think I have missed his daily presence in my life ever since.

Looking back, there are some aspects of this relocation that I am grateful for. The fact that I had been too young for questions of identity—tribal, non-tribal, Assamese, Khasi, Bengali—to kick in. I had escaped feeling like an outsider in Shillong, although I realised later, I must have been sometimes considered one. And in Gauhati, the city being almost contiguous to Shillong, I did not have to explain where I had appeared from. Finally, of course, being Assamese, I did not have to struggle to explain myself.

In the aftermath of the next move, I was not to be so lucky. Within a couple of years we were on the move again—this time to Delhi, to a place far beyond familiar shores. It was an overwhelming, terrifying yet paradoxically thrilling experience. That this was a city of immense significance and power—both historical and contemporary—of heart-stopping beauty and of ceaseless energy, I understood right away. We lived down the road from the tombs of the Lodi kings in the gardens named after them and were also within walking distance of India Gate. When my grandfather came to visit we would walk along wide boulevards lined by leafy neem trees to these monuments and I have to admit, something in my soul stirred every time I gazed upon them. On the way to school, our bus passed the residence of the then prime minister, Mrs Indira Gandhi. Very often, we were made to stop as her cavalcade left her gates. I will never forget the sight of her distinctive profile, as she gazed out from her white Ambassador car. What could she have been thinking? As a young child, I knew little of her politics or even cared, but I was to think often of those brief early morning encounters in later life when from a distance her politics did touch me after all. Further down the school bus route was Teen Murti Bhavan and then the bus turned left and made its way down Shanti Path flanked on either side by embassies of all the nations of the world. I could hardly escape the significance of where I was, even if I'd tried. Delhi inveigled itself into my skin and I grew attached to it. To its mangoes in season, to jalebis, to its lavish libraries and art galleries, to its gorgeous trees, to a certain way of looking at the world, to the energy its hardworking residents brought to life. And to good friends I made along the way. Despite the heat and dust, in spite of the constant awareness that personal safety was not to be taken for granted and last but not the least, in spite of how painfully Delhi forced me to examine myself. In this city, you could hardly escape feeling like an outsider.

In the late '70s in Delhi, I was a novelty, an exotic specimen from the other side of the world. With increasing frustration and very real sorrow sometimes, I sought to clarify that I wasn't Chinese, that Assam was indeed, a part of India, and yes, we had schools and roads there. We did not only eat meat, yes, we ate paneer too. No, I did not speak Hindi but was willing to learn. I had to convince a lot of people and at the end of that battle, I had to convince myself, too, that I was Indian. I am glad I was able to do so. I am glad I did not let this small matter of identity get in the way of my affection for this unforgettable city, an affection I still feel decades later.

After having to struggle to assert my identity as an Indian, imagine my surprise when in the middle of my ninth grade, thanks to another relocation we were whisked off to

Manchester where not only was there no doubt that I was Indian, I became the quintessential stereotypical Indian. At least, at first. This was not the era of the global village and the perception of India and an Indian was a one-dimensional one. It took a while to explain to neighbours and friends that while I was robustly Indian there were all kinds of Indians and I was a certain kind. The legacy of Assam tea helped; every time I mentioned Assam, eyes would light up. Ah, where the tea grows! In the very brief while we spent in the area of Sale in Greater Manchester, we made yet another new home. One that we carry on our backs until today.

From Manchester, we headed eastwards, back home. To Delhi we thought, but after only a few months there my father was summoned back to Assam, to a state simmering with unrest. The Assam Agitation was in full flow; schools, colleges, businesses had all stuttered to a stop. The mood across the region was turbulent. That is another story in itself, a remarkable one and requires another telling but in the midst of all this turbulence I faced my own personal battle. Having arrived home, at the beginning, in a sense, I now found I had to prove myself all over again. Not to people who knew me well, but to many others I was that curious thing—an insider who was now an outsider. I was judged not Assamese enough. True, I did not read or write Assamese fluently. I left in the fourth grade and had studied Hindi instead, but I taught myself to read and write enough so I could read my grandmother's letters and the Assamese papers too. I spoke as fluently and colloquially as the next man. Or woman. I had a passion for Assamese textiles and could identify by sight many of the motifs and patterns they were woven with. I read Assamese history, I watched its cinema, I dreamt of the Brahmaputra at night and although I did not know it then, would write and publish fiction that would be rooted in its flowing waters. My heart thrilled at the sights and sounds of this much loved place and once it was clear that my years away had not lessened the intensity of my bond with this soil, I was home.

Twenty-five years ago, I came to Bangalore to work and study in St. Johns Medical College. Armed with my experience in other relocations, I came prepared to be examined like a cell under a microscope. Imagine my surprise when beyond a few polite questions, no one put me under the grill. This was a reception I had not expected and it was probably in the first few months that I told myself this was a city I could live in. If I had to live away from Assam and Shillong maybe I could consider staying on here. I have to admit though, a few other things were in Bangalore's favour. There was a certain chill in the air—in those days!—that reminded me of Shillong, and a wind that blew faithfully through the year. There were also masses of Jacaranda and the smallness of the town lent it an intimacy that was all too familiar. Twenty-five years on, I am still in Bangalore, gathering some moss. In the early years, I was in and out of the city as my husband moved around on bank postings, but in the last decade and a half, I have been here steadily growing roots into the now familiar and loved soil.

Bangalore and the relative stability I experienced here have allowed me to examine a few things I did not have the time or inclination to earlier. The question of home, for instance. Where is home? Memory as I have said earlier, blurs and softens the edges. The handful of years I spent in Shillong have cast an inordinately long shadow and I can see why, fortified as they are with years of family history. Kamala Kareng still stands in Laban, testament to the family's life story, a hundred years old this year. My father works hard at keeping it in good repair—and this is a tough battle as the old house declines steadily—and it looks smart with its fresh coat of cream paint and a new green roof. The old rose bushes still flower as do the camellia and the magnolia, and the squash vine still yields abundantly. Two years ago, I went to Shillong, for the first time with my husband and son. My parents were with us, too, and together we visited three old houses. Of course, we stopped at Kamala Kareng first. I told my son this was this was his great-grandfather's house. Then, I took him to Laitumkhrah to another great-grandfather's house—this lovely house had been sold long ago and we parked outside, admiring it for a while. On the way back to Laban, we drove past the third house, built by yet another great-grandfather of my son's. Back in Kamala Kareng, we lit candles and lamps. By happy coincidence it was Diwali that evening and as I watched my father and my son light up the house, I felt my heart fill. As if we were celebrating—not houses, although so much has been said about them this is not about houses but homes—the many lives that have been lived in this beloved town. This will always be my first home.

But not my only one. Older now, wiser too, I know that home, at least for me, is not a singular, well-defined entity. Insidiously, surreptitiously, Bangalore has become home. I look forward to the trees changing colour, shadowing as they do, the turning of seasons, the yellow tabebuias and the cool purple of the jacaranda in February; the flaming red of the gulmohar soon after as summer sets in and later in the year, heralding winter the gorgeous pink tabebuias. I look at the older houses—the ones allowed to remain—and their red-tiled roofs remind of my early years in the city. Despite the incessant traffic jams, and the dust and noise and never-ending construction, I still love the gentle city that I know lives underneath.

Besides, my son is part of the soil of this city and where my family lives cannot but be home. For the same reason, Gauhati, where I spent many long years and where most of my family still lives, is always home. There has been a disproportionately heavy presence of family in my narrative and that is not without reason. Clichéd it may be, but home is where family is.

After I began writing and publishing, a curious thing happened. My early stories were rooted in Assam and there was curiosity in Bangalore about that far away place. In the gentle style of this city, people asked about this unfamiliar place and as I told them about it, I felt I was a bridge linking these two lands, these two homes.

Home is then that shawl woven with multi-coloured skeins that I draw across my shoulders on a chilly night. That shawl is redolent with the scents of Shillong, of magnolia and honeysuckle blossom and aromatic pine. In it the Brahmaputra shimmers a silver blue while the cries of my cousins as we play hide and seek twine around it. The neem trees and laburnum lining the gracious avenues of Delhi colour the shawl tender green and sunshine yellow while the black and red of Manchester United make a brief appearance too. The kuli, the koel, hides inside and calls out that spring and Bihu and Vishu and Pongal have arrived. As it calls out, I know the yellow tabebuias in the parks and streets of Bangalore are flowering. Somewhere in its depths, the shawl also conceals a night ridden with pain, a hot sweltering night in Calcutta many moons ago. When dawn broke that morning, I found my hands holding a treasure unparalleled. My son, my contribution to the story that began in Shillong. Then Calcutta was home too. How could it not be?

Six years from now, in 2022, the hundredth Assamese Durga Puja will be celebrated in Laban naamghor. My father has undertaken to bear the expenses for that year's protima, the idol of the Devi, and has asked all of us, his children and grandchildren, to be there. I will be there with my family, my son and husband. I look forward to coming home. And bringing all my other homes with me.

CHRONICLES OF A DEATH UNTOLD

Mahua Sen

Here's a little shrine of injustice for you, Gauri Dey. Your ordinary name, of no consequence, I overheard in family whispers when I was eight or nine, growing up in Shillong, the context out of reach for my age. I hold it up today, as I imagine it may have been your last wish. Bodies throbbing with the arrhythmic final palpitations do wish that someone would come to save them. Is it thirty years already? In these thirty years nobody came to grant you immortality in the inglorious book of India's marginalised victim stories or appropriate your faceless face in alignment with the cosmetic politics of poster art. The ink from the printing machine didn't spill or boil the blood of the nation's collective conscience to the benefit of your memory. If there was any outrage, it was as strong as a local underconfident whimper. This story had no takers in India. The night didn't burn in the fire of candles, no placards delivered low blows. You were inconvenient poster-girl material. Your own people were too weak and ill-equipped to break into a suitable uprising for you. The ground they stood on wasn't theirs enough.

When I moved to Delhi after college in Shillong, even though I was not conscious of it, I had come, to claim with all naiveté, the world as an equal. I may have deceptively crafted my position as the generic Indian youngster, seeking professional opportunities, pitching to skip through the barriers of urban class and privilege in the metropolitan promised land. I may have consciously concealed the context of my identity—which was filled with the echoes of the melancholic, dejected ancestry and community of my origin—should it hinder my shot at equality. If a benevolent humanity were to erect a symbolic sculpture of the refugee, wouldn't it be a poetic paradox to assign it a square piece of land in this world? Wouldn't it be more authentic and appropriate to host it at a temporary shelter, permanently? Once the homeland is inhospitable and for the sake of survival alone, people are forced to migrate to another land, they become guests in this world. Like they appeared out of nowhere or fell out of an unidentified round disk. As the entire idea of home turns to ruins, the reconciliation of loss mixes with caution, and in that a new genre of humanity is created. A breed that stands outside, never free enough emotionally to view themselves as equal inheritors of the earth. A breed of people doomed to be guests who overstay. The echoes of this recalibration of natural entitlement passes on, one generation to another. They are insiders on the outside and outsiders on the inside.

I am such an inheritor and I have tried, quite hard, to escape the ambiguous topic of home, for the most part of my adult life. I have never felt at home, anywhere, and I always feel others own the ground more than I do. It doesn't matter where I am or how much legitimate claim I have over the space I inhabit, the absence of belonging has always been ingrained in my wiring. This condition plagues most people of the community in my generation. We are the second generation of this lineage and it's probably too soon for us to construct an indestructible notion of homeland beyond the superficiality of the material.

I am of Hindu Bengali origin and hence, I may be seen as a part of India's majority population. It is estimated that ten million people were displaced in the partition on the east and west flanks of India. I am not sure if these figures include the migration that continued over the following decades. Once the term East Pakistan was coined and a line was drawn, it was a matter of time, before the majority of the Bengali Hindu population would have to say goodbye to their own homeland, everything they had owned, created and known as themselves. Amidst riots and communal violence, post 1947, a large section of that population fled to the north-eastern part of India. Shillong was prominent because of its proximity to Sylhet. In 1971, the war escalated the urgency for the remaining Hindu population to escape another round of genocide. The loss couldn't be postponed any further.

It would have been just another story of collateral damage in the creation of a secular country built after splitting the land on communal grounds. We could have lived with the irony. Unfortunately for us, the horrors didn't end there.

The Bengali Hindu population of Shillong is the only community in India to have suffered double displacement on communal grounds, twice within a generation. We inherited the collective fate of the Punjabi Hindus of West Pakistan and the Kashmiri Pandits. In the majoritarian spectrum, if Kashmiri Pandits are the acne of secular India, the Bengali Hindu of Shillong is the genital wart. Nobody knows you have one. Also, unlike Kashmiri Pandits, the Bengali Hindus didn't stand on the right side of land ownership. There was no legitimacy in our fight. For most Indians, we are part of a majority that had rightfully moved to 'our country'. In a country like India, 'minority and majority status' are not a national standard as they are conveniently made to be but a state variable. It is a dangerous oversimplification that overlooks the nuances that exist in a mixed populace, regionally. In situations where an apparently majoritarian population finds itself in a tight spot as a minority in a state, it is basically left to fend for itself.

Siding with a state minority, which is also a national majority, is equal to being up against a state majority, which is also a national minority. Nobody wants to stand up against a national minority community. Nobody. We know what the people who do that are called. This is a major design flaw, a trick question in itself, a conceptual trap, something no person worth their liberal salt would risk their image for. This giant discrepancy in the notion of secularism lives like a tumour inside the body.

Herein lies the reason why this story is untold and why it needs to be told now.

Communal riots and attacks had become the norm in Meghalaya since 1979, and remained prevalent through the 1990s.

Within a span of less than a decade since the 1971 war, people had barely adjusted and reconciled to the idea of a new life, livelihood still on shaky grounds for most, and the second nightmare began. From the point of view of the tribal population, this was their land and suddenly there were all these people from the plains, trunks on their heads, taking over what they believed was their land.

I was born that same year that was callously earmarked. 1979 officially opened a politicised era of unprecedented ethnic violence in Shillong. It would be fair to say that when I arrived on this planet, I slipped right into the cradle of xenophobia, as unsophisticated as it always is. What had started in Assam as an anti-Bengali movement spread like a raging fire to the forests of Meghalaya where it hit a spot—non-tribals, especially Bengalis, were taking away all the resources and employment and must be driven out by all means. The vital point deemed unworthy of consideration was that we were not conquerors. We were refugees with a right to citizenship.

The Khasi-led pogrom had set itself aggressively on the path of ethnic cleansing. Shillong, the hope for another chance at life, the panacea to the hard decades of migration, had turned into a replay of a nightmare still fresh in memory. Life for the community was anyway a desperate, half-alive effort at rehabilitation and reinvention with a complete loss of socio-economic and cultural stability.

I was probably a less than a month-old little animal, when the mobs arrived right at our doorstep. The community had prepared itself; there was a hideout ready in my uncle's bungalow, which could be reached from our still-under-construction house through the way of the drains in the backyard. The women and children slipped out in a moment's notice, while the grown men gathered and fought with whatever they had, rods and construction materials, knives and sticks. This story could have had many versions of outcomes. One of them could have been that I wouldn't be living to tell this tale.

Growing up in a typical Shillong East Bengali house, you wondered where that invisible, unspecific, home-shaped black hole was, because there surely was one. There was a shadow of morbidity, an aura of a troubled past, a loss of faith that slipped out like a bra strap, through all the laughter and signature dark humour, personal achievements and celebrations. There was something that no compensation could permanently dispel. Untreated Post-traumatic Stress Disorder and multiple reinforcements of the same ordeal, make up for a very grim inner community landscape. There was also, thus, this sense of urgency in the children of this trauma, to not just steal happiness from wherever it may exist, but bring it back like a magical cure.

The xenophobic persecution ran over two decades, from 1979 all the way to the late '90s. That is pretty much my entire childhood. All throughout, isolated violence was a big part of the lexicon, but 1987 was organised. It had a city to claim from the hands of 'foreigners' like us. 1987 was the year of holiday of my schooling life. Schools remained shut the entire year. The cycle was of communal violence, curfews, people selling their homes and leaving, more communal violence, more curfews and more people leaving. Children have a lighter experience of life events compared to adults. We were secure, in spite of what the environment was and nobody told us the worst details. I created my narrative by eavesdropping on adult conversations, solely with the intent of knowing whether school would be shut. My interest came with a simple and single-point agenda. I was eight years old and I didn't want to go to school. Two of the cool things that happened to me then were that I learnt phrases like 'President's Rule' and 'Flag March'. In hindsight, it all piles up in a corner for you to look at one day, when you cannot explain some irrational fear or mistrust that you cannot write off as a quirk in your personality. 1987 was that year for me, when the ink penetrated more layers than I would know for many decades.

What happened in the long-term exposure to an environment of violence happened below the surface. The element of mistrust in the surroundings and a sense of not belonging took hold slowly. We microdosed fear and customised the irrationality of 'something can go wrong anytime.' These things became part of our nature, the weirdness to our temperament, the self-deprecation in our assertion of identity. For me and others like me who grew up this way, the trauma wasn't a direct brush with death but a slow poisoning of an unequal relationship in the environment where we were forming ourselves. We carry in us the stories that we heard around us and we are in little ways the stories we carry. If you peep into my head, you will find this old Bengali man boiling sugar syrup in a large cauldron. A band of rioters break in and throw a living man in it, to boil to death. These things happened to people we know. Stories of people torched alive, burnt with petrol bombs, beaten up, driven out of burning homes in the middle of the night—these are the things our worlds were made of. To be beaten up on the street for no reason, except that one was non-tribal, was as normal as watching *Yes, Prime Minister*. There was confusion about male brawling and the communal context, and after such a long-drawn period of normalising, complaining was seen as a dent in manhood. If you got beaten up, you went home quietly and didn't make much noise about it. In two decades, isolated violence had become part and parcel of life in Shillong. We could live with it. Or leave. The hatred had lost its reason by then; it was absurd, as absurd as my favourite Herzog classic.

So, Gauri Dey, have you seen a movie called Even Dwarfs Started Small*?*

This unnerving and confounding Werner Herzog classic, for the uninitiated, is a film in which midgets in a remote reformatory, seek senseless fun through hedonistic destruction.

The film is a conduit as the midgets unleash their wrath, rampaging, blurring the line between destruction and addictive excitement. Their panicky cackle never leaves you, ever. Participation in acts of violence and destruction can and does trigger inexplicable euphoric release. The spark of hatred is washed over by more bombastic sensations of confused elation. To explain mob behaviour later, with ideology and politics, even if it may have been the instigation, is, in all truth, like a healthy man begging on crutches. Violence is inflicted more for the fleeting sense of heady ecstasy; hatred is a mere sanction.

Gauri Dey, the pregnant wife of a college professor in Shillong, was walking home with her husband one evening in 1987, the black year in the history of Shillong. In a stroke of bad luck, they were met with a group of men, who soon acquired the colour of a mob. Gauri Dey was gangraped, her foetus torn and her husband forced to watch the dreadful dance of racism, escalating into the destruction of his whole world. Ripples of utmost shock and horror spread through the Hindu Bengali community in Shillong. I was too young to have memories of it, but I remember that was the first time I was initiated into the world of rape. I didn't know what it was but I sensed it was something dark and unmentionable. I think there were some minor protests; that was all. There wasn't fair reportage. There was no national outrage.

I heard recently from a friend who, many years ago, happened to meet a guy who claimed to be in the mob. He had told my friend with nonchalance, that there was no personal vendetta. It was an unexpected adventure. The gang of men turned into a mob, the energy escalated fast and blood rushed and terrible things happened. In Shillong, terrible things had been happening for a while.

Let's go back to the great '60s, except that they were not so great for my father; they were quite terrible. By the late '60s, my father, then a bright young university mathematics topper, had come to understand that his opportunity to study at IIT Kanpur would have to be shelved. Home as it was, on the other side of the line was not going to hold steady for long. He reconciled with a job with the government and held fort for the fleet of people who were arriving for good, with nothing on them but grief. The only calculation that he needed to make was how to put thirty-six square meals on the table. There were eighteen dependents, of all ages, that needed not just food, but help and support to rehabilitate themselves. My mother hadn't experienced the mess of Partition directly before marriage. Her father, a retired British Air Force doctor, who worked at a tea estate in Assam, was already on Indian soil for most of his working life. Married at twenty-one, she came into a house where her first experiences were of community cooking. The situation peaked in 1971. My parents, left with no choice, completely surrendered to the care and recovery of anyone who showed up at their door. All the way into the late '80s, our home, on any given day, had a steady number of eighteen people. My parents adopted young relatives and raised and educated them along with their own kids. I cannot imagine the toll it takes, for this kind of selfless service, and yet, some duties cannot be abandoned. What does a person in that position blame if not the Partition, for ruining their past and their future?

The period and circumstances of the rehabilitation of the community as a whole was so short and so frugal that the intellectual and political leadership couldn't have been developed. As a result, the community stayed more under-represented, under-confident and, above all, without the luxury of a wider network within the larger fabric of India. There weren't any spectacular opportunities and the resignation, however unbearable, had become the signature of the community. The generation of our parents was busy rebuilding the idea of a home, holding our lives together, fighting with sticks, putting food on the table, and sacrificing their own comforts for the future of their children.

The community grew insular, more for self-preservation and out of fear, and we, as children, found enough room for play within that canopy. Schools, when open, bore no scars of the hatred outside and kids from all communities playfully coexisted, sharing the same joy over an untimely school bell. It was only when I went to college that the city opened itself up, with all its treasures and dangers, side by side. The rebellion of my age also readied me to officially disregard, for the first time, all the tacit territorial boundaries that had been agreed upon, at home. This is the time I invented my Shillong—bottle-green in colour, orange-grey skies, endless pavements to walk on, poets, and a cemetery no one went to. New friendships were forged and the friend circle expanded exponentially, both in size and in our desire for the world. The deepest ones formed over the exchange of copies of *Mad* magazine, poems and music. We wanted to be poets. The plot of the story had completely changed. With borrowed beatnik influences, the roughness of the land could be borne and used to construct a different imaginary world for the self. A world where I was not a Bengali Hindu.

The new young people, as the world always does deploy to right its wrongs—we had signed the rough peace treaty. This was the beginning of the Shillong that I have never lost since. The Shillong of my childhood, in spite of the violence outside, was a more benign, soft place. This Shillong of my youth was a more hostile version of it. It was a rewarding time to dilute one's identity and we all did it. I lived through it and I saw it happen. The Khasi Students' Union (KSU) that was at the helm of the pogrom was an organisation we all had grown to fear. In college, I befriended the head of the KSU as he befriended me, even if it meant just a polite acknowledgement of each other in the college canteen. The Kargil conflict was full-blown at that time and a captain called Clifford Nongrum had been martyred. A huge ocean of people landed up at the fire brigade football stadium in Shillong to show respect. Of course, I arrived there, too, and bumped into my friend from the KSU. In we walked, through the intimidating crowd, him behind me, his arms stretched out in protection. It was a good place already.

Over these years, there have been incidents of isolated violence, people being torched alive on communal grounds, multiple times. But Shillong is no longer an angry, hateful place. You do live with a strange dichotomy, an unkind history, on both sides, but it requires no attention. There have always been inter-community friendships and deep bonds and Shillong in the end is all about those little places of kinship and love. On my last trip home, I was returning from my morning run when it started to pour. Strangely, I was at the exact spot where I had once watched my friend getting thrashed for being Bengali. So, as I ran along, getting soaked, a voice called out to me, shyly offering to take me under her umbrella. History often rewrites itself, in the same spot. Shillong is home and there is no dispute in that. Yes, the whole psychological nervousness around the idea of home does continue, as a part of my nature, but if there were any place in the world that defined my belonging, it would be here. Over these years, I have reached a position where what happened in Shillong is less important than how the world chose to ignore it.

Eventually, brutality will always be outplayed only by one other thing—the indifference of others towards that brutality.

As descendants of refugees are bound to ask, who owns the land more than whom, and why?

Is it sufficient to lay claim first, and if that were true, then how can the migration of the partition be justified? Why does the liberal reasoning that swings in favour of Azad Kashmir despise the average Marathi Shiv Sainik for demanding Bombay for Marathis? Where is universality in that metric?

The narrative of liberalism is upheld by a thread that catalogues and references cases of minority atrocities, rightly, as a system of checking and ensuring that they aren't normalised or repeated. It is understood that the nature of media was different back then and in the absence of Twitter and Facebook, information spread and mobilised differently. However, there have been incidents in the recent past, at least three that I remember, of people being torched alive in Meghalaya. Those are incidents of communal violence. Those are incidents where people have been targeted and killed because of the community they belong to.

Doesn't the civil society of today, armed with its Twitter handles, require to question, catalogue and reference it for the same purpose of ensuring that such things are not repeated? If targeted Hindu communities with minority status do not qualify for the same consideration, is it not fair to ask, what is the narrative of secularism?

When concepts begin to show major design flaws and people are unwilling to admit them, address them, and rewrite them because somewhere they have built their identity around these concepts, and to acknowledge a crisis in a concept is to acknowledge a crisis in their identity, the concepts begin to fail. It is also a rather unfortunate outcome of the material age, that the importance of identity supersedes priorities of basic humanity.

Communism suffered and failed for the same reluctance towards introspection. Secularism stands vulnerable to the same fate.

It would be fair to oppose national minority communities and stand with national majority victims, when justice demands it. It is perfectly alright to speak for state minorities even if they are national majorities when they are lynched and killed. That would be an honest evolution of secularism. It is not just a matter of finding overpowering support on social media. The journalistic, artistic and intellectual ethic is very deeply defined by the same mechanism and in my view, the only way to save this ism is to step outside and analyse the concept.

Liberal India of today is conditioned to spontaneously deriving oppression on the basis of identity. The danger is in the propensity of denigrating any case on behalf of a marginalised Hindu community as a morally suspect right-leaning position. It is not that simple.

The story of why the story of Shillong Bengalis remained untold for three decades is the story of what secularism cannot see in the mirror. What use is secularism, if it lacks objectivity in standing up for the persecuted and adjusts its response in the fear of obscuring one's identity? What moral superiority does that position hold, when it knowingly manages its humanity? I don't know the world that is to come, but if it is a better, truer world, it will need to see a human being as a human being. And that, my friends, must include everyone. Including Gauri Dey, even if it's thirty years too late.

THE SEARCH FOR HOME

Mitra Phukan

Shillong in the late '60s of the last century. It was still, in those days, the capital of what is today known as 'Undivided Assam.' At that time, though, the divisions that were to break up the state still lurked in the future. There was an uneasy sense among sections of the people that this splitting up was going to happen, but nobody knew when. There were disturbances. Slogans were everywhere, telling the dkhars, the outsiders, to go away, back to the plains where they came from, to leave this beautiful city to the rightful inhabitants, who wanted a hill state of their own.

Meanwhile, the different communities continued to live their lives. What else was there to do, except carry on as usual, hoping that the stray stone being pelted would not land on their persons, or their houses? Those whose facial features revealed that they traced their ancestry to the plains came home early. It did not matter if their forefathers had come to this land two, three generations ago. It did not matter either if they were here only because of their jobs, because they worked in the Assam government or were posted here for a while. Many were Assamese who were reluctant to live in Shillong anyway, and were always escaping back to the plains whenever possible.

They had that choice. But there were many others who did not. Many who came in from the land south of these green mountains, known as the Khasi Hills, had settled here a generation or two ago, after Partition. They had come up from what was then East Bengal, which became East Pakistan. A few years later, this name, too, would change, and the land would become Bangladesh. But at the point at which we are speaking of, this was still in the future.

Among those who had left behind their lands and properties was a familiar figure in the homes of Assamese and Bengali music lovers in those days. Even in this place where a variety of physiognomies were seen on the streets, he stood out. Not that he was richly dressed or anything like that. Through the seasons, even in the cold of winter, he wore a simple *dhuti* and *panjabi*, with warmer though somewhat frayed woollens as the weather dictated.

But one did not really notice these things when face to face with him. He was tall, much taller than the average local Khasi. The fair colouring he had inherited from his Brahmin ancestors was enhanced by the cold of this climate, the golden hue of his complexion complemented by his aquiline nose and large, lustrous eyes.

The son of landowners in East Bengal, his undoubted talent for music had persuaded his father, a man of liberal ideas, to send this third child of his to Shantiniketan for a stint. The idea was that he would spend some years there, learning music and the arts, before coming back and taking up the responsibility of running the estates. This would be in line with what Rabindranath himself had done in his time. There was no question, really, of Khokon, as the boy was known, taking up music as a profession, as a performer or even a teacher. But it was the sign of a cultured person that he should know music, and the arts. A status symbol, the sign of a 'complete man.'

Even as a boy, he had stood out for his musical talent. In the *jalsa*s, which were regularly arranged at his home, he impressed even well-known ustaads who came in from Kolkata and Lucknow to perform. He was tutored in several instruments—the sitar, the esraj and the tablas—and also in singing. It was always his beautiful voice, deep and mellifluous, which caught the attention of listeners when they heard him perform.

At Shantiniketan, he blossomed. At that time, the place still had about it the fragrance of the Guru's presence. Those were the good years in his life. Often, he made the journey home by boat or train. Pre-Partition, it was as seamless as the flight of a bird that crosses man-made borders without any restrictions.

Partition ripped his life apart as it did the lives of many others. Like them, his family, too—his parents and two sisters—crossed over a newly created border. It was not a sudden decision. They had seen it coming, this Partition, and knew that in this new nation, things would never be the same for them. And so, winding up their homes, leaving their lands in the care of others, with their valuables securely tucked into bundles and boxes that they carried, they made their way into what was suddenly another nation. This land, and not the one in which countless generations of his ancestors had lived, would now be his.

They did not, like so many others, flee to West Bengal. Over the years, they had come over to a place that was just to the north of what was now East Pakistan. They had relatives there, even a small plot of land, which his grandfather had bought. In the past, they had sometimes come up through winding roads to summer in the cool climate of Shillong. It was an easily made journey, up to the north of East Bengal, crossing over at Dawki, and then taking a vehicle up through the beautiful hilly terrain to this place that was at the time the capital of a huge, sprawling state.

Shillong at that time was made up of a hugely heterogeneous mix of ethnicities. None of them had much in common with each other. It was, however, designated as the capital of Assam by the British administrators, who favoured the place because of its climate, and because its hillscape reminded them of home. For the British, Shillong was a home away from home. And now, after the British left for their actual home across the seas, it became the default capital of an Indian state. It was therefore not a natural coming together of places, people.

By the time the family reached Shillong, there was already a significant East Bengali population there. Though culturally and ethnically, there was a huge difference between the local Khasi and Jaintia population of the area and people like them, they felt, if not at home in this place that they now designated 'home' for themselves, at least safe. For yes, riots and unrest were shaking up the land they had left, and refugees were pouring in from the old country.

Their family, though, akin to others like them, did not really consider themselves to be 'refugees.' Even though their circumstances were now much straitened, they thought themselves to be 'middle class.' In any case, Shillong at that time was divided into several ghetto-like localities. The Assamese lived in places such as Laban and Bishnupur; the higher level bureaucrats in rather impressive houses beside Ward's Lake and in La Chaumiere; the people who had come in from East Bengal in areas such as Bhagyakul; while the pretty, flower-bedecked, lace-curtained houses of the local Khasis were in different localities.

It was in Bhagyakul that he lived now, in a small wood-and-plaster house that held more people than it was designed for. Over a few years, his parents, unable to withstand the shock of Partition, died, exiles in a strange land. He needed to get his sisters married, which he did, from the dwindling resources that they had managed to bring over with them.

He needed to find work. He had managed to bring across his beloved esraj and sitar with him. And he would still practice on them, even in the midst of all the turmoil around him. He did not feel like singing, though. What, in any case, was there to sing about? He was an outsider in a strange land, and it was only through his music that he felt a connect with his past life.

He did not have a formal degree, something that would perhaps have secured him a clerical job in the government, and security for life.

He took to practicing his music in the dawn hours, when the rest of the household was still asleep. With the doors to the inside rooms firmly shut, he would sit on the bed in the front room that was his bedroom as well as the drawing room, and play either the esraj or the sitar.

The cosmopolitanism of Shillong of those days included the Assamese, for whom Shastriya Sangeet was an aspirational genre. It was the sign of a cultured family to get their daughters to learn Raag Sangeet, as well as Rabindra Sangeet.

The twisty lanes of the locality where he played his sitar saw a lot of morning walkers. Many were Assamese. Day after day, the sounds of the sitar floating out from a particular house caught the attention of these walkers.

One of them was a senior government official of the Forest Department. He was, at that time, looking for someone who could teach his daughter classical music. He himself was not the musical kind, but it was his wife, a music lover herself, who was insistent that their only child should be taught Shastriya Sangeet. Where to get a teacher of that genre in this hilly land, full of migrants and temporary settlers who had come here for a few years on work? The local people had their own rich repertoire of music, as well as wonderful musicians who were making a name for themselves with their renditions of popular Western numbers, all around the country. But what the Assamese in general wanted was that their children, especially their daughters, should be adept in this other mode. It reminded them of home, and made them feel temporarily like an insider in this land that was so different from theirs, culturally, that they always felt like outsiders, no matter how long they had lived here. Home for them was symbolised through this music, these songs that spoke of the land they had left behind.

One day, the government officer knocked on the musician's door. The strains of the sitar came to an abrupt halt. The man who opened the door was young, with fine features and eyes that were already saddened with experience. The visitor knew of this refugee, he had made enquiries, and was reassured by the man's aristocratic bearing. There were many such in this town these days, people of good families who had had to leave everything and come here, and who were still trying to make a home for themselves in this land, trying to fit in as best as possible, so that they could feel like insiders again. A brief conversation later, the musician was hired. Not as a sitar teacher, but as a teacher of vocal music in which, too, the government officer learned, the man before him had many years of training.

From that day onwards, he was known as the Ganor Mastor. The Music Teacher. He was sincere, and he himself was a little surprised to discover that he was a good teacher. His student was a bright young girl, who responded to his teachings, and was soon singing the easy raags with confidence. He also taught her bhajans and Rabindra Sangeet.

His fame spread by word of mouth. Other officers, Bengali as well as Assamese, hired him to teach their daughters and sometimes their wives too. The music teacher appeared punctually after school hours at their homes. He became a familiar figure in the Assamese and Bengali parts of town. He always had a sense of purpose, even though, often, as he walked up hills and down again to reach his destination, he hummed a melody, distractedly.

Things began to look up financially too. He got married to a girl from the same caste as his own. She, too, was a displaced person—a delicate-looking girl who turned out to be a thrifty home manager.

The music teacher began to feel like an insider, at last. He was greeted with respect in the homes he visited, treated to sumptuous snacks. His students did really well in the annual Ananda Sanmelan competitions of music, which were held in the State Central Library Auditorium. Some of the senior students became approved radio artistes in the Guwahati centre of All India Radio. This was indeed a feather in his cap.

As for the comments of the local street urchins who sometimes jeered at him, and his dhuti as it flapped in the ferocious March winds, he learned to ignore them, humming melodies louder so as to shut out their taunts. In any case, he did not know their language, Khasi. He never bothered to learn it, though his wife had acquired a smattering of it.

His son and daughter, too, knew some of the language, even though they studied in the local Bengali High School.

There were many languages heard in the town in those days. Khasi, of course, because that was what the local people, the 'sons of the soil' spoke. But also a lot of English, Assamese, some strangely pronounced Hindi, and yes, definitely, Bangla, as well. Not so much the Bangla of West Bengal, though there was that too. But the Bangla heard most frequently at that time in that hill town was that of the various tongues of nearby East Pakistan, the sweet sounding Sylheti or the Mymensingh or the Dacca speech. This, even though East Pakistan was a totally different country, and culturally and linguistically so very different from this high plateau that was situated just to the north of that land.

Years, a couple of decades passed. Many of his students had grown up and gone on to pursue higher studies in other cities. But he kept going every Wednesday afternoon to the house of the forest officer who had first hired him. The girl, his first student, was now in Delhi, working. But her mother had continued the lessons. Her husband, by now a top officer, was often away, and she loved these afternoons when, after the lessons were over, she and the by now middle-aged music teacher talked of home. He spoke of the land he had left behind. And she, of the place, her parents' home, in Western Assam, on the border between East Pakistan and India, where she had grown up. She, too, was a migrant, even though she belonged to this country. For married women in most parts of the world had to leave the land of their birth and settle in another home. She would reminisce about how she had felt like an outsider in her husband's village after marriage. It was only here, in this wooden house with pine floorboards and a red tin roof, that she felt at home, an insider at last.

They cocooned themselves through the music and the talk against the dark clouds that were gathering around them, all over again. The local Khasis' demands for a hill state, where they could govern themselves, grew strident. After all, this was their land, an ancient plateau, which they considered home. The migrants from the plains, whether they were here on work, or had come as displaced persons and had settled here, lived in their own worlds, separated from the local Khasis by vast gulfs of language, culture, cuisine, and much else. The protests, the agitations, grew more insistent. The violence that followed was terrible. There were cases of arson, stabbing, murder. Non-locals lived in fear, hurrying home before dark. It was not unusual to find dead bodies floating on Ward's Lake, where they had been dumped after being stabbed in the back. People's ethnicities were written on their faces, literally. And the outsiders, the dkhars, remained alien to the locals, even those who had been there for several generations and could speak the local language fluently.

Full statehood was granted in 1972. What was, till then, the Khasi and Jaintia Hills and the Garo Hill districts of Assam became Meghalaya. Assam's capital was shifted down to Guwahati. Inevitably, all those who worked in the government had to uproot themselves and go down there, where the hot and humid climate was very different from what they had got used to. Those from the hills naturally shifted to the Meghalaya government.

It was the Bengalis, people like the music teacher, who were left in limbo. Suddenly, many of his students had to leave. Certainly, most Assamese left, and some of them were his best students. True, there were some Bengali students still there, but he could tell that they, too, would soon move away. They would go on to a university in a different city, perhaps

Kolkata or Delhi, and would, inevitably, settle there in their jobs.

Once more, after all these years, the music teacher began to feel the same fear and insecurity that he had in his youth. There were hooligans all around, young men who, emboldened by the fact that they now had their own state, assumed that they could do pretty much as they pleased. Anybody with features and clothes that marked them out as not being from those hills were taunted and jeered at. 'Go home, leave!' was the gist of their taunts. There was sometimes physical violence too.

The music teacher was an easy target. His dhuti and umbrella invited derision. But he never responded to the jeers, and moved forward with his habitual dignity up and down the hills to his students' homes. He never let the hurt that the cruelty of the barbs aimed at him caused show on his face.

His two children were grown up now. He had married off his daughter to a college teacher in Kolkata. And his son, unmarried still, was a medical representative who lived in the same city. The music teacher had sustained himself through his tuitions all these years, but now he felt the monetary pinch once more. He did not feel bitter, but often wondered where his home was. He had lived in this place for more than a quarter of a century, yet he felt that this was now an alien land. The land of his birth, too, was a place to which he was an outsider now, since he needed a passport to go there. Increasingly, the words of the Baul songs of that land would whirl through his mind:

'Where have you come from,
where are you going, O traveller?

You do but journey through this land,
For neither does this land belong to you, nor you to it.'

One of the people he missed most now was the lady, his first student's mother, who had, naturally, left too. He missed their Wednesday afternoon chats. Even though she, too, was a migrant, she had been happy here, he knew. This, for her, had been home.

In the beginning, after she shifted to the plains, she would call sometimes. His house did not have a telephone, though, and she would have to time it so that she could get him in another student's house. Gradually, the phone calls tapered off, but he had learned that she greatly missed her Shillong home. She would ask about her peach and plum trees, whether the hydrangea bushes were flowering, and did he cross her house on his way to his other students' homes? She and her husband had had to sell their property at a loss, for there were now stringent laws in place about the buying and selling of land in the tribal areas. She missed the climate, and hated her RCC house here in Guwahati. The heat and humidity made her sick, never mind that she had been born not too far away from here, in a similarly humid and warm place.

His own situation was gradually, in any case, becoming precarious. His wife, always frail, began to fall sick with increasing frequency. His son, now married and settled in a flat near his sister's place in Kolkata, had been urging him to shift. And so, one day, he did. He did not take much along, because he did not have much. But the sitar and esraj that had come here with him accompanied him once more to another city. He took with him also the harmonium, which had acquired a mellowness in its sound over the decades.

As for the house, this, too, was sold ridiculously cheap. If he felt the unfairness of it, he did not complain. As an outsider again, he did not feel that he had the right to do so.

The flat in Kolkata was small, poky. He felt suffocated there. True, he heard his language, Bangla, spoken all around him now, inside and outside the house. But it was not the Bangla of his youth, of his land. The bustle of the city around him, the dense crowds, made him feel uneasy, nervous even, whenever he went out. His sense of alienation only increased. There were many musical events here which would have interested him. But he felt too tired now. His body was unused to the heat, and he felt breathless all the time. His once erect posture seemed to crumple up, and he became bent and stooped. His complexion darkened, and he became, for the first time in his life, nondescript-looking. An old man, belonging nowhere.

A couple of neighbourhood parents who came to know of the music teacher and his fame as a trainer requested him to teach their daughters. They would come to his house once a week, and he would take out the old harmonium from below his bed, to teach them the Rabindra Sangeet that he himself had been taught so many decades ago, in a leafy place not too far away from here that had resonated with melodies. But his heart was not in it. He taught mechanically, without involvement. Often, he would think of his life back in Shillong. And to the life before that, some of which he remembered so very clearly even now. Indeed, as he grew older, those early memories seemed to become more and more vivid. He could hear the songs that the Bauls sang in his village, he could hear the tinkle of the temple bell, the calls to prayer from the mosque, as clearly as he had then. He remembered the melodies sung by the boatmen who poled their boats down the river at the edge of his estate. Tears came to his eyes easily now, and sometimes, he had to hold back sobs. He thought of the families to whose houses he had been such a welcome visitor, back in that hill town. Often, he thought of the lady, the forest officer's wife, who had become such a good friend. The two of them had made homes there, had tried to be insiders when they were actually outsiders, migrants, for different reasons, from the homes they were born into.

Sometimes, he got news of his students and their families. The uprooting from Shillong had hit all of them hard. They had become outsiders, once more, in the place where they relocated. In Guwahati, the forest officer's wife felt alien. And then her husband passed away.

When he heard the news, the music teacher did call her. But, she was too dazed still to speak much, and in any case there was nothing of importance he could say on the telephone, an instrument he was not used to.

To be a Brahmin widow, even in a society that considered itself comparatively enlightened, meant that once more, she was an outsider. There were many taboos, many restrictions that she had to follow. Indeed, her own mindset imposed restrictions on her. She had watched her grandmother and mother set aside their jewellery and bright mekhela sadors during their widowhood, and she felt compelled to do the same. Unlike them, she did not turn vegetarian, because her doctor told her that it would weaken her already frail body. But she felt a sense of guilt whenever she had a piece of fish or mutton.

She began to fall sick frequently. Her daughter, married and settled now in the US, decided, out of concern and love, to bring her over. It was no use arguing; in any case, the lady felt too weak to do so. All she could think about was the home she had left behind in Shillong, a home filled, to her mind now, with melody and happiness. She was definitely an outsider here, even though her citizenship status in this new country proclaimed her to be an insider.

In Washington, where her daughter lived, she was well cared for. She recovered her physical health, and tried to integrate herself to the life around her. But it was her hill home in that other country that she now longed for, when she thought of 'home.' Even her natal home, now bereft of her parents and brothers, did not call out to her in the way this Shillong home did. And yet, she was an outsider there now, definitely and quite firmly.

Gradually, she began to sink into silence. Soon, she stopped talking altogether. But she was, finally, happy. For her mind, oblivious to the concerned faces of her family and nurses and doctors all around her, had gone back to the place of happy memories, her hill home. And in this space in her mind, at last insider and outsider merged in a way they had not since she had left Shillong.

The music teacher's only consolation, in that tiny flat, was the little boy, his grandson. The toddler brightened up his days with his laughter and chuckles. Gradually, as he grew up, he became the old man's companion. The music teacher's wife had passed away soon after they had arrived in this crowded, congested city, unable to take this shock. In his loneliness, he began to tell the little boy stories about that time long ago, when he had not been an outsider in the land of his birth. The little boy was fascinated by what seemed like fairy tales to him.

Before long, he was beginning to sit in on the lessons that his dadu, his grandfather, imparted to the girls who came in. Soon, he was singing better than any of those didis.

Gradually, the little boy's fame grew, first in the para, the neighbourhood. In a city where musical expertise was taken for granted, and standards were high, it was a sign of how good he already was. He began to be invited to these musical gatherings that took place regularly in the para. His father was too busy with his office, his mother preoccupied with domestic concerns to accompany the little boy to these places. After all, he was only seven, and he needed somebody to go with him. The music teacher, whom everybody called Dadu, began to accompany him to these shows. As his teacher, he was the one who made sure that the mics were adjusted just so to his young student's height, that the accompanying instruments were placed right. He was the one whose feet the little boy touched before the curtains were opened. He was the one, now, who was escorted with honour to the front seat in the audience, as the boy's guru.

The boy began to be recognised as a prodigy. As his expertise and fame spread, the auditoriums to which his grandfather accompanied him became grander. He could no longer afford to be careless in his dressing. He began to dress on these occasions as he had, in those distant days in what was now another country. His son saw to it that his father's dhuti was of the finest cotton these days, with eye-catching borders, in typical *bhodrolok* style. His panjabis, too, were now of silk, or in summer of fine muslin with beautiful kantha embroidery.

The man, now old, almost in his eighties, revelled in the attention he was getting. As his grandson grew in musical stature, his own fame, and the respect accorded to him, too, grew greater. His name began to be mentioned in the papers, as the guru of the child prodigy. In the teacher's mind, the days of his youth, in Shantiniketan and in his own estates and home, merged with the sound of his grandson's sweet voice. His shrivelled appearance gradually gave way to the good looks of his prime. He was known as a handsome man once more. And though he himself never performed he was, finally, at peace.

As the boy grew older, though, his dadu realised that he needed to be placed under the tutelage of another guru, who would take him even further in his musical journey. After much thought, he finally honed in on a famed Rabindra Sangeet exponent and teacher.

But even after this change of teachers, the boy's respect and affection for his grandfather did not wane. His voice changed, became that of a man's. He was now invited to shows around the country. He began to earn tidy sums of money. His parents insisted that he acquire his BA degree, but it was as a musician that his path ahead was already charted. His father, too, had been promoted several times, and could now afford to buy a much larger flat. The music teacher's room overlooked the garden of the apartment complex, and fresh breezes soothed him as he sat by the window, looking at the greenery below.

Awards and accolades became routine for the family now. The young man's CDs became bestsellers. He began to tour the world, for the Bangla diaspora was everywhere. And they could not have enough of this young man's beautiful music. If the shows were in a nearby city, he would take his dadu along, and watch with his eyes misting over as the old man was made much of. He would have loved to have taken him to the cities around the world to which he was invited, but of course Dadu would not have been able to stand the journey. But he made it a point to call up his grandfather before and after every function, first asking for his blessings, and then discussing with him how his music had been received.

It was during one of these trips abroad that he got the news that Dadu had passed away. He was due to stay on for a month more in Chicago, conducting a workshop. Cancelling everything, he rushed back, to be in time for the funeral.

As he looked down at the body on the bed, now covered with garlands of *rajnigandha* and marigolds, the young man broke down. Weeping inconsolably, he sat down on the floor, at his grandfather's feet. He insisted on being one of the pallbearers on the way to the cremation ground.

The news that the young musician's dadu and first guru had passed away spread very fast. Musicians thronged to the cremation ground. The young singer performed all the funerary rites himself. As he stood back and watched the flames encircle the body, people came up to him, in little groups, to pay their condolences. And even later, when they went back home and observed the mandatory days of mourning, a steady stream of mourners and visitors came to pay their condolences. Many had met the deceased at the functions in which the young man had performed, and they had been impressed by his dignified personality. They came because they had truly respected this person, a man who had been buffeted by changes over which he had no control. And yet, through all these changes, he had lived with dignity, without a murmur of complaint. A couple of Bangla newspapers wrote small obituaries on him: Music Guru Damodar Chakravarty Breathes His Last.

At last, in the final years of his life, and in his death, he was an insider, part again of a society that accorded him respect, and love.

BOAT-BUILDING

Mona Zote

The question of being drowned or afloat
Does not really matter.

These days you can hear it
How everyone is building boats
How you can walk down the cramped streets
And hear above the everyday
The sound of someone deploying a hammer
Steadily as she goes
A sound soaring clear above all else.

I think, he's building a boat
He needs to go away
He wants to make sure everyone is safe
Because the water's rising
Maybe he needs to bring something back home
Things we need
Things he thinks we need
Maybe it's a shipment of warm sweatshirts
Maybe it's a good politician or two
Maybe it's all this gold everyone is so wild about
Maybe it's oranges from those other hills.

And sometimes, above the laughter of this man,
You see a startled cloud of birds
Bursting out from their sloppy nests
In a brief blind whirl of instinct
Ringing the air around the house that alarmed them
Forgetting soon, in their own way,
What they were afraid of
Just seconds ago
Because they are easily distracted.

So today or yesterday, I went shopping
I noted many things:
First, how the shopkeepers look up
With eyes that think they know you
Better than the last arms that held you.
Second, how there were so many girls
Walking from shop to shop
Stopping in the doorways
With vague powdered faces.
Third, how taking a dress out
Into the sunlight
Changes its colour and tone
Often it becomes friendlier.

Sometimes when I hold your hand
I think, how can you guide the tiller anymore
It feels small and not completely there
The skin thin as onion peel
I remember it being strong and healthy, Mother,
Holding my hand with assurance
Until I remember

As I know nothing about boats,
I cannot give the boat builder advice
I can only ask him questions
About the wind's speed, the drowsiness of being mid-ocean,
The snapping of sails, the urgency
Of sighting land when your barrels have run dry.
He frowns at the houses careening on their concrete stilts
And says something about clouds
How you can't trust them even if you love them.
At least they are consistently clouds.

I ask about provisions and if hardtack
Can make salt water taste better.

Here where the houses like to live dangerously,
Someone is building a boat for a river
Someone is building a ship for the sea
I look but I can only see many blue hills
Gold is spilling down the streets
The women are beautiful and the men are strong
I am sure their children will be angelic singers.
Boat-building is a child's endeavour.

This poem first appeared in *The Indian Quarterly.*

I, DKHAR

Paramjit Bakhshi

Ours is a story, rarely told: a tale so politically incorrect, it has no takers. Magazines never feature our plight, nor do national newspapers headline our troubles. We are invisible and unheard of—different 'strangers in the mist'—minorities but not of popular description, or ones who have suffered discrimination, down the ages. Ours is a relatively modern experience, so it remains an unspoken one. There is hardly a slot appropriate for our saga. The fault is admittedly ours too. For fear of making things worse we have hesitated in opening our mouths or putting pen to paper. We have spoken to each other in hushed whispers and dissuaded the other from speaking out aloud. Like the two Jews facing a Nazi firing squad, in the apocryphal story from the 1940s. When one of them kept howling about his innocence, the other told him, 'Stop screaming, you fool, you will only make things worse.' Things couldn't have gotten worse for them, but for us they surely can, because we all are not yet up for the kill. Not all of us together, though many of us have and still do get killed. It shakes us when it happens. Yet we have not ever dreamt of picking up a gun to start another insurgency. Also, unlike the tribal communities amongst whom we live, we cannot beat the drums, thump our chests, and raise a war cry.

This story is about being a *dkhar* in Shillong, a trifle unique but also largely universal of the hill states of the North-East. It is mine but it could also be the story of a *bangal* of Garo Hills, a *mayang* of Manipur, a *vai* of Mizoram and countless individuals assigned assorted tags in different hill states of the region. Our stories are different as every individual experience is bound to be. Yet the commonality, of experience, of being treated like an outsider, which is what all the terms at the beginning of this paragraph most mildly denote, runs through all of them. Commonly called non-tribals, by all tribes of the region, we are people whose origins lie in the plains of India. People who themselves or whose ancestors, by choice, or some weird twist of fate, came to commit the sin of considering these states their home. Of course, our other sins, too, are hardly discounted—the sin of looking different, the sin of being 'Indian,' the sin of somehow being responsible for everything that has and still goes wrong in these hill states. In my memory rings a popular phrase I heard as a child in Manipur: 'If you see a mayang and a snake, kill the mayang first.' As a mere *mayangmacha* (child of an outsider), I could not but be silent. One has also seen as an adult in Shillong, not many years ago, the graffiti—'non-tribal dogs get out in peace, or in pieces'—splashed on walls in Laitumkhrah, the most cosmopolitan part of Shillong. And again one has walked by silently.

As I sit writing this, another agitation against the entry of outsiders is gathering steam. Of course, state assembly elections are around the corner and such agitations are *nourriture normale* or normal fare, put out during these times for common consumption. Yet, just as the same daily fare numbs the taste buds, the same music jars the ears after a while, and familiar incense ceases to be pleasing, one's sensibilities rebel against the same cry which has resounded since 1979. This was the year I truly came to Shillong, a turning point in my life but also, I am aware, for the political and social fabric of the city. I had spent a brief one year here in 1976 studying for my pre-university. Thereafter, I had been selected to join the National Defence Academy. After two years of training as an officer cadet, I was boarded out owing to an illness, and returned to Shillong to do my graduation.

Strangely, one hardly remembers much about the trouble in 1979. One vaguely recalls that there was violence and perhaps for a period there might have been a curfew. This was the first agitation against dkhars but to be honest it did not affect me personally. I was then too busy discovering my own rebelliousness, post the loss of a childhood dream of joining the Army. The pendulum had swung to the other extreme. College life devoid of any ambition had become a saga of missed classes, binge-drinking and spontaneous parties. The laissez-faire atmosphere of the place which does not seriously condone such behaviour could have been my undoing. I was even considering dropping out of college, but fortunately another form of liberalism came to my rescue.

I fell in love with Catherine, a petite gentle Khasi girl who, like me, was an English Honours student, though a year ahead of me. She was in St Mary's College and I was in St Edmund's and we met accidentally when I was invited to her graduation party by a mutual friend. She radiated an energy which attracted me. She told me she really liked the poems I used to write for *Edmonthly*: a cyclostyled college magazine revived by a few of us from our class. I started visiting her regularly and her liberal family made me feel much at home. We would occasionally go out for walks, constrained, both by my meagre pocket allowance and the fact that a romance between a non-tribal boy and a Khasi girl was generally frowned upon by local boys. I had been especially warned by friends not to venture out to the 'wild west': an area comprising localities such as Mawkhar, Mawlai and Jaiaw, which were considered to be extremely intolerant of outsiders. We never did. I did, however, walk back most nights from Catherine's house to my hostel in Happy Valley, a distance of five odd kilometres. The public transport in those days would grind to a halt by seven in the evening. I would fill a brown paper bag with stones as I began my walk and empty it out most nights on arrival at the hostel. On this route I perceived no human threat to my safety, but the dogs on the way would occasionally want to get at me on the deserted streets. Were those stray dogs also non-tribal? If they were, they surely had a good run of Shillong. Better than us of the human variety. One had heard stories of drunks accosting and fleecing unaware pedestrians at night, but this never happened to me. I have always wondered whether they were really drunkards or just unemployed people seeking a way to brighten up their evenings.

Employment has been a major problem in Shillong for quite a few years. After my graduation when, with both sets of parents approving, Catherine and I decided to get married, the main hurdle to be overcome was finding suitable employment to sustain us. There was only one opening for a school teacher's job in a local school; the meagre salary from that would not have kept us going. I applied for a job in the tea gardens and was lucky to be selected to join as an assistant manager on one of Tata Finlay's tea estates in North Bengal. We spent seven years on the estates in Assam and Bengal. It was a life, which differed from our expectations. To begin with, I had romantic notions of leading a life close to nature and writing poetry with Catherine by my side. In reality, most of the years were spent inside a tea factory and the long hours at work left little leisure to write poems. For Catherine, too, life was lonely; I was hardly at home and the large secluded bungalows deepened her sense of isolation. When we saved a little money, we thought it would be a relief to leave the gardens and live in a city. Dehradun, where my parents had just settled down, finally constructing a house after retirement, was unfamiliar to both of us. Hence, to Shillong we returned.

In the absence of any corporate sector presence, I still could not get a suitable job in Shillong. I considered starting a business but nobody in my entire lineage had ever done so. We came from a Sikh family, which had either served in the police or the in Army for many generations. With little money and even less business sense, starting a business in my own name turned out to be a bureaucratic nightmare. When I finally went to the district council for the registration, a person who obviously disliked dkhars abused me and asked me to get out of the office. Unlike other non-tribals who had lived here for generations, I had no contacts and was unfamiliar with the concept of a bribe changing people's attitudes. The trauma of that experience stayed with me and I never returned to that office again. I survived by doing tea consultancy in places as remote as Vietnam and a little town in Arunachal called Roing. Catherine finished her B.Ed. and got a job as a teacher in Loreto Convent. With my travelling, we still did not have a proper family life. It was only after 2000, some eighteen years into our marriage, that things started to settle down financially. A couple of years before, we had begun a hostel in a premise rented for the purpose and that seemed to be paying off. A small venture marketing local agricultural produce also provided a healthy return during the winters. With the help of two bank loans and the money coming in from businesses, we constructed a house in Laitumkhrah and bought our first new car. We were happy at the fortunate turn of events.

Little did we know that our life would soon be thrown into turmoil. We now faced extortion—a completely unexpected threat.

Extortion has been a less spoken-about facet of business life in Shillong. Though not as rampant as it is in Nagaland where even government employees are forced to part with a portion of their salary every month, it has largely been collected from the business class in Shillong. Non-tribal businesses have been extorted from for decades, in some form or the other not only by militants but also by assorted NGOs and other so-called social organisations. The new development in the '90s was that extortion now came to be demanded from rich or assumed-to-be rich tribals too. Our encounter with extortion was a bit strange. The note came to my mother-in-law, who had no business connection with Catherine or me, demanding a certain amount of money but threatening to harm our children if the money was not paid. One hardly knew whether the note was genuine or just a jealous prank. Jealousy is a major factor amongst small communities and in Shillong, this assumes menacing proportions.

Somebody told me a very imaginative anecdote to highlight this aspect and it goes something like this. A woman is selling crabs in the local market. She has crabs in two containers—one covered and the other open. A customer stops by and is puzzled by the fact that though the crabs in both containers are identical, one of the containers is covered. He asks her the reason for this.

'Well,' she replies, the non-local crabs are covered because if I don't cover them, they will all escape.'

'Don't the local ones escape?' he persists.

'No, sir, they can't,' she responds. 'The moment any of them tries to climb out, all the others get together and pull him back.'

The strangest part is that relatives who are meant to be the ones wishing you well are most often the ones who wish you down in the well. This has been a sad part of our reality too. We got help from people we least expected to bail us out and were very often let down by people whom we considered our own. Sometimes, we have felt that relatives liked us better when we were down on our knees than standing on our feet. I have a name for this and call it the *bapli* syndrome. 'Bapli' in Khasi means 'poor thing' and somehow people just love pitying other people because it makes them feel superior. No rope is thrown to the drowning man but pity pours forth in a deluge. The actual process of a man escaping his misery is viewed with suspicion and envy.

To continue the story, whatever little we had was acquired through sweat and tears and we were in no mood to part with it. If payment had to be made, we would rather pay our creditors than hand over money to some goons. We informed the police who, to their credit, tried their best to help us. We received another letter threatening to harm our children for reporting the matter to the police. Though the police suspected some people from the locality, the culprits were never caught and the letters, too, stopped coming. Whether this was a good sign or not, we did not know. Our younger son was too small to be sent to any boarding and not wanting to endanger his life, we made a decision to leave Shillong once again. Shortly, with the help of a Khasi friend, a remarkable lady in her own right, my wife got a teaching job in an international school on the outskirts of Bangalore. She took our son and left. I stayed back to oversee the hostel session over till year end and sell the house. It took about four months and my wife had to fly in from Bangalore to sign the sale deed. The law prohibited me—her husband of twenty-three years but nevertheless a non-tribal—from becoming a power of attorney holder and signing the sale deed. Thereafter, for the next two years, all of us lived in the flat provided in campus by the school.

We returned subsequently, assured by friends that normalcy had returned to Shillong, the only home we knew. Staying outside and moving between the two cities, we spent up a big chunk of our money and with the rising real estate prices, found that we could no longer afford to buy a house in Shillong.

In Hemingway's *The Old Man and the Sea*, the protagonist is forced to go further out to the sea when fishing close by does not help. This is what we were forced to do. We moved some twenty kilometres away from Shillong, to a village called Umsaw, where we managed to buy a one-acre plot touching the Umiam lake. What a beautiful piece of land it was, with a lake frontage of two hundred feet and a small stream on the side, which ended in a waterfall. The view was spectacular too, especially the sunrise, and in winters, migratory ducks could be seen swimming close to the shore. With financial help from one of our friends, we managed to make a lovely four-bedroom bungalow on the lakeside. The idea being that we would run a small homestay for tourists. We ran the place for four years and somehow managed to pay all our bills. Catherine, now a principal of a reputed school in Shillong, often commuted between Shillong and Barapani. Though the distance was only twenty kilometres, on one occasion, thanks to the coal trucks, she was stuck in a traffic jam that lasted an astonishing six-and-a-half hours. The strain of running the place without trained help—no cook was willing to stay in this isolated place for the salary we could afford—started getting to us. Towards this, Catherine even resigned her prestigious but not very well-paying job. Both of us would cook all the meals for our guests and also entertain them, often till the wee hours of the morning. Still, the money that we earned was not enough to repay the loan we had taken. We also missed any social interaction since all our friends lived in Shillong. Though our village *dorbar* and the headman gave us all the support they could, the people from the neighbouring village, named Umbir, routinely caused a lot of trouble because they claimed that our place fell in their jurisdiction.

One night, when we were away in Shillong, they entered our house and started threatening our servants. We had to rush back in the middle of the night to solve the matter with the police following closely on our heels. Then once again began the familiar charade, this time under the guise of wanting the Inner Line Permit. Two dkhars were burnt alive in Shillong in broad daylight. There were many cases of arson, and night curfew was imposed by NGOs. There went tourism and there went our meagre earnings. Also, being the only non-tribal for miles around, I ended up feeling ironically like a sitting migratory duck, on a lonely patch of earth next to the lake. 'Laid Back Waters' was the name we had lovingly given our place but in actuality, we still found ourselves in deep and troubled waters. We were in our fifties now and wanted a bit of peace, leisure and company. We sold the place, lucky to find a buyer who gave us a decent if not a fabulous price. We now live in a little cottage in Shillong rented to us again by a friend who, like me, had spent years on the tea estates.

Will Shillong still continue to be my home forever? Even after thirty years of living in Shillong, I am not too sure. Most of my friends and well-wishers here have been Khasis. Some have looked after me better than people of my own community. They have stood up for me in times of trouble, often against their own people. I have known headmen who have treated me like their own and one who boldly berated a group of young boys when they abused me. And I will always remember and remain obliged to an elderly Khasi lady, who treated me like a son and loaned me a huge amount of money without interest and without setting any time frame for repayment. This is something my own brother would not have done. Tears rolled down her cheeks the day I repaid her loan after selling our house and she told me that the money had been given so that we would not sell the place. A Khasi traffic constable has stopped my vehicle and diverted me from heading straight into an on-going communal clash. In return, I have driven across the country with friends from this region and have felt responsible for them.

Sadly, all this bonhomie is still just one side of the coin. One has lived here on sufferance too. The realisation of being an outsider in your own country can never be a welcome experience. From being a 'Sahib', I have become an outsider of no consequence, and a generally unwelcome 'dkhar'. My features brand me an outsider and no amount of intermingling will make me an acceptable local. Even if I were to attend church, wear a *tapmohkhlieh* (a traditional Khasi shawl) and chew *kwai* (local betel nut) habitually. Some stranger would just have to say, '*wat krendkhar*' (keep quiet, outsider) and I would have no acceptable retort. In a car accident involving a local and I, the fault is and will always be mine. This has been my experience. I have been threatened by individuals and by people banded together as an organisation. This has happened in my own house, on the road, and even as a result of a golf game. Till now, I have stood up to every fight, but will not be able to as I grow old.

In addition to the economic struggle, I had also lived through the trauma of various agitations such as the ones in 1987 and 1992 and the subsequent dark days of militancy, which reached its peak in the late '90s. With my own eyes I have seen a mob of students attacking dkhars on the streets of Police Bazaar, the commercial hub of Shillong. I have taken refuge in the high court building and watched with disbelief the violence perpetuated under what seemed like the protection rather than the inaction of the police. And I have narrowly escaped mob fury in front of the district council. I have witnessed outsiders gunned down in their shops for not paying extortion.

And though militancy and agitations come and go, I do not see any end to our discrimination. Unlike Delhi, where a proposed law would punish people calling North-Easterners 'chinki' or 'momo', no such decree is envisaged here to prevent us from being called 'dkhar' with other dirty suffixes. We are minorities of a minority, but no concessions will ever be made for us. The traditional durbars have no room for us and we are not allowed to take part in any proceedings even though our fate is decided by them. In the Meghalaya Assembly, out of the sixty seats, fifty-seven are reserved for the majority, for the Khasis, Jaintias and Garos. The other three seats are open for all but now rarely held by non-tribals. So we have no political representation. In certain villages around Shillong, a Khasi woman married to a non-tribal is not permitted to stay. We are, like the name of the famous movie, 'inglorious bastards', with no father or godfather to look after our wellbeing. National TV channels organise debates when a maid, who happens to be a Khasi, is asked to leave the Delhi Golf Club, but plains people being burnt alive in daylight do not even make national news. *Times Now*, even under Arnab, a North-Eastern lad now with a *Republic* of his own, had no time for us. And Barkha has never rained her attention on what has happened here a single hour of the twenty-four seven. Do you all know that the murders of non-tribals have never been solved and not one person has ever been convicted for them? All cases against all communal troublemakers are routinely withdrawn by whichever government is in power.

The karma philosophy establishes a link between cause and effect. What is happening here must have a cause. One has heard stories of how in the old days, non-tribal traders cheated people here. Sometimes, a cloth sold to a tribal villager would be measured both in length and breadth and the tribal would be fooled to pay for that total measurement. Others took advantage of people's simplicity and naiveté and cornered government businesses by bribing and by cunning. Some old settlers behaved like brown sahibs and looked down on the local people. Somewhere this must hurt in the collective conscious of the local people. What is happening today is perhaps some form of historical revenge. I really don't know. But what I do feel is that I cannot be held accountable for the actions of other people. I consider myself an individual and not part of some collective communal narrative. In my personal capacity, I have loved at least one person from Shillong and have stuck by her just as she has stuck by me for thirty-five years. I have also maintained a set of ethics and not robbed anybody or looked down on them. Just as it is wrong to blame the tribals living in other parts of

India for what is done to outsiders here, it is wrong to paint all dkhars with the same brush.

One thing, though, is certain. If the inner line becomes a reality, I will certainly leave Shillong. I do not trust lines. A somewhat similar line was also drawn by Radcliffe when India was partitioned. This line was responsible for the displacement of millions of families. One of them was ours. Perhaps they took the line too lightly. From the stories my grandfather and my father told us, everything changed overnight. Sadhu Singh, my grandfather, a police *thanedar*, was away on duty far away in Sialkot, a distance of 220 km on Google Maps, the night a neighbour chose to fire on his house in Rawalpindi. The same neighbour who had for years exchanged pleasantries, with my grandparents, every morning. My uncle, then eighteen, responded to every volley, but realised that fighting was useless, surrounded as they were by people who had suddenly become 'others'. Sometime in the early hours of the morning, the family consisting of my grandmother and her six children, three boys and three girls, quietly slipped out of their house carrying just a few belongings. Fortunately, they made it across through the mayhem and murder that Partition unleashed. What it felt like for them to leave a land where they were born and brought up, to leave a home where they had even lovingly constructed little canals to water the garden, to leave everything which they loved and cared for, I will never truly know, in spite of all the stories told to me. No first-hand story, no movie, can capture the pain they must have felt and endured. It could not be cured by any balm or washed away by any subsequent joy. I know it never left my dad. He may have made Dehradun his home, but in reality, the only community he knew comprised army officers settled there in Defence Colony.

We, on the other hand, have no community to call our own. I am an outsider here and my wife will be an outsider in small-town India elsewhere. Apart from large metros, the proverbial India of 'unity in diversity' is a piece of fiction. As I submit the final proof of this piece, a new bill is being passed by the District Council, a sub section of which states: 'Any Khasi woman who marries a non-Khasi as well as her offspring born out of such a marriage(s) shall be deemed as non-Khasi who shall lose the Khasi status and all the privileges and benefits as a member of the Khasi tribe who cannot claim preferential privileges under any law.'

It is a reality that in this country, and especially in the hill states of the North-East, there is no space to be just Indian. One remembers the lines by the Sufi poet Bulleh Shah, who wrote:

> *'Chal Bulleya chal utho chailye,*
> *jithe lokia kal de anhe,*
> *na koi sadi jaat penchane,*
> *no koi sanu manne.'*
>
> 'O Bulle, let us go to that place,
> Where people have not too much intelligence,
> For there, nobody will ask of our roots and look
> down upon us,
> And nor do we desire that they look up to us.'

The challenge for people like us is to find that space. If at all it still exists.

POEMS BY R.G. LYNGDOH

THE MIGRANT LABOURER

As I peer into your bloodshot eyes,
The contours of your soul
Lie hidden behind a glassy haze.
The crease of wrinkles,
Encircling your eyes,
Spiral around the misty depths.
Hardship has been your companion,
And you have seen so much of it
That now pain only bemuses you.
Is it just a defence mechanism?
Or is it a manic streak developed
And honed by too many battered times?
Each furrow on your leathery face
Tells a tale of endless dark days and sleepless nights,
When hunger gnawed your innards into a bloody pulp.
You have touched rock bottom so many times,
But still no blow has knocked you out, and
You always rise up stronger from each painful fall.
Fate may have dealt you a cruel hand, yet
You never fail to hope and your faith never dies,
Humbled, I can only stand to salute your resilience.

JUSTICE

'What you do to others has a way
Of coming around and happening to you.'

The tension in the air was thick
As shadowy figures furtively crept about
Looking to dole out 'revenge' in the dead of night.
They could see the targets huddled together
For security around the flickering bonfire,
Peering timidly, trying to see into the darkness.
Without a thought he drew his baseball bat,
As they stepped in, swinging out at the crouched men,
Their blood charged by alcohol-fuelled emotions.
He saw the terrified face pleading up at him,
And he felt his arm rise high above his head
Then, he heard the sickening crack of breaking face bones.
Suddenly they heard the tramping of boots,
As the enforcers of the law rushed into the scene,
They barely escaped as the uniformed figures swooped in.
He rushed into his house gasping for breath
To be greeted by the midwife holding up his newborn child,
And he was shocked to see the deformed face of his first son.

EQUAL CITIZENS

The Delhi street was packed
As they converged from all over.
They even held hands in solidarity
As they shouted out in protest.
'We are citizens of the same family,
Deserving equal treatment and opportunity.'
Then they dispersed to crawl back
Into their own little ponds again,
Their bonds were untied and forgotten,
The hands began to point in accusation,
And equal treatment and opportunity
Were shelved to become mere phrases once more.

HOW WE GOT HERE

A Brief history of Being Dkhar in Shillong

Samrat

By the time I was around seven years old, my world was already divided into groups. In school, there were the boarders, rough chaps from elsewhere that stayed away from their parents, and day scholars, who were good boys like me that stayed at home. It was a boys' school, but the absence of girls was at that time a matter of satisfaction rather than regret. It was only several years later when we hit our teens that greater knowledge and rampaging hormones caused most of us to change our views.

As we grew up, we gradually became aware of other lines of difference. Language was obviously one. Though we were under strict instructions to speak only English in school, we knew that we did not all speak the same language at home, or even during lunch break. Some of us were dropped off to school in cars, while others took the bus or walked. During moral science class, some boys would be shepherded off to the school chapel, but others would not. Even the humble tiffin box was an education; it would open to reveal different kinds of food, and some of us would happily share lunches, eating whatever was in the boxes, while others would not.

The process of being socialised into gender, class, linguistic and religious identity and food taboos began early.

It was perhaps inevitable. The power of existing structures and categories is one reason. Human nature, if such a thing exists, may be another. Identifying ourselves with others to form groups based on shared characteristics or interests seems a very human trait. Psychologists have a word that goes some way to explain this tendency to form in-groups and out-groups. It is called 'belongingness,' a fundamental human urge to belong. It explains the completely natural way in which diverse strangers thrown together into tour groups, training groups, or even a train compartment, band together—and why the odd person who plugs in his headphones and keeps aloof from the group is viewed with some distaste by its remaining members.

In Shillong, in those years, we found that the line of belonging and not belonging had been decided for us by the accident of birth. There were frequent bouts of violence by local Khasi groups against local minority populations, the non-tribal peoples who were derisively called 'dkhars' and treated as unwelcome outsiders that did not belong in the place. School friends and trusted neighbours apart, we dkhar kids learned early on to be wary of 'them'—the Khasis.

The danger 'they' posed revealed itself in little ways at first.

During school breaks, we would sometimes wander down to the school gates to buy peanuts and *jhal muri* from the scrawny Bihari street hawkers. We knew we had to pay money for these things, but it was common for Khasi boys only a little older than ourselves to take what they wanted without paying, and to punch or kick the hawkers if they dared ask for money. We were a little higher than the hawkers in the power hierarchy; our school uniforms afforded us some protection. Walking the streets was, however, a risky matter for us as well. At any time, a bunch of Khasi boys might come up and deliberately bump into us. They would then stop and pick a fight. We would be expected to run away from the fight, or get beaten up. Those were the safe options. The Khasi boys might belong to, or have support from, powerful organisations. We had no such organisation to back us.

The organisation that was a particular source of terror to us was the Khasi Students' Union (KSU). This group was famous for its agitations that frequently turned violent. The violence was not always restricted to mere beatings.

In 1987, the KSU demanded that all foreigners—a word that in actual practice referred to all dkhars or outsiders from communities seen as belonging to the Indian mainland—be ethnically cleansed out of Meghalaya by the government. The crucial distinction was between hill tribes and the rest; tribals from any of the numerous tribes in North-East India were safe. Non-tribals, except the Meiteis of Manipur who have East-Asian features, were not.

The KSU began a series of bandhs that brought the town to a halt. The Congress government of the time, led by Captain Williamson Sangma, tried negotiation and compromise, but matters got out of hand. For forty-eight hours, mobs clashed with the police, attacked local residents and village shops and set ablaze ten vehicles, including the police superintendent's jeep. The arson and police firing left four persons dead and over three dozen civilians and policemen injured.

The violence was the direct result of a festering anti-foreigners' movement launched in 1985 by tribal students under the Khasi Students' Union banner and abetted by a section of opposition politicians. There were still a few non-tribal Congress(I) state politicians then, and one told *India Today* magazine that the agitation 'has the tacit support of the majority of tribals and unfortunately, even our party has indirectly been playing along with it.'

'Tribal students, led by the militant Bull Lyngdoh, have ever since the signing of the Assam accord in August 1985, been clamouring for the accord's extension to Meghalaya. They empathized particularly with the clauses relating to the detection and deportation of foreigners,' *India Today* reported at the time. The state government tried compromising with the students through negotiations and, encouraged by the Centre's silence, took several policy decisions aimed at assuaging their fears. In response to the catchy students' slogan 'No detection, no election,' the state acted in February 1986 by abruptly deporting over 10,000 Nepali-speaking residents of the state without bothering to check if they were indeed foreigners.[1]

The concessions only made the students demand more. The crunch came in May-end, when two Nepali students of Shillong College were brutally beaten up by a few tribal students. Something remarkable happened—a police case was lodged. In those days in Shillong, cases of dkhars being attacked would rarely result in police First Information Reports.

Even more surprisingly, the police acted against Bull Lyngdoh, the chief of the KSU, and arrested him. Lyngdoh refused bail. The KSU demanded his unconditional release. This was a demand the government could not fulfil. The KSU called for blackouts. The darkness that descended on the town was punctuated by violent mob attacks against dkhar

---

[1]Banerjie, Indranil. 'Identity Crisis,' *India Today*. 15 July 1987.

homes, shops and even cinema halls. Schools and colleges shut down. The state government seemed unwilling or powerless to end the violence. Many dkhars left. For those who remained, life revolved around curfew relaxations, when everyone rushed about to buy food, medicine and other necessities of life.

It was not altogether a bad life. For a school kid, to have months of holidays and no exams is a wonderful thing. I have fond memories of the curfew holidays, as we called them. It was a whole year of play; the violence was just how life was. It was unremarkable. The only bad memory I have of it was from the time I was set upon by two boys on the street, complete strangers, who punched me in the face for being a dkhar. I was then twelve years old and on my way to the library to return my books.

The politics of ethnic cleansing went deep, affecting children and adults alike, but even in the worst times, some basic elements of civilized interaction remained largely intact. The ethnic divide did not break any of my friendships. Personal relations continued largely unaffected by the wider turmoil. Even between strangers, human decency generally trumped ethnic identity.

One day, trouble broke out suddenly, as it was prone to. Those were times before mobile phones. News spread by word of mouth and the whole town shut down. School had reopened briefly—eventually it would shut down for the whole year—and I was in class. My mother rushed to bring me home. We did not have a car, and by the time she got there, the streets were empty. Buses and taxis had gone off the roads. I had been packed off with a classmate whose parents had come to pick him up in a car. Mother remembers she found herself stranded at the school. It was another parent, a Khasi lady, who happened to be the deputy commissioner at the time, who dropped her home.

The house we used to live in then was close to Police Bazar, a short distance from the old state assembly building. The KSU would occasionally hold some agitation near the assembly, and the police would occasionally respond with force. If the CRPF was around, there would be severe beatings for any protester who got caught. They were infamous for wielding their sticks with indiscriminate force.

During one of those skirmishes near the assembly, Bull Lyngdoh, the KSU chief, jumped over a wall and raced into the doctor's clinic adjacent to our house to seek refuge. The security forces were on his tail. The old Bengali homeopath, who wore a dhoti and wooden slippers till his last days, sat him down and saw off the policemen.

In the years that followed, ethnic violence and rioting were a recurrent occurrence. The worst incidents happened after 1987. A young woman, Gauri Dey, was pulled out of her home by a mob, raped and killed by having a stick inserted into her vagina. Another young woman died when a petrol bomb was flung into a taxi during Durga Puja in 1992. Her death was followed by rioting and mob violence. A businessman travelling from Guwahati to Shillong was burnt to death.

There was never any expectation of justice for the dkhars or non-tribals from the state government. I am not aware of any convictions in any of the cases of rape or murder. Nor was there any outcry of the kind that has attached to riots and ethnic cleansing in other parts of the country such as the 1984 Sikh riots and the 2002 Gujarat riots. The forced exodus of Kashmiri Pandits is well known. The forced exodus of Bengalis and Nepalis from North-East India is forgotten.

The relative silence, particularly in the case of the Bengalis, is somewhat odd, since this is a community from which many journalists, writers, academics and filmmakers have made a mark at the national and international levels. Perhaps the silence is because this is also the community from which many have suffered extreme violence for three successive generations. It is the silence of the repeatedly oppressed.

The Bengali Hindu community of North-East India includes a large number of families that migrated there as refugees from erstwhile East Pakistan. Partition, the holocaust of the Indian subcontinent, drove them from their homes. A succession of riots leading up to the Bangladesh genocide of 1971 by the Pakistan army under dictator Yahya Khan—one of the worst in world history in which an estimated 1-3 million Bengalis, mostly Hindus, were killed—destroyed the community[2]. Those who survived the riots and genocide in their lost homeland then faced violence in their new homes as their unwilling hosts across North-East India rioted to drive them out. Scattered and leaderless, these people who had contributed more than any other as a group to the cause of India's independence found themselves destroyed by the very freedom they had fought for.

It was said of the colonial British Raj that they used a policy of 'divide and rule.' The divisions they created far outlived their empire.

Division of people and lands by religion, starting with the partition of Bengal in 1905 and leading eventually to the

---

[2]The figure of 1-3 million is from the *Encyclopedia of Genocide,* Vol. I. The assertion that the victims were mainly Hindus is made on the basis of numerous reports and books including *The Rape of Bangladesh* by Pakistani journalist Anthony Mascarenhas who broke the story of the genocide in 1971.

partition of the Indian subcontinent along religious lines into a predominantly Muslim Pakistan and a predominantly Hindu India in 1947, is only one example of an enduring divide that originated in colonial times. The broader role of the census and colonial cartography in creating lasting divides between linguistic communities is largely forgotten even by its victims.

The root of our troubles in Shillong that lasted around twenty-five years starting 1979—a year marked by the outbreak of riots between Khasis and Bengalis—can perhaps be traced to 1790, when the British East India Company drew the first borders between the Khasi Hills and the Sylhet plains, and between Khasi and Bengali identities. Historian David Ludden, in an essay titled 'The First Boundary of Bangladesh on Sylhet's Northern Frontiers,' wrote: 'This period in the expansion and demarcation of Sylhet territory punctuated a long process of geographical change that involved the interaction of five very old, dynamic, and overlapping geographies—of nature, land use, markets, culture, and governance—which had together defined Sylhet historically as a region with indefinite boundaries and shifting substance.'

According to Ludden, each of these geographies had a distinct composition. 'Nature's geography set the physical framework for livelihoods in mountains, uplands, and floodplains,' he wrote. This expanded and contracted depending on natural factors such as floods and the changing course of rivers.

The social space of ethnic and cultural identity was one that had, according to him, emerged during centuries of migratory mobility across southern Asia, from Arabia to Vietnam. 'Eighteenth century ethnic spaces held mixtures of Persianate, Sanskritic, Bengali, and disparate tribal cultures; and mixing was still ongoing. Rajas in Cachar and Jaintia had embraced Hindu ritualism to spawn tribe-and-caste societies that spread around the northern mountains. Conversion to Islam increased and diversified the Muslim population. Tribal groups mingled and assimilated with Hindus and Muslims. Bengali Muslims and Hindus controlled most of the lowlands, but Afghans and Turks were also important. Migrations into Sylhet of all its many ethnic and cultural groups continued throughout the eighteenth century,' Ludden wrote. 'Geographies of nature, land use, markets and culture had no strict boundaries; they remained open to limitless mixing and mobility.'[3]

It was this unbounded fluidity—marked in the case of the Khasi and Bengali peoples by the presence of a community of Khasi-Bengalis who shared characteristics with both groups—that was permanently destroyed over the next few decades by colonial processes aided by the proliferation of certain relatively new technologies that the colonisers and missionaries brought with them. The printing press was prime among these. Its role in creating the modern imagination of hard boundaries—between ethnicities, between lands—was critical.

To understand how, a bit of a flashback is necessary.

Meghalaya's story starts with Assam, from which it was carved out following a movement for a hill state. Tribal aspirations that had led to the demand for the hill state, centred on control of jobs and resources by the local tribal groups, were, however, inadequately met by the creation of the state in 1972. The first major riots, in 1979, began when the KSU launched an agitation against 'foreigners' jointly with

---

[3]Ludden, David. 'The First Boundary of Bangladesh on Sylhet's Northern Frontiers', *Journal of the Asiatic Society of Bangladesh.* 26 June 2003.

the All Assam Students' Union and other students' unions in the North-Eastern states, according to an article in the *Shillong Times* by Michael N. Syiem, a former president of the organisation. The event that sparked off the rioting was the killing of a Bengali MLA from the Garo Hills, Manik Das, in Boko, Assam, during this agitation, which brought out mobs of the MLAs mainly Bengali supporters and their largely Khasi opponents on to the streets of Shillong[4].

There was by this time a history of violence against Bengali speakers in Assam that stretched back to at least 1960, when the Assam state government of the Congress party led by BP Chaliha was pressurised by an agitation powered by students and backed by the Assam Sahitya Sabha to make Assamese the sole official language of the state. This sparked protests in the Barak Valley, which had a Bengali majority.[5] The police responded with disproportionate force, shooting dead eleven protesters. Meanwhile, across the newly drawn border separating the state with East Pakistan, the Bengali Hindu minority had been under attack almost since the birth of that country. There had been severe ethnic cleansing in 1947 and again in 1950. A further round of rioting and ethnic cleansing followed in 1964. There was evidence of state complicity in the rioting, with at least one minister of the Pakistan government, Abdus Sabur Khan, being directly involved.

The 1960 move to impose Assamese in Assam, a state with significant populations of diverse linguistic groups, all of whom had their own areas of influence, was seen as some sort of payback for the imposition of Bengali as the official language of Assam by the British in 1837. The genesis of

---

[4]'Old Wounds Reopened,' *Shillong Times*. 2 April 2015.

[5]'Bongal Kheda Again,' *Economic and Political Weekly*. 30 July 1960.

conflict between these two linguistic identities can be traced to that year.

Assamese, Bengali, Oriya, Magahi, Maithili and Bhojpuri are all descendants of a language known to linguists as Magadhi Apabhramsa. Linguist Suniti Kumar Chatterji classified Bengali, Assamese and Oriya as Eastern Magadhan. According to him, Oriya branched off first. The common dialect in North Bengal and Assam continued as one speech, as a member of the Bengali-Assamese group of dialects. 'In the 15th century,' wrote Chatterji, 'it split up into two sections, Assamese and North Bengali, when Assamese started on an independent existence of its own by not acknowledging the domination of literary Bengali, already established in East Bengal as well.'[6]

The centre of Assamese culture in those times was in western Assam, in the territories that had once been part of the ancient Kamrup kingdom. This was a kingdom that finds mention in Chinese Buddhist pilgrim Hiuen Tsang's account of his visit there in the seventh century AD. The king at the time was described by Hiuen Tsang as a man named Kumar Bhaskarvarman, of the Brahmin caste. 'From the time that his family seized the land and assumed government, there have elapsed a thousand generations,' Hiuen Tsang wrote. The site of the capital of this kingdom, Pragjyotishpura, which was already ancient during Hiuen Tsang's time, is not certain. It is now identified with Guwahati but Gait, in his magisterial history of Assam, speculated that it was either in Goalpara or Cooch Behar in present-day Assam and West Bengal, respectively, or somewhere near Rangpur in Bangladesh.[7] No sign of it has been discovered yet.

---

[6]Chatterji, Suniti Kumar. *The Origin and Development of the Bengali Language*. Calcutta: Calcutta University Press. 1926.

[7]Gait, Edward. *A History of Assam*. Guwahati: EBH Publishers. 2017.

Assam from ancient times was known as Kamarupa till the end of the Koch rule in the seventeenth century, according to renowned Assamese linguist Upendranath Goswami. In his research paper (later published as a book) 'A Study On Kamrupi: A Dialect Of Assamese' published in 1958, Goswami wrote: 'The Aryan language spoken first in Assam was the Kamrupi language spoken in Rangpur, Cooch Behar, Goalpara, Kamrup district and some parts of Nowgong and Darrang districts.'

'It is in this Kamrupi language that the early Assamese literature was mainly written,' writes Goswami. 'Up to the seventeenth century, as the centres of art, literature and culture were confined within western Assam and the poets and writers hailed from this part, the language of this part also acquired prestige.' The most noteworthy Assamese poet of the pre-Vaishnavite period in Goswami's estimation was Madhava Kandali, who belonged to the present district of Nagaon, and rendered the entire *Ramayana* into Assamese verse under the patronage of King Mahamanikya, a Kachari king.

'The golden age of Assamese literature opened with the reign of Naranarayan, the Koch king. He gathered around him at his court at Cooch Behar a galaxy of learned men. Sankardev, the real founder of Assamese literature, and his follower Madhavdev worked under his patronage,' wrote Goswami. Sankardev and Madhavdev's Vaishnava devotional songs are performed to this day. They are in a literary language called Brajabuli, first popularised by Maithili poet Vidyapati in the fourteenth century.

It was only after the decline of Koch power by the seventeenth century that the centre of literary importance shifted from western Assam to the Ahom court in eastern Assam.

The standardisation of the Sibsagar dialect as 'correct' Assamese occurred with the arrival of the printing press, brought by Baptist missionaries keen on preaching the Bible.

The spoken language of the common people, however, remained local dialects until mass media and mass education began to change that in the twentieth century. On ground, Assamese and Bengali merge into one another along a dialect continuum even to this day. A traveller travelling from Sibsagar to Kolkata by boat—the old method of travel between these two places—would encounter a gradual change in the spoken language, with Assamese changing by degrees into Bengali. En route, the traveller would hear Kamrupi dialects such as Goalpariya and Rajbongshi that have elements common to both standard Assamese and standard Bengali.

The gap between the two standard languages became an issue for the first time only after the advent of British colonial rule. The trouble started with the popularisation of the Gaudiya dialect of West Bengal as standard Bengali. That this was not the very definition of Bengali until the nineteenth century is evident from the fact that Ram Mohan Roy, the first Bengali to expound on the grammar of the language, called his book *Gaudiya Vyakaran*—not Bangla or Bengali Vyakaran.[8] It was first published in 1826, the year the British extended their rule to Assam following the conclusion of the Treaty of Yandaboo. Initially, British rule extended only to Lower Assam. Their rule reached Upper Assam in 1833, when they installed Purandar Singha as king in the Ahom territory.

A debate on language policies was then on in the corridors of colonial power. The language of administration at the time was still Persian, a remnant of Mughal rule. The

[8] Samrat. 'Kamrupi, A Language With No Army,' *Mint.* 23 Oct 2017.

language of religion was Arabic for the Muslims and Sanskrit for the Hindus—an important consideration in a world where only a minuscule percentage of the populations acquired literacy, primarily for reading the scriptures. (Even in 1901, the literacy rate in India was only 9.8 percent for men and 0.6 percent for women.[9]) In 1835, after much agonising, the British finally decided to replace Persian with English as the official language. That same year, Lord T.B. Macaulay presented his infamous 'Minute on Education' in which he argued for the replacement of Arabic and Sanskrit education with education in the English language.

In 1837, Persian was replaced as the language of district courts by local vernaculars, and Urdu and Hindustani. Hindustani was the Sanskritised Hindi vernacular that according to historian Arnold J. Toynbee was 'actually manufactured by British Protestant missionaries to provide the Hindu population of northern India with a counterpart of the Persianised Hindi vernacular, known as Urdu, which the Indian Muslims had already manufactured for themselves.' In the case of Bengal, to which Assam had been appended upon its conquest, the shift was from Persian to Bengali, for which the Gaudiya version was taken as the definition—even though the dialects of Vanga, from which the province and the language get their name, correspond to those of eastern Bengal.

This gradually gave rise to a debate in Assam where the Baptist missionaries had set up their printing presses in Sibsagar. 'In 1836, two remarkable members of the Amcrican Baptist Mission, the Rev. N. Brown and O.T. Cotter, with their families, first set foot on Assamese soil. Among other things,

[9]Census of India, 2011.

a printing press was part of their missionary equipment. The missionaries made Sibsagar the centre of their activities and used the dialect of Sibsagar for their literary purposes,' according to Upendranath Goswami.

These missionaries published, from their press, the first Assamese grammar text and the first Assamese-English dictionary. 'Under the influence of the missionaries, a set of native writers grew up, and books and periodicals in the language of eastern Assam multiplied. Thus, the traditions of the Ahom court, supported by the mission press, established the language of eastern Assam as the literary language of the entire province,' Goswami wrote. 'The differences between the standard and Kamrupi dialect are not insignificant. They range over the whole field of phonology, morphology and vocabulary.'

The standardisation of Bengali and Assamese languages and the use of Gaudiya Bengali as the language of courts set them on a collision course. This collision took a while to develop. Animosity between the two linguistic groups did not express itself immediately after the imposition of Bengali as the common court language of Bengal and Assam in 1837. The first public protests of note occurred in 1853 when A.J.M. Mills, a judge of the Sadar Dewani Adalat, visited Assam on an inspection tour. He also received a letter on the issue from a missionary named A.H. Danford.

The matter simmered till 1872, when a petition entitled 'The Humble Memorial of the Assamese Community at Nowgong, Assam' was placed before the lieutenant governor of Bengal, Sir George Campbell, seeking the removal of Bengali and its replacement by Assamese. The author of the petition was the president of the committee and author of the first Assamese dictionary, Reverend Miles Bronson from the American Baptist Mission.[10] The following year, the British finally replaced Bengali with Assamese as the language of courts in Assam. Another year later, in 1874, Assam, including Sylhet, was separated from Bengal and became a province of British India with Shillong, then ten years old as a town, as its capital. The largely Bengali-speaking areas of the Barak Valley and Goalpara, along with their populations, also came to Assam during this redrawing of maps.

By this time, school and college degrees from the educational institutions established by the British authorities had become important for securing government jobs. In this matter, the Bengalis had a head start over their neighbours. Of the 938 students who matriculated from Calcutta University in 1872, only 4 graduated from schools in the Brahmaputra valley. As late as 1898, the number was only 32. Sylhet had a relative advantage in the matter, and 68 students from there obtained BA degrees between 1888 and 1900 compared to 29 from the Brahmaputra Valley.[11]

The result was that the Bengali boys—work outside home was still a male domain—began to corner a lion's share of the jobs. The Bengali clerk became the face of the British sarkar at the level of painful daily interaction across North-East India. The sahibs themselves were distant, exalted beings.

Shillong being the capital of Assam, a lot of people from all over the province migrated there. When, in 1905, Bengal was partitioned for the first time by Lord Curzon's administration, the town became the summer capital of the

---

[10]Fishman, Joshua and Ofelia, Garcia (eds.) *Handbook of Language and Ethnic Identity*, Vol. 2. Oxford: Oxford University Press. 2011.

[11]Sharma, Jayeeta. *Empire's Garden: Assam and the Making of India*. London: Duke University Press. 2011.

new province of Eastern Bengal and Assam, a vast territory that included almost the whole of today's North-East India and Bangladesh. Dhaka was the winter capital.

The Bengal partition was revoked in 1911, and the capital of the Raj shifted from Kolkata to Delhi, but Shillong's cosmopolitan character remained. In fact, the town's interactions with the world increased with the First World War that began in 1914. The Empire began to recruit labour and cannon fodder from all its farthest reaches. Labour corps were raised and sent to distant lands from the Khasi and Garo Hills to die on behalf of their colonisers.

The Indian struggle for independence was on. In 1919, the year of the Jallianwala Bagh massacre, the first Indian to win a Nobel Prize, Rabindranath Tagore—he was the literature laureate in 1913—came to Shillong, having returned his knighthood. He stayed in the house of a Bengali officer in the British administration, who was then assistant commissioner of Chittagong. In 1938, the then president of the Indian National Congress, Subhash Chandra Bose, visited the town to work on government formation in the province. His efforts resulted in the installation of a Congress government led by Gopinath Bordoloi.[12]

During the Second World War years, soldiers and airmen from distant parts of the world arrived in North-East India. There were the English, Irish, Scots and Welsh, of course, but also Americans from the US Air Force, and Chinese Kuomintang soldiers. Shillong, already a melting pot, became a temporary home to people from these various nationalities.

---

[12] Hazarika, Sanjoy. 'Subhash Bose and the "special" case of Assam,' *The Sunday Guardian*. 22 Jan 2012.

The imagination of Shillong as provincial town rather than cosmopolitan 'hill station' began in the 1960s with the efforts of Assamese chauvinists to evict Bengalis from the state of Assam of which it was the capital. It picked up pace with the hill state movement that led to a lot of Assamese and Bengalis eventually being forced out, as the local Khasis and Garos wrested control of the new state of Meghalaya, and Shillong became its capital. By the time the '80s rolled around, which is where I began this essay with my personal memories of growing up in Shillong, the town had become a battleground between Khasis and dkhars.

On whom, then, should we lay blame for the transition from a world where, in the words of historian David Ludden, 'Geographies of nature, land use, markets and culture had no strict boundaries; they remained open to limitless mixing and mobility', to a world where both land and cultural identities are marked by sharp boundaries?

It would be tempting to blame the colonial British and the evangelising American Baptists whose efforts ultimately caused the transition, but perhaps the blame belongs rightfully to a combination of factors. The proliferation of printing presses in the nineteenth century triggered the standardization of languages and hence of linguistic identities. The proliferation of printed political maps with vast territories coloured into ethno-linguistic identities—Assam for Assamese, Manipur for Manipuris and so on—exacerbated the problem. Diverse territories with rainbows of cultures were reduced to monochrome representations following European notions of nationality and race that were then popular. The Census deepened the sense of unitary religious and linguistic identities and froze what had formerly been fluid into a rigidity akin to rigor mortis. Urbanisation and the rise of mass education, with a resulting dependence on the job economy, exacerbated the ensuing clash between the newly created ethno-linguistic 'nations'.

It did not take long for our ahistorical peoples to forget their shared past.

Notions of 'purity of blood' and assertions that only 'pure Khasi' or 'pure Assamese' had the right to live there were heard in Shillong and Guwahati during their troubled years, several decades after the West had moved on from these toxic notions following the Holocaust of the Jews in Nazi Germany. These statements were seen as expressions of 'jatiyobadi' politics in Assam, and provided inspiration to armed insurgent groups that carried out massacres of unarmed civilians with origins in 'mainland' India.

Multiculturalism is now all the rage in polite Western societies, and has been for a few decades. It is contrasted with the white nationalism now regaining ascendancy across Europe and in America for the first time since World War II.

The Europeans and Americans, like most Indians, tend to think that their present will someday—if we behave ourselves and work hard—be our future. On the contrary, I believe that their habits of counting, measuring and classifying everything on earth with the eventual aim of monetising it all has created many of our problems. Nature was reduced to natural resources by taxonomy and the periodic table. The human world was reduced to human resources by a similar process. Time and space were monetised. The processes of state formation rigidified borders and identities. We have had two World Wars to remind us of the problems these can cause. And yet... we must now hope that economic interests will save the world they have created.

Today, despite occasional flare-ups such as the mob

violence in June 2018 against a Dalit Sikh colony after a brawl in which two Khasi boys were beaten up, the dkhar is no longer a target of open hostility in Shillong. Economics has trumped divisive politics for the moment. Whether the resumption of identity politics sparked by the National Register of Citizens in Assam, and the proposed Citizenship Amendment Bill, will allow this state of affairs to persist is moot. Across North-East India, it will take only a little communal foolishness for a return to the bad old days.

INSIDERS, OUTSIDERS AND THOSE IN BETWEEN

After All, There's Much in a Name

Sanjoy Hazarika

Over the past years, one of the issues that has engaged my attention in terms of that theme's very contemporariness and contrariness relates to the perceptions of and understanding of the 'outsider' and the 'insider' in the narratives flowing in and around the North-Eastern region. It has a major bearing on the way the region is not just perceived but also how it is shaping itself into a larger narrative, while retaining the strong chords of discord and consonance, which are the heart of its own history and cultures.

Thus, for example, ethnic groups that may feel themselves viewed with prejudice and suspicion in one part of the region also face discrimination on grounds of skin colour and facial appearance—not to mention the way they dress and speak (not all are fluent in, for example, Hindi). They have faced it over decades and at times it does not appear to have diminished. Yet, what is changing is the way people engage with this approach, speak, collaborate, resist and mobilise over it—whereas in times past, many incidences of racial discrimination and abuse may have been suffered in silence.

In large metros, despite their obvious striking difference in terms of looks, professionals from this area are increasingly absorbed into the legal, administrative, media and other professions. Competence matters as do social skills. They merge seamlessly into the larger population in other parts of the country, and find that they are treated with greater level of equality than back 'home'. Thus, an 'insider' of the region may feel that he or she is regarded by a neighbouring community or group in that very region as an outsider. Examples of these are too many to enumerate, and abound in Meghalaya or Assam, Manipur or Mizoram.

There are horror stories, too, among those who come from the 'mainland,' as travellers and settlers have found, and who face discrimination and prejudice in the North-East. There are specific names for the outsider in virtually each state—*bahirormanuh* (outside people) or *bidekhi* or *deshwali* in Assam, *vai* in Mizoram, *dkhar* in the Khasi hills of Meghalaya, and anti-outsider campaigns across the region have been sharp, ugly and many times bloody.

But I have friends who are from the Sikh and Punjabi Hindu, Sindhi and Marwari communities who have lived for generations in places like Shillong, Guwahati and Imphal. These towns are home to them. Some of the younger generation have stayed on, others have moved. In Shillong's Police Bazar are stores like Uncle's Shop, Mohini Stores, Lila Brothers and many more, on either side of the bustling road and jostling each other into the depths of the bazaar, a bazaar which is never still but filled with shoppers. The sidewalks are crowded with sales at tiny shops while hawkers, calling out in a babel of languages and accents, cry out their wares.

It's where I also grew up, in a place that I still call home, of clear skies in the sharp winter sun and bracing clean air. My father settled in Shillong when it was a part of the composite state of Assam soon after Independence and as a health professional in government service, rose to head the then Reid Chest Hospital for TB patients before he passed away, very young. My mother stayed on, unlike thousands of other Assamese families who packed bags and baggage and went down to the steamy plains to begin the burst of building and investment in Guwahati and Dispur, the new capital, when Assam was sundered to create Meghalaya for the Khasi, Jaintia and Garo tribes.

The Orientalist and multiculturalism advocate, the late Edward Said, has influenced my thinking while trying to understand contesting identities and collaborative proximities. Of the need, in complex regions as the north-east of India, to think out of the box, outside the classroom, challenge the orthodox and ordinary. As we know, Said opposed the 'mainstreaming' of knowledge, people and ideas.

He abhorred the model of intellectual work 'as something you do for a living, between the hours of nine to five, with one eye on the clock, and another cocked at what is considered to be proper, professional behaviour—not rocking the boat, not straying outside the accepted paradigms or limits, making yourself marketable and above all presentable, hence uncontroversial and unpolitical and "objective".'

Said's model of public intellectual work envisioned the intellectual as 'someone who considers that to be a thinking and concerned member of a society one is entitled to raise moral issues at the heart of even the most technical and professionalised activity as it involves one's country, its power, its mode of interacting with its citizens as well as with other societies.'

These points are central to this discussion for they are built around the life experiences of people from and in the region, which shape attitudes and approaches, of governments and communities.

There is a chain of connectivity between insiders and outsiders, of perceptions and distances. This is something with which we are familiar in my home state of Assam. In Mizoram, Nagaland and Manipur, many speak of their encounters with a law that enshrines impunity, inequality and injustice and embeds discrimination. These are rules and laws for 'locals' or 'insiders' designed and enforced by 'outsiders'. One speaks here of the Armed Forces Special Powers Act (Assam and Manipur), 1958, which was aimed at putting down an insurrection in the Naga Hills district (now Nagaland) of Assam. These experiences are woven together in a fabric of blood and fear written with instruments of torture, verbal, physical and legal.

T.S. Eliot put it powerfully:

Your shadow at morning striding behind you
Or your shadow at evening rising to meet you;
I will show you fear in a handful of dust.

Our region has seen a war with China and conflicts with Pakistan. But above all, it remains both combative, embattled, cloistered and divided about the 'differences' among its many constituents, such as between Nagaland and Manipur or between the Naga and Kukis or in Assam between Assamese speakers and other groups, including the Bodos and Muslims of Bangla origin. Often, we casually refer to the latter as Bangladeshis, a word that has become more of a pejorative than anything else. The prism of identity continues to define us.

How is an outsider defined? Is it by law and citizenship; is it by ethnography, economy or sociological and political norms? Or is it also by appearance (i.e., 'North-Easterners' in Delhi and other metros), by circumstance and increasingly by the *nazar* that is stamped in the eyes of the beholder. The gaze, which says, 'This is what I think you are, whether you like it or not and that is the place you belong, the place where I locate and place you.'

The nazar can be deadly as Syed Shafiddun Khan found out to his cost in Dimapur. Khan, who was accused of rape, of being a Bangladeshi, which he was not—his larger family lives in Karimganj, Assam, and his sibling and father worked in the Indian Army—and also branded an IBI (Illegal Bangladeshi Immigrant). The IBI is a new acronym to typify Muslims of Bengali origin.

We are not getting either into the details of the sexual assault case in which he was enmeshed, with sharply contradictory 'facts' emerging about the nature of that event, or the way he was dragged out of a supposedly high-security prison by a huge mob, beaten, stripped, tied to a motorcycle and dragged for kilometres before his dead body was propped up in the centre of Dimapur, a crowded, dusty town, that bakes in the humid heat of the Assam plains during summers and is cooled by the hill breezes from the Naga range in winters.

Dimapur is a commercial town, the heart of the tax collection of various armed wings of the Naga movement, the business centre of Nagaland where it meets the Brahmaputra valley, the place where the rich and powerful in government, both politicians and bureaucrats, those in business, the 'underground' professionals and major scholars of the state have built splendid mansions. Business appears to thrive. Different communities live cheek by jowl here and there is also a group called the Sumias, where Sumi Nagas have intermarried Muslims of Bangla origin. Khan's was one such family; he was married to a Naga woman.

Here as in many complex situations in the region, the 'truth' lies in a strange and tortuous middle ground between fact and fiction and the mixed narratives which flow about the issue of immigration. It lies in the gaze of the beholder, the holder of opinions and those who drive public mobilisation on such sensitive issues, centred around the idea of what or who constitutes an 'outsider' which we so often tend to stigmatise as a 'foreigner' or a 'Bangladeshi.'

We cannot but remember that anger against alleged Bangladeshis has been reflected in sporadic incidents across the North-East. Protests against 'illegal migrants' have also rocked Manipur and Meghalaya.

So the question that needs to be asked here is: who is being identified as a foreigner and more so as a 'Bangladeshi'? Even senior figures in Delhi were unaware that the man who was beaten to death was an Indian national, assuming, obviously and mistakenly so, because of his religion that he was a 'Bangladeshi.' This is an issue that time and again rears its head especially in Assam, and, as we have noted, in other states of the region as well.

Representatives of many 'indigenous' groups in the North-East look at Muslims of Bangla origin with suspicion. Issues are driven by rhetoric, suspicions, concerns and even hate.

Public opinion is moulded by those in high places of politics and government and some in the media who continue to push stereotypes and old ideas of homelands and identities without considering research and field data let alone the views of 'the other' side.

In a state like Assam and its neighbouring states of the North-East, where a range of ethnic and religious groups live next to each other, this is a heady cocktail, an explosive recipe. Even a few words or acts can trigger a cycle or cycles of violence as we know and as we have seen, time and again.

Thus, we totter at the edge of a precipice, so often, without completely falling in. Who then is this ubiquitous 'Bangladeshi' that many seem to hate so passionately? Surely, the definition lies not so much in what one is in so much as what one is not. Thus, by the very nomenclature, a Bangladeshi can't be someone who migrated to India in 1947 or 1961 but only after 1971, the creation of the nation by that name. The National Register of Citizens (NRC), which was published in July 2018 and which is supposed to have the authentic list of Indian citizens in the state—and exclude those who were there illegally—has been mired in controversy. To widespread consternation, an estimated four million did not make the cut—these included former officials, well-known families as well as people from families whose siblings had made it to the list! The process was continuing at the time of this book going to press. In one decision, the Supreme Court ordered a 10 percent sample survey of those left out to check for discrepancies.

Many adhere to the belief that most people of Bangla origin, especially if they live in *chars* and *saporis* (or sandy islands) of the Brahmaputra valley, are illegal and therefore Bangladeshi. Few care to understand that while char populations are often temporary, yet there is a permanence in that temporariness: they do move from char to char, especially when *char bhanga jai* (when the chars break) at times of flood and acute erosion. This is not the same as moving seamlessly from nation to nation.

There is no doubt that there has been migration from Bangladesh into Assam and the North-East. This is a fact. But this appears to be ebbing, not necessarily growing, as home conditions improve in our neighbouring country. And indeed, people from our region are looking West, to other parts of India, as our own economic conditions here stutter along.

Few are looking at this: in many social indices, Bangladesh scores over many states of the region and other parts of India! Look at facts, not at rhetoric. Many who speak of it as a basket case have not been there. Go there, I often say, your eyes will pop—it is a robust nation, democratic and industrious. One of their achievements is a lower population growth rate than any part of South Asia, barring Sri Lanka, and it has been described as moving up to a middle economy out of the impoverishment that marks its once fellow LDCs (Least Developed Countries): Laos, Cambodia and Sub-Saharan Africa.

The many different competing groups of the North-East may be strangers to each other but we are no strangers to history. History is a close and at times a terrible and unforgiving companion.

Attitudes are formed by experiences and narrated in stories; these stories become texts, are embedded in books and taught to generations who pass on the word. The volume of words become a torrent of cement and brick, building high walls of division. Those inside the wall are privy to special information, or so they believe. Those outside are the *bahirormanuh,* the outsiders. Let me share one such story.

In the 17th century, when the Mughal army came to Assam under Mir Jumla to fight the Ahoms, it had a Persian chronicler. His name was Shahbuddin Taalish and although Taalish talked extensively of the courage and tenacity of their opponents, he also said of Assam:

> *It is another world, another people and other customs;*
> *Its land is not like [our] land, its sky is not like [our] sky.*
> *Its sky sends rain down without the [originating] cause of clouds;*
> *On its ground the green grass sprouts up without any aid from the soil.*
> *It stands outside the circle of the Earth and the bowels of the*
> *[enveloping] sphere.*
> *It has been separated from the world, like the letter aliph.*
> *The seasons all begin [here] at the time of their conclusion [elsewhere];*
> *Here there is heat in [our] winter and chill in [our] summer.*
> *The Rajah of Assam brought to the field an army*
> *Whose large number became a cage on earth;*
> *[They are] tumult-raising and sudden [in attack] like the eyes of the fair sex,*
> *Hurling arrows and [other] missiles, and making a [firm] stand in the battlefield*
> *Its rivers are deep*
> *Like the thoughts of a wise man*

So, from times past, we've been on the outside. But we, too, have our own vocabulary: for those we regard as the outsiders although they may think of themselves as the *mukhyadhara*, we have special names as I noted at the start. These include 'vais' in Mizo, 'bangal' in Axomiya, 'dkhar' in Khasi, 'bahira manuh' in Nagamese—although, often these words are also directed at each other

But move to the 19th century and the coming of the British empire to the lands of the Nagas, Mizos, Manipuris and Assam apart from the Khasis, Garo and Jaintia. The British colonial adventure was essentially one of commerce and expansion. They defined several of these areas as Excluded or Partly Excluded and brought in laws to enforce distance between hills and plains. Colonial law created one set of divisions.

It is not that the hills and plains were particularly well connected, but they had barter agreements, trading posts and markets or haats, which were established at regular intervals.

Some haats in Assam attracted traders from Tibet and Bhutan. All this existed before the British who created the Chin Hills Regulation Act and brought in a system of permits for 'outsiders' from beyond the area. They would need an Inner Line Permit (ILP) to conduct business, visit and travel within areas such as the Naga and Lushai or Mizo hills.

Today, the Inner Line Permit is enforced in three states of the region and there are efforts to make it a law in Manipur. So colonial law today is still the basis of defining the outsider, one who cannot settle although there are no restrictions on individuals and communities from any of these states moving or settling in any part of India as part of their immutable rights.

The ILP is not an issue for me. But what fascinates me is that there is another rule which actually creates a joint citizenship of Indians and Myanmarese.

In 2015, I travelled to Burma through Mizoram, a brief visit to Chin state through stunningly green, cool and beautiful landscapes and a horrendous road, one of the worst I have driven on.

With the most elementary of identity cards or identification, people living on the 2,000-odd km border especially in Nagaland, Mizoram and Manipur can move fifteen kilometres into each other's territory, into sovereign lands, without travel papers. Because they have kin here. They share a common language, faith, families and traditions. So how does one explain this?

On the one hand you have the ILP by which an 'outside' researcher, a businessman or a traveller cannot travel within the states of Arunachal Pradesh, Mizoram or Nagaland without a special pass. And on the other, you have citizens of India and Myanmar who can visit each other and even live in each other's countries under what could be defined as a loose joint citizenship.

While colonial laws have divided people from each other and created separate nations, there is also an inherent quiet flexibility within the Indian state that recognises the fungibility of borders.

My journey from Aizawl to Champhai and then to the border town of Zokothar on the India-Myanmar border on a slushy and broken road, with vehicles lurching along at speeds of less than ten-fifteen km, was a good schooling.

One experience was striking: In a little bamboo shack in the middle of nowhere, surrounded by the lush green of the countryside, was a small shop. There were pumpkins and bitter gourd, handfuls of herbs and tender bamboo (used for pickles and cooking). But there was no store-owner around, there was no sign of any nearby home or village. The presence of the owner was marked by the existence of a collection box which urged the purchaser to put the money in it. In most other parts of South Asia, such an advertisement of trust and honesty would be seen as plain stupidity and the goods for sale as well as the money box would have been happily seized by passersby, without a moment's hesitation.

That shack with its green goods holds a valuable lesson for all of us: it says something about the self-belief of the Mizos and the value that they place in trust, especially these days when the social, print and visual mediums, and our minds have been peppered with twisted tales of love, betrayal, mistrust, embezzlement, abuse and murder most foul.

Being Indian these days is no easy task. But it takes great courage to do what many young people from the region are doing. Whereas an earlier generation—perhaps some of their own elders and relatives—staunchly opposed the idea of India and held onto perhaps an impossible dream of freedom and separation, many younger people are engaging with the idea of India and reshaping it to their comfort and conviction. They have not embraced it as much as people in other parts of the country. But they are engaging with it every day of their lives in metros and other locations.

Perhaps, this is how it should be.

Thousands of people, a majority of them young, from the North-East, many of them from the largest state of Assam, move every year outside the region in search of jobs, better lives, opportunities and education. They hold a range of jobs, from the basic to high-level positions, seeking education, conducting research, and leading the way in sporting events such as boxing, participating in high-skill group activities such as soccer or leading the way with music performances—if you take any major football team in India and counted the number of players from the North-East, there would be more than a handful, at least one-third to half the team!

Yet, despite all this, there is the bitter sting of discrimination that many face, and it has everything to do with appearance. I haven't faced it so far. But many others have. What is important now is that instead of quietly accepting the humiliation and nastiness heaped on them, younger people are courageously fighting back, forcing governments, employers, institutions and other civil society groups to take cognizance and lend their support. The most vulnerable are women, who face molestation, harassment and verbal abuse. But they are battling on. Why do they come? They are moving away from insecurity both political and economic, from lack of opportunities, from poor education facilities. India's metros and centres beckon to them. And despite discrimination, taunts and occasional violence, they are asserting their rights to access the equality and opportunities before all Indians.

However, there is another side to this—if economic prosperity and political equality is the goal, then we need to be aware that equality and prosperity cannot come if discrimination is institutionalised by the state. I speak of five letters: an acronym, which is a statement of that discrimination—AFSPA.

AFSPA is a bare, six-section act, which basically gives national security forces, especially the armed forces, powers to function with impunity. Its critical clauses are those which permit security forces to destroy suspected arms dumps, hiding places and shoot and kill but without the risk of criminal prosecution. In its fifty-eight years, not a single legal challenge to these sweeping powers has been sustained even in the Supreme Court of India. It has been found to be constitutional, but I have said that what is constitutional may not be just. It creates different classes of citizenship—between those who are protected by it (the security forces) and those who suffer its consequences, which is the general public apart from armed groups.

For decades, this law has been used and abused to suppress people, harm innocents and make them disappear in no less than four states of the region—apart from fighting insurgents and armed rebels. The list of the disappeared goes on, in every state where it has been deployed. Even UN special envoys have commented on the unjustness of using such laws as AFSPA.

The Supreme Court recognised a petition by a human rights group from Manipur that brought before it the disappearance or deaths either in custody or incidents of 1,528 civilians in the state. It ordered the investigation of seven random cases listed in the petition by a committee headed by former Supreme Court Justice Santosh Hegde. The committee found each case to be one of calculated killing by the security forces and police.

A final verdict is awaited but when we can be sure of is that impunity strengthens inequality and injustice, it also ensures that the insider-outsider divide remains unaddressed despite the occasional bridge.

It basically goes back to the shack on the road to Champhai in Mizoram: a question of trust. Does Delhi trust the state governments or not? The people of the region?

Activists such as Irom Sharmila, who was on hunger strike for over a decade, have long demanded the repeal of the act. Former Prime Minister Manmohan Singh appointed a committee of which I was a member to review AFSPA after national uproar following the rape and killing of a young Manipuri woman who was in the custody of a paramilitary unit.

The committee's findings were robust: repeal AFSPA and replace it with more humanitarian laws. But it has not been tabled in Parliament, not published, not implemented. The Defence Ministry and the Army oppose it. In addition, what is often forgotten is the trauma of civilians caught in the crossfire, that has not been healed, and incidents which are still denied. A study that a team did a few years ago on the impact of conflict in Nagaland and Assam turned up the recurring nightmares that people face even after the conflict has abated. There is much to be done with Post Trauma Stress Syndrome counselling.

The insider-outsider syndrome is not just about being Indian. It's also about accountability. It's about equality and the need to assert that those who act criminally cannot have the protection of law. That is why AFSPA must go. The other side of discrimination is that of injustice, impunity and inequality, embedded in law. It is this that needs to change. I am not sanguine but I take hope from the words of two senior retired army officials whom I have interviewed.

Ideas in action are the best way of making democracy work, effectively and sustainably. I've found that in the experience of our boat clinics, which my team and I have designed and which reach more than 400,000 persons every year with basic health care in the Brahmaputra valley.

Democratic struggle requires space for dissent and protest. In the poorest areas, this space is often threatened by multiple forms of repression, deceit and violence.

The future of India, one could argue, lies not just in the

defence of its sovereignty but in the defence of its democratic spaces, in all parts of the country, especially our own borderlands.

GROWING UP MIYAH

Shalim M. Hussain

When I ran away from my boarding school in Barpeta Road in 1993, there were no telephones in my village. The village police outpost was sent a telegram instead. The distance between my village Sontoli and Barpeta Road is a little less than fifty kilometres and can ideally be covered in an hour and a half. However, the river Brahmaputra passes between Sontoli and Bahari (the nearest bus stop) and it takes a motorboat ride of more than an hour to complete a one-way trip. Today auto-rickshaws and electric rickshaws ply between Sontoli bazaar and Sontoli ghat but two-and-a-half decades ago one had to cycle or walk to the ghat and wait for one of the two 'line' boats or country motor boats to ferry us to the other side. When the telegram with my missing report reached home on a January evening in 1993, my father hired a motorboat and immediately left for Bahari. He had booked an entire motorboat only thrice in his life—once when he brought my mother home in 1986, then when my maternal grandfather passed away on 21 March 1991 (on the same day that Prime Minister Rajiv Gandhi was assassinated) and in 1983, almost exactly ten years before I went missing, on a fact-finding mission after the Nellie massacre.

The day the telegram was sent, my friend Rose[1] and I decided that we had had enough of boarding school. We were both a little over five years old and had been at school for only a month. His parents and my grandmother lived in Kalgachia, a village twenty-seven kilometres south of Barpeta Road, and our families knew each other quite well. I don't remember who suggested the idea but we decided to run away one Saturday afternoon. National Highway 27 connects Barpeta Road to Sorbhog. From Sorbhog a narrower, almost perennially potholed road leads south to Kalgachia. I had very little knowledge of the roads then but my companion was street-smart and said that he could easily take me to my grandmother. We dressed in our 'outing dress'—shorts, shirt and sweater vest, socks and black school shoes—and waited for the school gate to open. At around twelve in the afternoon, when it was time for our nap, the washerman came with the laundry. He usually bundled the clothes in a large bedsheet and pushed it to the school gate on a handcart. He then opened the gate, carried the bundle on his head and walked into the school building. It took him about an hour to sort out the clothes and this was our window of opportunity. Rose and I waited until the washerman was in the hall and then casually walked out of the gate. We walked hand in hand through the market and took the right turn from Simlaguri. We were now on the national highway and on our way to Sorbhog. I have very vague memories of what happened next but I remember a lot of rain and lightning. The first showers of the year were upon us and we were not properly clothed for a walk, much less a daring escape.

[1]Name changed.

Rose was smart. He suggested that we walk slowly if there was a flash of lightning or if there were cars on the street. When the road was empty, we could run. Because of the heavy downpour our clothes were soon wet and our shoes squishy. The streets in Sorbhog didn't have streetlights, so there were long stretches of dark nothingness when our imagination took over. I am not sure if it's a fake memory but at one point, I might have seen lightning hit a cow. I vaguely remember the cow jumping in the air and falling on its back and a large red spot forming on its belly. Back in school, in 1994, someone noticed the white birth mark on my right arm and asked what had caused it. I told him that on a dark evening in February 1993, a lightning bolt had grazed my arm. That was also why I had straight stiff hair, I said. Anyway, we got as far as Sorbhog, close to where Jawahar Navodaya Vidyalaya now stands. There we suddenly felt strong hands on our shoulders and turned around to see a man standing behind us.

Apparently he had been following us for some time and our lack of an older companion and our clothes, particularly our shoes, made him suspect that we were runaways. He held us firmly by the shoulders (at this point we were too tired to run any more) and asked where we were from and where we were going. We told him about our relatives in Kalgachia, and then because we were so cold and scared, we gave him the name of our school. The gentleman, Mr Sadananda Das, put two and two together and took us home. He lit a fire in the cowshed and made us take off our wet clothes. His wife gave us blankets and served rice and boiled eggs while Mr Das cracked jokes to make us feel more comfortable and hung our clothes on a string over the fire. We had walked almost twelve kilometres and it was eight at night. Our legs were swollen and we were running high temperature. At night when I woke up to pee, Mr Das was awake. He remained awake all night so that we couldn't attempt another escape. In the morning he took us to the police station. The telegram to my parents had already been sent from the Barpeta Road police station and as we were walking to Mr Das's house from Sorbhog, we saw a car stop on the highway. My grandmother, great-aunt and aunt, and Rose's parents came running out of the doors. Our great escape was over.

I remember February 1993 with great fondness (though my memory of the actual events gets foggier every year) to remind myself that there is good in the world. The night Sadananda Das took Rose and me into his home, there was a small commotion in his locality. His prudent neighbours said that it would be better if we were taken to the police station immediately. Some of them said that it might not be a good idea to let two Miyah boys (our accented Assamese was a dead giveaway) stay in his house for the night. Communal tensions were at an all-time high in India then. The fear and distrust caused by the Babri Masjid demolition and the Bombay riots had travelled to Assam too. The Assam Agitation had ended only eight years ago but the wounds still remained exposed. Besides, there was another practical fear. The neighbours were scared that if Rose and I took seriously ill at night or worse, Mr Das would be in trouble. The good gentleman stood his ground. He would take us to the police station in the morning after we had had dinner and a good night's sleep, he said. Had Mr Das not rescued us from the street, had he not shown us basic human decency, Rose and I would have had to walk the remaining fifteen kilometres to Kalgachia. I don't know if we would have survived the long walk.

My parents kept me home for a few months and after repeated requests, the school decided to take me back. Rose's parents admitted him to a school in Kalgachia. We haven't met since. In 1993, the fragile peace in Assam began to unravel. In October, around fifty people were killed in ethnic violence between the Bodos and the Muslims in the nearby district of Bongaigaon. In July 1994, violence erupted between the Muslims and Bodos in Barpeta. Around a hundred people were killed, including many Muslims who had been sheltering in a relief camp in Bansbari, just twelve kilometres north of Barpeta Road. As school children in the sheltered atmosphere of boarding school, we didn't get wind of the violence that was happening almost literally outside the school campus. Our minds were occupied with more quotidian concerns—the school was being moved out of its temporary premises to a new location close by. Every Sunday after mass at the colonial-era St Joseph's Church, we walked in line to the construction site of the new school building. We ran around the half-completed corridors, carried bricks, and established a close friendship with Hazrat and Shabkhatun, two of the labourers. Since we were not allowed to go outside the school campus or interact with the people of Barpeta Road (except during the annual sports week or during festivals when we were chaperoned by the warden), the only Bengal-origin people I met during the early years of my schooling were these friendly labourers. Hazrat worked off and on as the school was slowly built, storey by storey, over the next five years but Shabkhatun became a permanent fixture. When she was not doing manual labour, she was appointed as a cleaner. My brother, who joined me at school in 1995, developed a very familial relationship with Shabkhatun and she would share her lunch with him. It was very plain stuff, usually rice and mashed brinjals, but it tasted like home, he said.

It was during my final year in school that I understood the seriousness of the 1994 violence. Ten years had passed and many of the children who had memories of that turbulent year were, like me, appearing for the Class 10 board exams. Some of them had lived 'beyond the railway lines'. The railway tracks cut Barpeta Road into two parts—the town and the rural suburbs. On one side was our school and on the opposite side, hidden behind a thick row of betel nut trees, was the great beyond. All we knew about the village beyond the railway tracks was that terrible things had happened there. During my final years at school I had started quizzing, and it was for a quiz competition that I crossed the railway lines and realised for the first time that civilisation didn't end at the station. In August and September 2017, I was travelling to Barpeta Road after a gap of almost a decade. I was meeting poets from the Bengal-origin Muslim community who had decided to call themselves 'Miyah Poets' and were writing remarkable poems on their lived experiences of poverty, exclusion and disillusionment. These were intensely political poems, guided by a deep feeling of angst and desire for self-expression. One of the first poets I met and interviewed was Abdur Rahim, a young school teacher who lived beyond the railway lines.

Rahim asked me to meet him at a printing press his friend and fellow Miyah poet Shahjahan ran at Barpeta Road. I wanted to get their poems on tape, so we travelled to his house deep in the village. The monsoon was receding but the earth was still soggy. The road that led to Rahim's hamlet was unmetalled and it was a little difficult for Rahim to guide his motorcycle through the mud. The house was built on a raised plinth, almost one-and-a-half metres high, and looked new.

There, seated in his front yard, Rahim told me about October 1994. He was six years old when many houses in his village, including his, were set on fire. All the members of his family abandoned the burning house and took shelter in the tall grass. They couldn't salvage much, except some valuables and their 'documents.' These documents—land revenue receipts, identity cards and land deeds—were the only proof that they were genuine citizens of India, and like all Bengal-origin Muslims who live under the constant ignominy of being called illegal migrants in their own country, they valued these strips of paper as much as their lives. The family remained hidden in the grass without food and water while their world burnt around them and it was only after the violence had subsided that they returned and started rebuilding their homes and futures. When crowds of arsonists walked by the tall grass, Rahim's parents stuffed his mouth with a *gamcha* to stop him from crying. At one point, Rahim's father went to their neighbours, begging for food. Most of the neighbours, Bodos, were scared of taking them in, but one family offered them a plate of soaked leftover rice.

Rahim said that it was necessary to talk about witnessing mob violence at such a young age and growing up with a constant feeling of dread and uncertainty, even if only through the medium of poetry. Rahim writes his poems almost exclusively in Assamese, though a few of his Miyah poems are written in the dialect he speaks at home. In 2016, when Miyah poetry started taking shape on Facebook, many of the poets wrote in Assamese or their regional dialects. It was a novel step, given the linguistic status of the Bengal-origin Muslims in Assam. We record Assamese as our language in the census reports and all documents, are educated largely in Assamese medium schools (English medium schools in the villages are a recent phenomenon, having started only in the early 1990s), and use Assamese for correspondence, though we continue to speak our local dialects at home. This creates a great divide. Uneducated Bengal-origin Muslims are repeatedly harassed by the state authorities as suspected 'illegal migrants' based on their lack of familiarity with the Assamese language while their educated cousins can evade such discrimination. However, accepting the Assamese language or being fluent in it doesn't necessarily allow Bengal-origin Muslims to belong to the 'mainstream' Assamese community. Sometimes this attempt at assimilation is mocked as insincere. 'Our use of Assamese in public and our own dialects in private is sometimes viewed as double-facedness,' said Rahim, 'and that puts us in a dilemma. What do we do? A couple of generations ago when we were all illiterate and couldn't speak Assamese, we were accused of clinging on to our Bengali roots. Now that we have grown into and whole-heartedly accepted Assamese language and culture, we are accused of putting on a show.'

The fear and uncertainty Rahim had faced in 1994 was faced by my mother and her family in 1983. She was still in college and the Nellie massacre had just happened. On the morning of 18 February 1983, more than 2000 Muslims of Bengal-origin were massacred in fourteen villages of the Nagaon district of Assam. Nellie was one of the villages. Unofficial sources place the number of casualties at around 10,000. All sorts of rumours started spreading in Kalgachia–arsonists were coming to the village looking for Miyahs, counter attacks were being planned, opportunists were going from village to village collecting protection money, etc. Not knowing what to believe, my grandfather took his wife, children and his old father and hid in the fields at a distance from his home. They remained there for two days until my eldest aunt's husband proposed a better idea. He would take them to his place in the evening and bring them back very early in the morning. It was important for people to know that the house was not abandoned, or it would be taken over by arsonists. A small stream of the Beki River separated my mother's village from her brother-in-law's, so the journey had to be made on my grandfather's fishing boat. For the next fortnight, as the situation in the state went from bad to worse, this was their regular routine. My mother had just begun college but classes were cancelled because of the violence, and it took her four years to complete a course which usually took two years then. My mother and aunts hardly talk about that frightful fortnight in 1983 but when they do, they always refer to it as the year of 'gondogol' or chaos.

The events of 1993 and 1994 are in the distant past and since I didn't witness either of them personally, I can't write about them from a personal point of view. What I do remember quite vividly was the first time I took the word 'Miyah' seriously. It happened in the summer of 2007 when I was house-hunting in Guwahati. This, however, was not the first time I heard it used as an insult. When my father was alive and my siblings and I were in boarding school, he would sometimes take us to school after our vacations. On one journey after the summer vacations, Abba bought three bus tickets—my brother and I had one seat each and my sister, who was five or six years old then, sat on my father's lap. Now, public transit etiquette in rural India dictates that children should always sit on the lap or on someone's knee. An old gentleman boarded the bus at Chenga, the bus stop after Bahari, and asked my brother or me to vacate our seat for him. This was our first adult experience of feeling the plastic seat under our butts and we were obviously not too eager to part with the honour. The man got angry and said in a low voice, 'Look at these Miyahs! They breed so fast that their children are like a bunch of coconuts!' I had never seen my father so humiliated in his life. He stood up and demanded an apology. The older gentleman raised his voice. The other passengers stepped in and broke what would probably have been a fight. Thankfully the old man got off the bus soon, but my father sat through the rest of the journey with a terrible sadness writ large on his face. Abba had spent most of his life battling the odds. The son of an impoverished farmer, he had educated himself, worked odd jobs (including a long stint as a field reporter during the Assam Agitation), earned some wealth and respect, and yet, the look on his face that afternoon, as I recall it now, was of a man in his forties who had suddenly realised that it was all for nothing. My mother, when she heard the story, took it quite lightly. 'Thank God we have only three children,' she said, 'or the man would have called them a bunch of litchis.'

I joined a degree college in Guwahati in 2007 and my brother moved from boarding school to the big city to continue his studies at an expensive private school. We had no experience in grocery shopping or cooking, and since my brother's school didn't have a hostel, we decided to stay at a private hostel. After about a month of searching for a suitable place, we managed to find accommodation as paying guests in a large establishment which hosted over sixty boys. On the first day of our stay, my brother and I were called to the common room for the ritualistic hazing or ragging. When we entered the room, a boy was seated on the dining table; another was standing with his head bent low in front of the table. There was a stark difference in their clothing. The seated fellow wore comfortable shorts and a vest while the submissive one was in a formal shirt buttoned at the cuffs, formal pants and leather shoes. It was July, the height of summer in Assam. It was apparent that the boy in the vest was a senior (not in age though; he was a senior simply because he had joined the hostel the previous year) and was exercising his ragging rights on the poor guy in formals. The victim was asked to recite the national anthem and the poor fellow was so scared that he went straight from the opening 'Jana Gana Mana' to 'Punjab Sindh...' The ragger shouted, 'Are you a Pingladesi?' I was paying very close attention. Having just graduated from the great ragging laboratory of Cotton College, which either turns a teenager into an unfeeling soldier or reduces him into a sniveling worm, I was eager to know the severity, or lack thereof, of ragging in the outside world. The word Pingladesi sounded odd. Wait, what did he mean? The boy was speaking in an unfamiliar accent. 'Are you a Pingladesi?' he repeated, 'Are you a Miyah?' Ah, Bangladeshi! In Assam, the words Miyah and Bangladeshi are used interchangeably for 'illegal immigrants' from Bangladesh. More often than not, 'Bangladeshi' and 'Miyah' are words spat at Assamese Muslims of Bengal origin. The poor junior was almost on the verge of tears. Thankfully, the warden was informed about the events in the common room. He stood at the door and waited until the assembly had dispersed. No actions were taken, no apologies were made and the matter was allowed to pass.

There's much to be said about the senior-junior relationship in educational institutions, but it usually begins with casual violence and bullying on one side and seething anger on the other, and slowly sublimates into friendship—in some cases, into long and fruitful friendship. The senior might treat the junior as a dog but let someone say a word or lay a hand on the dog and there will be blood! One of my seniors at Cotton College, who later became my roommate in Delhi and is currently working in the Indian Administrative Service, was one of the few people who could call me Miyah and get away with it. He earned the right in Delhi, far away from Assam, where the word didn't mean anything. Moreover, he used it sparingly and with deep affection. When we were boarding together in Delhi, he was a silent, studious (and almost comically frustrated) civil services aspirant, but I had seen his raw side just as I had seen the raw side of other boarders in Cotton College. One afternoon in 2005, the future civil servant and the older boys decided to chase 'illegal Bangladeshis' from Guwahati. The pavement in front of our hostel had turned into a line of temporary hutments. A group of impoverished Bengal-origin Muslim encroachers settled there one evening. Soon, they put up tarpaulin-roofed temporary huts. All of them worked as menial labourers, some as grass cutters in our college. The day the hostel boarders attacked the squatters was the day I learnt a valuable lesson in human character. The boys were not random thugs with a penchant for violence but educated, normally mild-mannered boys who went on their task with glee (almost as if they were on a picnic), beating, cursing and spitting on the people on the pavement, smashing their pots and pans and tearing their tarpaulin shelters. Suddenly, the fact that they were students of Assam's most respected educational institution didn't matter. Reasoning with them, telling them that the squatters were in all probability poor villagers who had just moved to the city in search of jobs wouldn't have mattered.

The problem with socially normalised bigotry is that it has the power of directing all minds in the same direction. I will forever be ashamed of the one incident where I participated in the same kind of bigotry I had begun to detest. In my second year in college, my brother and I found a room very close to his school. The only problem was that it was very far from my college. I had to change two city buses to get to Guwahati Club. Between Guwahati Club and my college was a flyover. One had the option of crossing the flyover on a tempo but it was a very short distance and the tempos charged an obnoxious amount of five rupees for a half-kilometre drive. So I usually walked. One morning as I was walking down towards Guwahati Club, I heard the tinkling of a cycle bell and turned. It was someone I knew—the adopted grandson of my great-aunt. We had grown up together but since he had not had much education, this cousin of mine used to work odd jobs. While in the village, he worked as a farm hand on my great-uncle's fields. Then when he felt that the village was too small to contain his ambitions, he came to Guwahati as a labourer. Now he was on the driver's seat of a cycle rickshaw and pushing at the bell furiously. I didn't know when he had taken up this new job.

'Where are you going? Let me give you a ride,' he said. I grudgingly sat in his rickshaw while he rose from his seat and applied all his strength on the pedals. When we reached the upward slope of the flyover, I asked if I should get down and push the rickshaw but he was adamant that I remain seated. We soon reached the top of the flyover and the easy slope downwards began. He told me about his life in the city. He had come with a labour contractor to work on a construction site. 'How was it?' I asked. 'Oh, plain rice and dal day in and day out. One day, they took all of us in a truck and put us in the police lock-up.' When I asked him why they had done so, he said that he didn't know. He remained in the lock-up for a week and returned to the construction site after his release, only to learn that the contractor had already employed another batch of labourers. He looked for a job at other construction sites but after being turned down a couple of times, he visited a friend who referred him to a 'mahajan' who was looking for rickshaw drivers. He got the job. My cousin paid the mahajan a certain amount of money every day and the rest of the earnings were his own. We slid down the slope and I asked him to stop at the foot of the flyover. 'But let me take you to your college,' he said. I didn't allow him. He understood, turned the rickshaw and cycled away. I walked to college in shame. The reason I stopped him from dropping me off at the college gate was that I didn't want my friends to know that there were rickshaw-pullers in my family. I didn't want to introduce this emaciated, ill-dressed, foul-smelling, crass-talking cousin of mine to my friends. All my fancy education had taught me nothing and in a way, I was no different than the boys at Cotton College who could be so gleefully brutal to the pavement dwellers.

When I came to Delhi for my Masters in 2010, I realised that the perfect anonymity of the city suited me. I loved Guwahati; it was the first city I had ever loved, but it was home and one always expects more from home. The great beyond may be frightening and cruel but home should be cosy and nurturing. I didn't have to worry about being ashamed of Delhi. It was still difficult for me to find accommodation there. As a Muslim, I had to either stay in one of the Muslim ghettos or have a non-Muslim roommate who could vouch for me. I had to explain to my friends at the university why I didn't know Urdu and commit blasphemy by acknowledging that I had never had biryani at home. But the feeling of not belonging was extremely liberating. For the first time since boarding school, I could speak in English instead of accented Assamese and my Hindi was as bad as everyone else's. I didn't have to worry about singing the Assamese national song out of tune or missing a word here and there. Distanced from the judging crowd of Assam, I could remember with fondness the kindness of Sadananda Das, recreate rosy memories of my days in Guwahati and the small town of Barpeta Road, and gain perspective on the decades of violence and heartbreak in Assam. It was the unfeeling capital city that made me decide to return to Assam and belong, but this time on my own terms.

CHRONICLE OF FORGETTING

Sonal Jain

It has finally stopped raining.

It rained for fifteen days straight. Sounds subdued by that of the rain are now slowly re-emerging yet wary that the rains may return to take over once again. The earth seems to be awakening after a long watery hiatus. (Or is the world really all water like they tell us with 75 percent of our bodies, too, made up of water?) The birds have begun chirping insolently—making sharp, loud, tweeting sounds. They are hungry, and tired of the incessant rains.

In front of me, partially hidden by a tall, ugly building that has cropped up recently, lies a landscape of a city on a hill. More houses mushroom out of it every year. The top reaches of the hill are protected, so the trees remain so far.

The continuous sound of the rain drops thundering on the tin roof, on the concrete, grass and trees, alters the mind in a strange way. No, it is not depressing (depression has enough sources), but gives rise to what Orhan Pamuk calls *huzun*, 'the melancholy of Istanbul.' Cities, melancholy and rain are some of the ingredients in this story. This city is Shillong and though it is the centre of *my* universe, it is referred to as the *distant* city in many accounts.

In another city, there was a man who sat paralysed, mute on a chair for nine long years confined to the courtyard within a crumbling house. He was the family patriarch and even in his immobile and almost mute state kept tabs on the running of the household and affairs of the family. Time must move differently when you are incapacitated, powerless and no longer in control of your motor functions but your brain still moves at its original speed. There must be a disruption of the *normal* pace of time.

Now the rain comes down again, even harder than before, almost mocking the people who had come out to enjoy the brief respite. The thunder and rain make everything inaudible again, including my own thoughts. It is a relief from them in any case. I stare at the pages of *his* diary and wonder what parts of his body he could feel and what parts moved even a little. Did he remember the diary and its entries from 1936 as he sat immobile for the better part of the 1970s? Different times and different places—1936 in Lahore, Pakistan, and 1970 in Meerut, India. In Lahore, he was a young man at the beginning of his life and getting an education unaware of what awaited him. While in Meerut, he was awaiting his impending death in a state of forced silence. The stereotypical sound of *tanga*s comes to me as I think of him in Lahore (like in a bad period film made on the British Raj).

Another time, another place. The pages from his journal have been kept safe by Sameer Jain, my elder cousin and the first grandson of the man in Lahore, the man in Meerut. Sameer was an investment executive on Wall Street for many years and now yearns ardently for the Shillong he grew up in. He is the messenger who has sent these lost dairy pages to me from New York.

In pre-Partition Lahore, my grandfather, Mehar Chand

Jain, was studying at DAV College. On 17 January, he makes a note of his expenditures from June 1935 to January 1936. He writes, 'Oh, it's my birthday.' It saddens me as a voyeur to bear witness to the loneliness of a man I know so little about. I do share his loneliness today, eighty long years after that lonely birthday he spent in Lahore. Does the shared experience of a deep loneliness bind us or am I just *projecting* my dull but stratified sadness onto him? I also witness (though not as a voyeur this time) an endemic of loneliness today. A whole population of lonely people unable to connect to each other. Recently the British government has appointed a 'Minister for Loneliness,' after a twelve-month investigation into the prevalence of loneliness in the UK, and concluded that nine million Britons suffer from loneliness: 14 percent of the population.

But on 9 February 1936, a Sunday, *he* did note spending four rupees on a cinema show with Raj, Manmohan and Indar. He was probably less lonely on that day. His love for cinema is a side of his personality that is never talked about in the family. Was cinema frowned upon as a decadent indulgence? I wonder if the four friends spent the four rupees to see *Devdas* (in Hindi), starring K.L. Saigal, that was released that very year.

Devdas is the story of unrequited love that more or less underlies the history and flavour of romantic love in the subcontinent, forming the collective unconscious of lovers. It is the story of a rich boy and a poor girl who were childhood sweethearts. The boy is sent off to study to the big city and the girl in the mean time is married off to a very wealthy older man as a retribution to an insult inflicted by the boy's father on the girl's family on account of their being of a lower financial status. He does not approve of the match.

On his return the boy is heartbroken and goes back to the proverbial *big city* and finds comfort in the arms of a prostitute. His final attempt to meet his lost love ends with him dying outside the tall walls of her husband's mansion.

This of course was the 1930s, when there was dignity in dying for one's country or from a heartbreak. I tell myself that the pain of heartbreak is a cultural construct and we as a people do seem to revel in it. Although the pain I experience, too, feels like many small deaths.

Did *he* in his lonely life in Lahore have a lover, or maybe a whore he loved?

Some people always find themselves on the edge of history.

There is the damned sound of the *tanga* again.

Flash-forward to the Welsh Mission, Dr H. Gordon Roberts Hospital, Shillong—nestled neatly on the edge of a hill in a busy little residential neighbourhood with small cottages and many flowers. The hospital is on the edge of the hill that the family once owned in Jaiaw.

I was born there in 1975, in room number 46, on a cold wintery morning with bright blue skies. My parents were apparently alone in this birth, no relatives fussing around or bringing almonds or *halwa*. My mother tells me the reason for this was that one grandfather sat paralysed on a chair in a courtyard of a crumbling house while the other had recently been brutally murdered by dacoits on a farm on the edge of Meerut—hence the conspicuous absence of grandmothers fussing around on my birth. My mother was taken to the hospital in my father's Willys Jeep (as if that can ever make up for the lack of grandmothers).

Sameer Jain
18 May 2016, 11.23 p.m.

Circa 1970. In Jaiaw Langsning, there were two houses and a hill that sloped to a factory. Apparently, after division in property, the two houses went to Dad and Janak chacha and the factory and jeep went to Ramesh chacha. Apparently, it was a very difficult time for Pitaji (grandfather) who was paralysed, Maati (grandmother) who like Nirupa Roy, was caught between sons (think *Deewar*), and everything (the family) fell apart.

The rain is so heavy now. It feels like it is permeating through my skin and pores into my organs. Do our organs have a waterproof membrane covering them? When a body is cut open, everything collapses into each other? It is a gooey mass of red and pink, so it's difficult to tell. Recently on the highway from Shillong to Guwahati, I saw the brain of a young biker splattered on the road. It was a gooey pink mass.

Did *he* know true love in his life? The kind of love that tears your heart into bits and the pain is so intense that the sound of the rain thundering down becomes one with you. You dissolve with the crashing of raindrops on the tin roof and hope never to be put back again. Water has it easy that way; from the blue skies and white glaciers it moves—changing, dissolving, disintegrating and merging with the ocean. Never a moment to reflect on the nature of the 'I.'

29 May 1936, Friday
Yog Raj left Lahore for Pandu

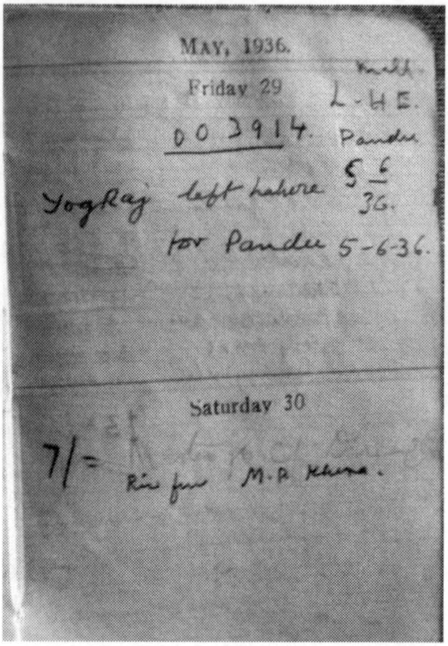

Another landscape. Pandu, a port on the southern bank of the river Brahmaputra, an ocean called a river. It is older than the mighty Himalayas that gives rise to it. The Himalayas are 450 million years old. So how old is my river? It begins in Tibet where it is fondly called Yarlung Tsangpo, and Tashi, my guide on a trip to mount Kailash, proudly tells me that in Tibet, the river is considered to be the mother. Here in India, it is the son of Brahma, the creator god.

Yog Raj would have arrived on the northern bank of the river. The train route in those days was from Lahore to Amritsar, where one would have to take another train to Avadh (now Lucknow) and from there, the train *Avadh Assam* to Amingaon. The entire journey took forty-eight hours. From Amingaon (on the northern bank of the Brahmaputra), Yog

Raj would have crossed the raging river on a ferry to come to Pandu. From Pandu it was another two-day-long journey to Shillong. It cost four annas. The stench and grit of those endless train journeys on the Tinsukia Mail or the Assam Mail comes back to me. A stench that embeds itself into the very fabric of the dull blue synthetic seat covers of the trains, the gaps in the windows full of moist black muck. By the end of a three-day journey, it enters your clothes, your hair and skin, and remains embedded until recalled again, even after twenty years.

In the village of Amingaon, I've always been struck by the disused bright red railway warehouses with the word 'ABANDONDED' written across in bold. There is also a large dilapidated railway platform with a tin roof largely overtaken by the bright verdant green that does seem to be the ruling colour of the land—the land of the son of Brahma. While the goddess perched atop a blue hill bleeds a rich, moist menstrual blood every year, the rains religiously wash it down to the red river, which takes it down to the formless oceans.

The damned sound of the tanga once again; prodding slowly up the steep climb of the ancient Shillong plateau. Clippity-clop and bells. A journey that would have taken two days then now takes only two hours. This plateau was formed due to the same tectonic process that gave rise to the Himalayas a few hundred million years ago. Below, to the south-east, lies the Burmese plate and to the north is the Tibetan plate. Words like Precambrian gneiss complex and Proterozoic intracratonic are used by geologists to describe the plateau. The age of the land was something I became aware of a long time ago. Its black crystallised translucent rocks had to have taken a very long time to form even in my twelve-year-old mind.

18 June 1936, Thursday

A great shock of an earthquake
Reminded of the future and of the past

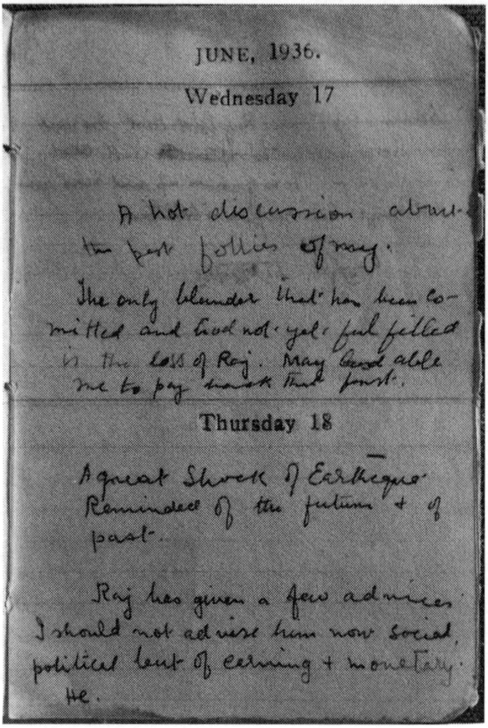

JUNE, 1936.

Wednesday 17

A hot discussion about the past follies of mine.
The only blunder that has been committed and God not yet fulfilled is the loss of Raj. May God able me to pay back that fast.

Thursday 18

A great Shock of Earthquake
Reminded of the future + of past.

Raj has given a few advices I should not advise him now social political but of earning + monetary. He.

Why did this earthquake remind him of the future and the past? Was it an existential musing or related to the previous day's entry?

17 June 1936, Wednesday

A hot discussion on past follies of mine.

The only blunder that I have committed, and God has not yet fulfilled is the loss of Raj. May God enable me to pay that back fast.

We now seem to have a larger sense of invincibility and immorality. He did meet Raj (Yog Raj Chandhoke) again, and they did build two beautiful homes on a hilltop in Jaiaw, Shillong.

On 5 June 1936, a Friday, *his* journal entry notes the fare to Pandu, '18-4-0'. 18 rupees, 4 annas and 0 pies. This would have been the train fare from Lahore to Pandu. The porters cost 3 annas and 6 pies. So he did travel a distance of 1787 kilometres (air distance) to Pandu to join Raj.

In 1661, the Mughal general under Aurangzeb, Mir Jumla, occupied Pandu and Guwahati for a short two months. In spite of repeated battles the Mughals largerly failed to annex Assam from the Ahoms. Mir Jumla's occupation of Pandu and Guwahati was the rare time that a single monarch ruled the vast geography from Lahore to Pandu.

So while in Lahore, Mehar Chand was forging friendships that would last a lifetime and waging wars with himself, history was catching up with him. The subcontinent was waging its own war against the British imperialist rule. His family was back in Uttar Pradesh in Garhi, a small village near Saharanpur. He was part of a group of freedom fighters led by the most charismatic revolutionary, Bhagat Singh. Bhagat Singh was a socialist and his violent dramatic attacks against the British occupation have served as raw material for many films. His unique method of resistance, allowing for his own arrest followed by a long legal battle in order to draw public attention to the atrocities and flaws in the British political and judicial system, was historic and effective. He was finally convicted and hanged at the age of twenty-three. He immediately became a hero, a martyr and an inspiration to the people of a country in revolt.

After the arrest of Bhagat Singh, Mehar Chand Jain and

Yog Raj Chandhoke fled from Lahore to avoid incarceration. They made their way to Rangoon (Yangon) and stayed in hiding for some time.

The air distance from Lahore to Yangon is 2740 kilometres.

Pluviophile: A lover of rain; someone who finds joy and peace of mind during rainy days.

The rains continue, relentless.

Time in relation to plateaus and caves is different. Can our minds conceive spaces of time spanning a few million years? There is an old man here in Shillong who is obsessed with caves. He has discovered and mapped over 1500 caves in Meghalaya, some of the longest in the country. Entering an undisturbed cave for the first time has to be like going into another space-time dimension or even outside of it.

This man has another passion, apart from caving, and that is making bonsais.

He is also a manager at a local bank and the last time I went to visit him, he was reading a novel in his office.

19 June 1936, Friday

Solar eclipse.

Raj told me that he used to... (struck out) with... (struck out again) but he is grown up now and realises his responsibilities.

I should not advise him now on (the) social and political but only on earning and monetary matters.

Sameer, my estranged cousin brother, tells me they parted ways eventually, after many long, eventful years of being friends and business partners, and lived atop the hill next to the hospital in Shillong.

10 September 1936, Thursday

No profitable business unless own capital.

Soap—an investment of 5000/- would get an income of 150/- only.

11 September 1936, Friday

A proposal to go to Patna.

Capital 5000/-

12 September 1936, Saturday

A proposal to go to Shillong.

The same difficulties would come in our way, which the other had.

The story continued in Yangon where they went into hiding. Their days in Yangon were irretrievably lost. Gone with the two men, and probably will never be known again. From Burma/Myanmar the two friends made their way back to India. Still fugitives in the British Raj, they could not go back home or to Lahore. So, via what is now Bangladesh, they made their way to Kolkata (Calcutta as it was then called) and on to Guwahati.

Subsequently, the two friends moved to Shillong. My father tells me they first set up a tailoring shop in Shillong. The shop was a front for the two men still in hiding from the British authorities.

The rain is coming down in sheets now. It blows in with the wind in long, sweeping dance movements. It is the middle of the night. The electricity is out and the howling winds outside feel like the waves in a Japanese ukiyo-e painting in shades of grey and black. Many a night and morning, I have awoken to these different ukiyo-e paintings.

He asks me if I had written down the lines from the previous night. I say I had not and that it is alright even if the lines evaporated into thin air. I question our obsession with remembrance and memory.

He has an obsessive need for permanence and therefore says, 'They will evaporate and fall back on you as rain.'

18 May 2016, 02.01 p.m.
Sameer Jain

About Jaiaw, Maati told me a story. It seems that one Hari Singh, a Khasi guy, left them a pot of gold during the war for safekeeping. After the war, Pitaji returned it to him. Impressed with his honesty, the Khasi guy gave Pitaji some money. Apparently, the entire Jaiaw hill was bought with the Rs. 35,000 he gave. It was a huge hill if you remember from Robert Hospital to Mawlai G.S. Road (Guwahati-Shillong Road) divided between him and Yog Raj.

13 September 1936, Sunday
Settled a problem.

We do not expect now what we had in mind.
The world is selfish—one and all.

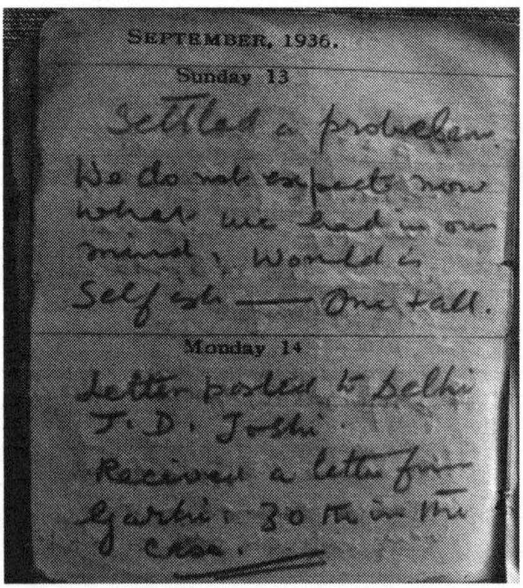

I have been trying in the last two years to give dignity to grief, disillusionment and pain. Not just to my own but to others' too. Haruki Murakami asks if a perfect grief exists. It has to be a dignified grief.

Tonight, the rain is particularly harsh. There are strong winds lashing out at everything. The windowpanes are banging constantly and the tin roof rattles on and on—incessant. I have been crying for a long time. And only the unending nature of the rain seems to justify my tears. The sound of the rain drowns out the otherwise pathetic sound of the weeping, giving it some much-needed 'dignity'.

I am not sure about what I am crying for this time. Most times I know, most times it is for myself; sometimes it is for someone else too. But right now, I am not sure. Is it for lost loves, potential loves, disillusionment, the words in the diary or the words never written? Is there dignity in grieving for someone you never knew or crying for a fictitious character in a book who lived with you in your room for days as you plowed through, bleeding alone in your room (like the goddess perched on the blue hill).

15 September 1936, Tuesday

Malikji has gone to Calcutta.

Letter from Man Mohan Lal.

Raj and I settled that I should go to Lahore.

He would come later.

We do not hope for anything here.

Later the two friends set up a factory to manufacture soap in Shillong. They called it the Assam Soap Factory. This was well before the state of Meghalaya was formed in 1972, so it was technically the first and only soap factory in the state of Meghalaya later. Apparently, it did well; and they began to supply soap to adjacent East Bengal too. They expanded the business and Mehar Chand set up another factory in Calcutta. My father was born in Calcutta.

Notes, dairy page
Golden Soap Factory
171 A Harrison Road
Calcutta.

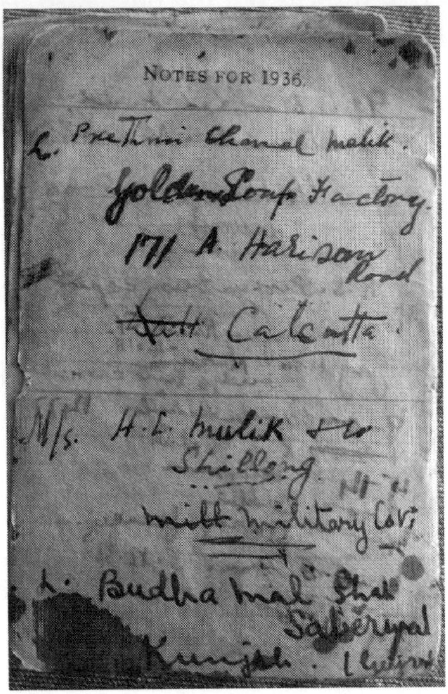

19 May 2016, 04.30 a.m.
Sameer Jain

During the riots in Calcutta (Hindu-Muslim riots after the partition of the subcontinent into India and Pakistan), they were trapped in a Muslim building in Harrison Road in Calcutta. Tarawati (our grandmother) told me that my dad was a year old in her arms. All the women were hiding on a rooftop, ready to jump off to save their honour in the eventuality that Muslims were to make it till there. A Muslim friend saved them by sneaking them to a police outpost in a van. It was a very narrow escape. They then lived in a refugee camp in Calcutta and later went back to Guwahati and from there onwards to Shillong.

So with history as a constant companion (and mostly not a welcome one), Mehar Chand traversed different geographies, sometimes hopeful and at other times hopeless. The Partition once again tore apart the life he had created in Calcutta. The soap factory was looted and the family barely escaped with their lives and dignity. The factory was in a Muslim-dominated area and there was no going back to that area given the post-riots divide between the Hindus and the Muslims.

So the nation was born through blood and gore. It was now taking shape and its new boundaries were being drawn. The lives of individuals are mere collateral in this process of myth-making. Mehar Chand, too, gets caught up in the nation-building socialist zeal and decides that business is not a noble profession. He concludes that he can contribute to the infant starving nation through agriculture and mechanised farming. This zeal takes the family on another adventure, uprooting and taking them to Kashipur in Uttar Pradesh. Mehar Chand and his family thus spent many years in the Himalaya Terai region on a farm surrounded by forests inhabited by tigers. My father has memories of tigers and snakes amongst other jungle beasts. One rainy season he was trying to help his mother save the firewood for the next morning and instead of putting it out with water, he brushed it against the wall. Little did the five-year-old know that the wall was made of thatch. It caught fire, burning the kitchen down. After this misadventure as well as commercial failure at farming, the family returned to Shillong. They eventually lived on the beautiful hilltop in Jaiaw for many years.

Sameer, my cousin, tells me that the closest of friends, Yog Raj and Mehar Chand, parted ways many years later, unable to reconcile their irrevocable business and personal differences.

Around 1970, after the two elder boys and the two girls were married off, the house and property were divided in acrimonious dispute between the three sons. All was later sold when the sons moved on to other localities and cities. All but my father, the middle son, who built another house on another hilltop in Shillong. Many years pass by in setting up a new business and starting of a family with my mother. Three children are born. Life is passing by when again in the 1980s, there is a massive anti-outsider movement by the Khasi Students' Union. Everything comes to a standstill. Schools, offices, shops are closed and when they, the brave catholic Loreto nuns, do try to open the school one Monday morning, the window panes are smashed in. This brings an abrupt end to the resistance put up by the sisters.

We are young and failing to understand the larger implications of the 'movement,' and are happy with the sudden disruption in our mundane school-going lives. We embark upon new adventures when not in school. A couple of girls and I join a karate class and enter the world of Shaolin warriors and Bruce Lee. It is a fascinating world. We dismiss the adults' worry about our academic regression as days turn into weeks and weeks into months. On the way to the karate class is a Chinese-owned shop, *Golden Stores*, from which we are rewarded with sweet easter eggs on some days. The sweat, muscle pain, resilience and valour derived from the world of Shaolin warriors was not the worst way to enter puberty. Life lay in front of us as it must have for Mehar Chand in Lahore.

We were now suddenly dkhars (derogatory term for outsiders in Khasi) in the land Mehar Chand Jain had come to decades ago. The violence of history catches up once again. Suddenly fear punctuates the everyday experiences. 'Don't go out,' 'come back home before dark,' 'keep the front door closed,' 'don't just open the door,' became operative phrases. My elder brother began to carry a *nunchaku* hidden under his leather jacket whenever he went out.

My father, Ramesh, and his friend were associated with the Guwahati Stock Exchange in those days. They frequently went together to Guwahati and returned the same day. On one such day, a friend came to ask if my father would like to accompany him. My father was not feeling too well and so he declined to go. On the way back that evening, his friend's car ran into a violent mob in Mawlai (close to Jaiaw). The mob surrounded them and set the car alight with his driver and him inside. The driver managed to escape somehow but my father's friend was charred to death that unfortunate night.

Now, many, many years later, the violence has died down. But the fear has taken a different form—a stubborn resistance as well as subtle modifications in behaviour, routes and timings. The violence, too, has taken subtler forms of discrimination, exclusion and subordination. These take on different forms, sometimes manifesting in clearly stated exclusion from electoral processes while at others unstated discrimination in job eligibility and patronage of businesses of the so called 'outsiders.' Threats are common. This systemic 'othering' is something that any group, community, caste or gender throughout the world seems to become very efficient at very quickly. Giving rise to a differentially privileged and marginalised class of people which may be independent of their position in the national or global stage.

After many departures, to study, to work, sometimes to be away from the violence, I come back here—to Shillong.

Perhaps the many gaps in this story could have been filled in by an aunt, the elder daughter of Mehar Chand who lives in a town in Uttarakhand. Unfortunately, she is suffering from dementia and forgets everything very quickly. Maybe some among us subconsciously choose to forget as some memories are too difficult to carry with, as you lie alone on a bed.

Others block out the pain and never let anyone or even themselves near it, lest it oozes out of their chest like an alien baby trapped inside, happy to rip apart the rib cage, tissues and muscles to come out. For some, the past is a place of endless pain and the future only impending death. As it may have been for Mehar Chand when he lay paralysed for nine long years.

It is still raining; its intensity has decreased. It is now a slow, lazy drizzle with large drops on the tin roof. It seems like brief relief until it regains strength and comes back down with a vengeance, out to get anything in its path.

The average annual rainfall in Lahore is 628.8 mm, while in Shillong, it is 3385 mm.

(*This story is part of a larger work in progress.*)

OUTSIDERS IN THEIR OWN LANDS

The Chakmas of the North-East

Suhas Chakma

The 'Insider-Outsider' debate in the North-East is not only about the right to freedom of movement inside one's own country but also about special measures for protection of the identities and rights of certain racial or ethnic groups. Partition of India and migration as a consequence exacerbated the debate but the British Raj had to deal with this issue during its early days of suzerainty in the Indian subcontinent.

Following the Sepoy Mutiny of 1857, the direct rule by the British Crown in the Indian subcontinent started under the Government of India Act of 1858. In 1873, the British Raj introduced the Bengal Eastern Frontier Regulation to provide for 'inner line permit' for entry of non-native persons in erstwhile areas such as Kamrup, Darrang, Nowgong, Sibsagar, Garo Hills, Khasi and Jainta Hills, Naga Hills, Cachar, Goalpara, the Sadiya Frontier Tract, the Balipara Frontier Tract, the Lakhimpur Frontier Tract the Lushai Hills district, Chittagong Hills, etc.[1] Many of these areas were gradually taken off the list

[1]Bengal Eastern Frontier Regulation of 1873 is available at http://www.mdoner.gov.in/sites/default/files/silo4_content/entry%20restrictions%20in%20NER/Bengal%20Eastern%20Frontier%20Regulation%2C%201873.pdf

while the Chittagong Hill Tracts (CHTs) 1900 Regulation was introduced separately to provide for the same protection. The Government of India Act of 1935[2] further legalised natives vs. non-natives in certain territories by defining excluded areas and partially excluded areas under Section 91 and Section 92 of the Act.

One of the largest movements of refugees in the twentieth century during the Partition affected demography in North-East India and shaped its sub-nationalist politics. While the Hindus and Sikhs who fled from West Pakistan settled in North India, which was inhabited by people of the same stock, those who fled from East Pakistan, current Bangladesh, mainly settled in the North-East, which was inhabited by people of different ethnic, linguistic and religious origin. Tripura bore the brunt of refugees fleeing East Bengal and witnessed a decadal population growth rate of 78.71 percent during 1951–1961 and 36.28 percent during 1961–1971 against a population growth rate of 24.56 percent during 1941–1951. The immigrants soon became the rulers in a democratic setup in Tripura. By 1975, Sikkim, too, merged with India following a referendum in which Hindu Nepalese played a critical role in facilitating the merger. Anti-foreigner sentiment became the most dominant, omnipresent issue.

By 1979, Assam was engulfed by the anti-foreigner agitation led by the All Assam Students Union (AASU) while the radical elements went to form the United Liberation Front of Assam (ULFA). The anti-foreigner agitation in Assam went on to influence an entire generation of leaders in the North-East and shaped both the underground and overground ethno-politics of the region.

---

[2]The Government of India Act of 1935 is available at http://lawmin.nic.in/legislative/textofcentralacts/GOI%20act%201935.pdf

Origin of the Chakmas

The Chakmas had inhabited areas in India (Assam, Tripura and Mizoram), the Chittagong Hill Tracts region (CHTs) of Bangladesh and Myanmar (Arakan) from time immemorial. The actual origin of the Chakmas is unclear but the Chakmas are the only tribal group in the North-East whose linguistic origin is Indo-European.

Throughout history, the Chakmas maintained their Buddhist religious identity and did not convert to Hinduism or Islam. The Chakmas were the first tribe in the North-East to have been brought under the direct control of the East India Company in 1781, but they did not convert to Christianity.

Chakmas in Independent India

No other community in undivided India has been as devastated by the partition of India as much as the Chakmas. The Chakmas and other non-Muslims constituted about 98.5 percent of the total population of the CHTs during Partition and sought to be a part of India. Yet, for reasons known to the rulers, the CHTs were awarded to Pakistan. Though Pakistan became independent on 14 August 1947 followed by India on 15 August 1947, the inclusion of the CHTs in Pakistan was announced only on 17 August 1947.

Though the majority of the Chakmas were settled in the CHTs, Chakmas had been living in undivided Assam, including present-day Mizoram and Tripura for a very long time. Indeed, the Advisory Committee on the Fundamental Rights of the Constituent Assembly constituted 'Excluded and Partially Excluded Areas Sub-Committee' under the chairmanship of Shri A.V. Thakkar and the only member from the North-East in this committee was Sneh Kumar Chakma. The provisions relating to 'Scheduled Areas' and Tribes Advisory Councils under the Fifth and Sixth Schedules to the Constitution of India originate in the recommendations of the 'Excluded and Partially Excluded Areas Sub-Committee'.

Further, the Constitution (Scheduled Tribes) Order, 1950 that identified the tribes or tribal communities, or parts of, or groups within, tribes or tribal communities, in the localities specified in relation to them listed the Chakmas as Scheduled Tribes in Assam, Meghalaya and Mizoram, West Bengal and Tripura because of the inhabitancy of the Chakmas in these areas.

Enduring Effects of the Assam Anti-Foreigner Agitation on the Chakmas in Mizoram and Arunachal Pradesh

The leaders of the AASU who went on to form the Asom Gana Parishad and shifted from the hostel rooms of Guwahati University to Ministerial Bungalows following the elections in 1986 today share power with the Bhartiya Janata Party (BJP) that decided to grant citizenship rights to the minorities who fled Bangladesh, Pakistan and Afghanistan till 31 December 2014. The ULFA which went underground against foreigners in Assam went on record to recognise the contribution of the immigrants following pressure from the Directorate General of Forces Intelligence of Bangladesh. The Aurobindo Rajkhowa faction of the ULFA has effectively been seeking Scheduled Tribes status for the Assamese while Paresh Barua has become a Chinese stooge. Even though the anti-foreigner agitation is dead and effectively buried in Assam, the Chakmas continue to face institutionalised and state-sanctioned discrimination in Mizoram and Arunachal Pradesh.

The Chakmas of Mizoram: Foreigners in Their Own Land

Chakmas are often targeted as foreigners in Mizoram and history is of particular pertinence to examine the origin of the Chakmas and Mizos in current-day Mizoram.

As per the state government of Mizoram, 'The earliest Mizos who migrated to India were known as Kukis, the second batch of immigrants were called New Kukis. The Lushais were the last of the Mizo tribes to migrate to India. Mizo history in the eighteenth and nineteenth century is marked by many instances of tribal raids and retaliatory expeditions of security. Mizo Hills were formally declared as part of British India by a proclamation in 1895. North and south hills were united into Lushai Hills district in 1898 with Aizawl as its headquarters.'[3]

The CHTs had come under Mughal control by conquest in 1666 and used to pay taxes. In 1757, the East India Company established its rule in Bengal after defeating Nawab Siraj-ud-daulah in the Battle of Plassey. In 1787, the East India Company made the region its tributary after defeating tribal leaders.[4] The British Crown took over from the East India Company under the Government of India Act of 1858. In a notification issued by the government of Bengal, dated 30 June 1879, the boundary of the CHTs to the east was defined in clear terms as: '...runs along the whole course of Sajek river to its junction with Karnafuli River, a little north of Demagiri; thence it continues eastward along this stream up to the junction of the Tuichawng River, after which it follows the

[3]http://www.mizoram.nic.in/about/history.htm

[4]Gupta, Aman. *Human Rights of Indigenous Peoples: Comparative Analysis*. Gyan Publishing House. 2005. p6.

whole course of this river....' It took over another hundred years for the British to bring the Lushai Hills under its control. As per the government of Mizoram, 'Mizo Hills were formally declared as part of British India by a proclamation in 1895.'[5]

The eastern parts of the Chakma king's territory in the CHTs, including Demagiri (which Mizoram renamed as Tlabung), were transferred from Bengal province to the Lushai Hills district under Assam province on 1 April 1898. The Chief Commissioner of Assam, Mr W.E. Ward, in his letter No 149-P dated 17 July 1897 submitted to the Government of India stated: 'The station of Demagiri is not situated within the present area of the South Lushai Hills. It is topographically within the area of the Chittagong Hill Tracts. But, under Sir Charles Eliott's [Lieutenant-Governor of Bengal] orders, passed in 1892, it was declared that, for administrative purposes, Demagiri should be considered to be part and parcel of the South Lushai Hills.'[6]

It is pertinent to mention that when the Bengal Eastern Frontier Regulation was promulgated in 1873, the Lushai Hills were not even part of the British Raj. There is no doubt that the whole western belt of Mizoram has been inhabited by the Chakmas and Reangs/Brus. Indeed, the Chakmas had little problem in Lushai Hills in post-independent India. In 1972, when the Lushai Hills district was upgraded into a Union Territory, the Union of India also created the Chakma Autonomous District Council along with Lai Autonomous District Council and Mara Autonomous District Council.

It was only in the 1990s that the anti-foreigner agitation became a means to target non-Mizo minorities. The state

---

[5]http://www.mizoram.nic.in/about/history.htm

[6]Reid, Sir Robert. *History of the Frontier Areas Bordering on Assam 1883-1941*, p.40.

government of Mizoram in an all-party meeting organised by the then Chief Minister Mr Lal Thanhawla (who is also the present chief minister) on 15 April 1993 raised the need for identification of so-called 'foreigners' in Mizoram and used the voter lists to identify the alleged foreigners. The Mizo Zirlai Pawl (MZP), the students union, set 26 January 1950 as the cut-off year to identify the alleged foreigners and urged the political parties in the state to take initiatives. On 26 September 1994, the State Election Office declared 25 January 1950 as the cut-off year for identifying the alleged foreigners. On 30 January 1995, the MZP served 'Quit Notice' to the Chakmas who entered Mizoram after 26 January 1950 to leave Mizoram by 15 June 1995. Thousands of Chakmas who were included in the 1980, 1983, 1991 and 1993 electoral rolls were deleted from the subsequent electoral rolls published in 1995 and 1996. In Aizawl district alone, a total of 2,886 Chakma voters were deleted from the Final Assembly Electoral Rolls published on 2 January 1996. The entire populace in some villages recognised under the Lushai Hills District (Village Councils) Act, 1953 were deleted from the 1995/1996 electoral rolls on the basis of complaints by a few individuals. The forcible identification of Chakmas as foreigners was finally stopped following NHRC directions that 'any adverse decision by the Mizoram authorities shall be communicated to the Commission and may not be given effect to, except after bringing the matter to the notice of the Commission.'[7] However, thousands of Chakmas deleted from the 1995 electoral rolls were not enrolled.

At present, the electoral officers summarily reject claims of

[7]Annual Report 1996-1997, National Human Rights Commission, available at www.nhrc.nic.in

Chakmas for inclusion in the electoral rolls despite claimants submitting all supporting documents like birth certificates, educational certificates, electricity bills, PAN card, etc. The electoral officials interview Chakma claimants, testing them on general knowledge at the time of hearing, and reject their applications when they cannot answer.[8] Chakmas above the age of twenty-five years are also not being enrolled though there is no such age bar for inclusion in voter lists. In Tuichawng-I under Lunglei district, 122 claimants (Chakmas) had submitted claims (Form No 6) in 2015 but only 32 persons were enrolled, which means that 74 percent of the claims were rejected without any reason in 2015.[9]

The Brus, who were also deleted from the electoral rolls during 1995, were not lucky. In October 1997, thousands were forced to flee to Tripura after being identified as foreigners and over 30,000 continue to languish in the relief camps in North Tripura at the time of writing.

The Chakmas of Arunachal Pradesh

Unlike the Chakmas who have been living in undivided Assam, Tripura and parts of Bengal, the Chakmas in the North-East Frontier Agency (NEFA), current Arunachal Pradesh, were settled following the 1962 Indo-China war debacle. The then advisor to the governor of Assam in charge of NEFA, Shri P.N. Luthra, sought proposals from the political officers for resettlement of people in the vacant border areas along the

---

[8]The author has video clips where the electoral officials were asking general knowledge questions to Chakma claimants during hearing in Lunglei district of Mizoram in the summary revision held in 2016.

[9] Memorandum submitted to Dr Nasim Zaidi, Chief Election Commissioner, Election Commission of India, by All India Chakma Social Forum (AICSF), dated 22 September 2016.

Indo-China border in order to strengthen the frontiers and their defence.[10] As part of this, about 2,902 Chakma and Hajong families comprising 14,888 persons who were fleeing from East Pakistan were given settlement in Changlang (formerly Tirap), Namsai (formerly Lohit) and Papum Pare (formerly Subansiri) districts of Arunachal Pradesh. The Chakma and Hajongs were not treated as outsiders in the NEFA throughout the 1960s and 1970s; they enjoyed all the rights, and many were given government jobs including ones under the then NEFA administration. The Chakmas actually did not feel the need for citizenship till 1980 when the state government of Arunachal Pradesh passed a resolution prohibiting employment of the Chakma refugees. This policy of the Arunachal Pradesh government was shaped essentially by the anti-foreigner agitation in Assam.

The denial of rights since 1980 forced the Chakmas to demand citizenship under the banner of the Committee for Citizenship Rights of the Chakmas of Arunachal Pradesh, formed on 2 October 1991. The pressure to force the Chakmas to flee Arunachal Pradesh began in earnest. As the Chakmas were caught between the 'Quit Arunachal Notice' of the state government to leave the state by 30 September 1994[11] and a 'shoot at sight' order issued by the Government of Assam to prevent Assam from becoming a dumping ground for all outsiders, the National Human Rights Commission (NHRC) moved the Supreme Court of India to protect the lives and liberties of the Chakmas in November 1996. The Supreme

[10]Letter No. 17/64 dated 21 April 1965 written to all political officers/ additional political officers of NEFA by Shri P.N. Luthra, advisor to the governor of Assam.

[11]http://dspace.nehu.ac.in/jspui/bitstream/1/4978/1/Susmita%20 Sengupta.pdf

Court in its judgement[12] dated 9 January 1996 directed not to evict the Chakmas and Hajongs, and to process the citizenship applications. This judgement remained unimplemented, and the Supreme Court passed another judgement[13] on 17 September 2015, issuing directions to implement the judgement of 9 January 1996. A fresh petition[14] is pending seeking compliance with the judgement dated 17 September 2015. Over a half century after migration and two Supreme Court judgements later, not a single citizenship application of the Chakmas has been processed.

There are about 55,000 Chakmas in Arunachal Pradesh and over 90 percent of them are citizens by birth under Section 3 of the Citizenship Act. However, they are still discriminated against as foreigners and not included in electoral rolls, 'mainly for the reason that they belong to the Chakma tribe and race, which is violative of the Constitutional mandate of Article 325'[15].

Misinformation about the Chakmas

Misinformation against the Chakmas is one of the root causes that perpetuates xenophobia against them in India. It is not only ethno-centric politicians but even academics who contribute to the xenophobia.

Joy L.K. Pachuau of Jawaharlal Nehru University and Willem van Schendel of Amsterdam University in a recent publication wrote that Chakma migration into Mizoram had been taking place and it suddenly exploded in 1964 when

---

[12]1996 AIR 1234, 1996 SCC (1) 742

[13]Writ Petition (Civil) No 510 of 2007

[14]I.A. 4/2017 in Writ Petition(s) (Civil) No(s) 510/2007

[15]Order No23/ARUN/2003 dated 4 March 2004 of the full bench of the Election Commission of India.

tens of thousands of people in the Chittagong Hill Tracts (then East Pakistan) displaced by the Kaptai hydroelectric project settled in Mizoram.[16] It is true that Chakma migrants on the way to the then NEFA passed through Mizoram. However, that Chakma refugees from East Pakistan settled in Mizoram as alleged by Pachuau and van Schendel is a fallacy. As per Census reports, the Chakma population in the Lushai Hills (Mizoram) was 11,435 in 1951, 19,377 in 1961, 23,236 in 1971 and 39,905 in 1981.[17] That the population of Chakmas increased only by 3,859 persons during the period between 1961 and 1971 when the Chakmas migrated to Arunachal Pradesh disproves the contention of Pachuau and van Schendel. Obviously, Pachuau and van Schendel did not access the decisions of the Government of India on the settlement of the Chakmas in the NEFA during 1964–1968. The then governor of Assam, Vishnu Sahay, in his letter no. GA-71/64, dated 10 April 1964[18] advised the then chief minister of Assam, B.P. Chaliha, not to settle the Chakmas in Mizo districts in view of the trouble between the Mizos and Chakmas. Instead, he suggested the Tirap Division of the NEFA, and the Chakmas were accordingly settled in the NEFA. Obviously, reliance on general perception to raise xenophobia against the Chakmas in Mizoram contradicting the official records per se is not limited to student leaders of the North-East with little exposure to basic research

---

[16] Pachuau, Joy L.K. and vad Schendel, William. *The Camera as Witness: A Social History of Mizoram, Northeast India*. Cambridge: Cambridge University Press, 2015. pp 367.

[17] Sources: Census Reports, Library of International Institute of Population Sciences, Mumbai. Chakma, S.B., MA Dissertation, Tata Institute of Social Sciences, Mumbai.

[18] Letter available with the author.

skills to differentiate between facts and fantasises; more disconcertingly, even well-known academics with subject expertise fall prey to fake news to cover up sloppy research.

In Arunachal Pradesh, both the state government and the All Arunachal Pradesh Students Union (AAPSU) consistently raised the issue of Chakmas posing threat to 'indigenous peoples' because of the disproportionate increase in their population. The Arunachal Pradesh government in its affidavit before the Supreme Court in *NHRC vs. State of Arunachal Pradesh*[19] raised the contention of 'unbridled growth of refugee population' while the AAPSU focussed on the Chakma refugees outnumbering indigenous peoples.

The official records of the growth of the Chakma population in Arunachal Pradesh speak otherwise. As per Census records, in absolute terms, a total of 14,888 Chakmas/Hajongs were settled in Arunachal Pradesh by the Government of India during 1964–1969. Their population increased to 47,471 persons as per the 2011 Census. This means, in 47 years, the Chakma and Hajong population increased by 218 percent. The growth rate of the Chakma/Hajong population is almost the same as that of indigenous peoples of Arunachal Pradesh (Scheduled Tribes) whose population increased from 2,99,944 persons in 1961 to 9,51,821 persons in 2011, i.e., by about 218 percent. In comparison to the Chakmas/Hajongs and indigenous peoples of Arunachal Pradesh, the population of other non-tribals such as Adivasis, Assamese, Nepalese, Muslims, Marwaris, Biharis, etc., increased by 955 percent during the same period. The decadal growth rate of these non-Scheduled Tribes was 125.40 percent during 1961–1971, 100.12 percent during 1971–1981, 70.74 percent

[19]1996 AIR 1234, 1996 SCC (1) 742

during 1981–1991 and 24.08 percent during 1991–2001.[20] The Chakma issue has been politicised to such an extent in Arunachal Pradesh that the growth of non-Chakmas by 1000 percent against the growth of the Chakmas by 218 percent is overlooked.

Chakmas Face Discrimination in Mainland India by Student Groups from Mizoram and Arunachal Pradesh

North-Easterners facing racial discrimination in mainland India is a rampant phenomenon. What is little known is that the Chakmas often face acts of racial discrimination at the hands of the same student leaders from Arunachal Pradesh and Mizoram in mainland India.

On 11 February 2017, 'Chakma Dance—Arunachal Pradesh' was cancelled by the organiser, i.e., RSKD Memorial Charitable Society, Delhi, at 'ONE-One North-East Multi Cultural Show & Musical Event' held at Indoor Stadium, University of Delhi, after an official from the Ministry of Home Affairs verbally directed them not to allow the Chakmas to perform. Later, it emerged that a group of students from Arunachal Pradesh led by the then Delhi University Students Union (DUSU) Cultural Secretary Romjir Rakshap had written a letter seeking personal intervention of Mr Kiren Rijiju (Union Minister of State for Home Affairs of India) to cancel the 'Chakma Dance—Arunachal Pradesh'. This is not an isolated incident. Earlier, the Chakma dance from Arunachal Pradesh was initially cancelled at 'Xperience North-East-Connecting Cultures' held from 4-5 February 2017, co-sponsored by the government of Karnataka,

---

[20]'Arunachal Pradesh: Not the Chakmas/Hajongs but other non-tribals pose bigger threat to indigenous peoples', Asian Centre for Human Rights, 26 November 2015, available at http://www.achrweb.org/Review/2015/249-15.html

allegedly following objections by the Ministry of Home Affairs (MHA). However, following intervention from some activists hailing from the North-East, Chakma students were allowed to perform their folk dance as 'Chakma Dance from North-East.'[21]

In November 2012, the Mizo Students' Union, Delhi, opposed the nomination of two Chakma students to represent Mizoram at Delhi Police's Special Cell for the North-Easterners whose tasks were to coordinate with the Delhi Police to look after the welfare of North-Eastern people living in Delhi. Rejecting their demands, the North-East Students' Forum (NESF) said in a statement that all North-East student organisations were invited during the selection process for the coordinators but the Mizo Students Union, Delhi, failed to respond and hence they had no right to protest against the selection of Chakmas representing Mizoram.[22]

Is There an Anti-Chakma Policy at Work?

In a country of 1.2 billion people as per the Census data from 2011, the total population of Chakmas in India stood at 2,26,860 persons with 96,972 persons (19,554 families) in Mizoram; 79,813 persons (18,014 families) in Tripura; 2,032 persons (430 families) in Assam; 466 persons (211 families) in West Bengal; 106 persons (44 families) in Meghalaya, and 53,721 persons in Arunachal Pradesh. Even at the state level, their population is minuscule. The Chakmas comprise 8.83 percent of the total population of Mizoram (10,97,206), 3.88 percent of the total population of Arunachal Pradesh

---

[21]Information provided to the author by Chakma student leaders of Bangalore, Karnataka.

[22]http://www.misual.com/2012/11/16/chakmas-representing-mizoram-will-not-resign-nesf/

(13,83,727), 2.17 percent of the total population of Tripura (36,73,917) and 0 percent of the total population of Assam (3,11,69,272), West Bengal (9,12,76,115) and Meghalaya (29,66,889). There are only three Chakma MLAs with two MLAs in the 40-member State Assembly of Mizoram and one MLA out of the 60-member State Assembly of Tripura.[23]

As the Chakma headcount is too microscopic to matter in electoral politics, they have often been targeted and the Union of India has failed to even implement the Supreme Court judgements to process their citizenship applications of the Chakmas of Arunachal Pradesh. This has led to the development of a policy that smacks of racism and xenophobia against the Chakmas practiced by the Government of India at the instance of state governments. All the minorities who fled to escape persecution in East Pakistan and West Pakistan pre-1971 were granted citizenship en masse. The Chakmas are the only group of people who came prior to 1971 but are being forced to apply for citizenship.

The treatment of the Chakma refugees vis-a-vis other refugees in India in the post-1971 period explains the discrimination. In Mizoram, there were 63,000 Chin refugees as of 2005[24], but no en masse repatriation of the Chins ever took place. In Arunachal Pradesh, there are about 7,530 Tibetan refugees as of 2009[25] who are welcomed because of their proximity with the Monpas, while Chakmas despite

[23]'Survival and Development of the Chakmas in the Twenty-First Century,' All India Chakma Social Workers Convention 2016 (8th-9th September 2016) available at http://www.chakmasocialforum.org/ConceptNote.html

[24]'Chins of Myanmar in Mizoram: A Fact-Finding Report,' 2005, Human Rights Law Network available at http://hrln.org/admin/issue/subpdf/Chins_of_Myanmar_in_Mizoram_1.pdf

[25]Starred question no. *69 to be answered on the 29 April 2015 http://mha1.nic.in/par2013/par2015-pdfs/rs-290415/69.pdf

being Buddhists are often targeted. There are 64,144 Tamil refugees staying in 107 ordinary camps in Tamil Nadu in addition 36861 Tamil refugees staying outside the camps after getting themselves registered at the nearest police station[26], but not a single Tamil refugee has been sent back to Sri Lanka even after the resolution of the armed conflict and complete elimination of the LTTE in May 2009. About 88 percent of the 8,000 Afghan refugees in India are of Hindu or Sikh faiths and the Government of India is ensuring their naturalisation.[27] The Government of India currently allows even the Rohingyas to stay.

In contrast, each time Chakma refugees from Bangladesh fled to India to escape atrocities, they were housed in camps and repatriated back to Bangladesh. All the Chakma refugees from Bangladesh who sought refuge in the camps in Tripura, India, from 1986 were repatriated back by 1998. As the US Department of State's 'Country Report on Human Rights Practices for 1998' reported: 'In February, the last group of tribal refugees returned to the Chittagong Hill Tracts region from camps in India. This completed a process initiated in 1997 of repatriating more than 60,000 refugees who had fled the internecine violence of tribals and Bengali settlers in the Chittagong Hill Tracts. The repatriations were part of the peace agreement between the government and tribal leaders signed in December 1997.'[28] Even though all Chakma refugees

---

[26]Unstarred question no. 1175 to be answered on 4 May 2016/Vaisakha 14,1938 (SAKA) available at http://mha1.nic.in/par2013/par2016-pdfs/rs-040516/1175.pdf

[27]http://www.sikhiwiki.org/index.php/Afghan_Sikhs_return_in_mass_to_India

[28]US Department of State's 'Country Report on Human Rights Practices for 1998' is available at https://www.state.gov/www/global/human_rights/1998_hrp_report/banglade.html

in the post-1971 period had been repatriated to Bangladesh, the Chakmas have been targeted as foreigners in Mizoram and Arunachal Pradesh.

Conclusion

The increase of the non-tribal population by 955 percent from 1961 to 2011 in Arunachal Pradesh is not an exception but indicative of the irreversible trends of migration in the age of globalisation. Mizoram will witness more challenges than Nagaland once the Bhairabi to Sairang broad gauge railway connection and Kaladan Multi-Modal Transit Transport Project get operationalised. That the BJP came to power in Assam after issuing notification to grant citizenship to minorities who have entered India on or before 31 December 2014 speaks volumes about the increasing political irrelevance of the insider-outsider debate there. Yet, make no mistake—Chakmas, who originate from the very areas that the British identified under the Bengal Eastern Frontier Regulation, shall continue to be the victims of the insider-outsider debate in Mizoram and Arunachal Pradesh.

Targeting vulnerable minorities for political purposes is nothing new.

ABOUT THE CONTRIBUTORS

Anindita Dasgupta is Associate Professor and Head of School, School of Liberal Arts & Sciences, at Taylor's University, Malaysia. She is the book review editor for *Millennial Asia: An International Journal of Asian Studies.* Anindita has been the recipient of a number of international research grants including SEPHIS postdoctoral grant of the International Institute of Social History, the Netherlands, South Asia Fellowship of SSRC, New York, among others. Multidisciplinary in her approach, Anindita has carried out intensive fieldwork-based studies in India, Bangladesh, Nepal, Sri Lanka and Malaysia in the last fifteen years. An expert on identity, diversity and culture, she has extensive experience in consulting for regional universities, and has held several visiting fellowships in Southeast Asia. Anindita is the author of two books, one monograph and more than thirty publications.

Anjum Hasan is the author of the novels *The Cosmopolitans, Neti, Neti* and *Lunatic in my Head,* the short story collection *Difficult Pleasures,* and a book of poems titled *Street on the Hill.* Her books have been nominated for various awards including the DSC Prize for South Asian Literature, the Hindu Best Fiction Award and the Crossword Fiction Award.

Ankush Saikia was born in Tezpur, Assam in 1975. He has worked in journalism and publishing in Delhi, and is presently based in Shillong and Tezpur. He is the author of the Detective Arjun Arora series (*Dead Meat*, 2015; *Remember Death*, 2016; *More Bodies Will Fall*, 2018).

Binayak Dutta is a faculty member in the Department of History, North Eastern Hill University, Shillong. He is the author of *Religion in Politics* (2009) and co-author of *History of the Judiciary in Assam* (2013). His main areas of focus in his published works are modern India and Partition Studies.

Jahnavi Barua is a writer based in Bangalore. Her first book, *Next Door*, a collection of short fiction, was published in 2008 to wide critical acclaim. Her second book, *Rebirth*, was published in 2010 and was shortlisted for the Man Asian Literary Prize and the Commonwealth Book Prize. She was awarded the Charles Wallace Trust Fellowship for Creative Writing in 2006. Her books are on the syllabi of universities such as Jamia Millia Islamia and Mysore University and her short fiction has been widely anthologised. She is currently working on her third book.

Mahua Sen is a visual artist, musician and writer. Born and raised in Shillong, she currently lives in New Delhi. She had a career in broadcast media and she continues to play strategy-based communication roles in a parallel universe. Apart from her multidisciplinary artistic practice, she is mostly lost to the holy cause of pontification.

Mitra Phukan is a writer, translator, columnist and trained classical vocalist who lives in Guwahati, Assam. Her published literary works include four children's books, a biography, the novels, *The Collector's Wife* and *A Monsoon of Music,* and a collection of fifty of her columns titled *Guwahati Gaze.* Her latest works are a translation of an Assamese novel, *Blossoms in the Graveyard,* and a collection of her own short stories, *A Full Night's Thievery.* Her column 'All Things Considered' in *The Assam Tribune* is very widely read.

Mona Zote lives in Aizawl, Mizoram. She describes herself as a poet 'disguised as a government employee'.

Neeta S. Singh is a senior lecturer at Sunway University, Malaysia. While teaching English literature at various institutions of higher learning, Neeta pursued her interest in legal studies, and upon being called to the Malaysian Bar, practiced as a lawyer for several years before returning to academia.

She is a keen observer of Malaysian political developments and a passionate advocate of democracy. As a writer, she has published articles on a variety of topics such as democracy and civil society movements, migration and displacement of human populations, and a number of book reviews.

Paramjit Bakhshi studied across the country, finally finishing with BA (English) Honours from St. Edmunds College, Shillong. His work life has been equally varied—he started his career as a tea planter in North Bengal but also worked in Assam and Vietnam. After leaving tea he has donned many hats including that of an entrepreneur, a personality trainer, and a columnist. A rolling stone by temperament, he believes that not only does a rolling stone gathers no moss but also gets a shine.

He currently lives in Shillong with his wife Catherine and their two sons Zoravar and Aidan.

Preeti Gill is the co editor of this anthology and is an independent literary agent who has more than twenty years of experience in the publishing industry as a commissioning editor and rights director. She has travelled extensively in the North-East of India and written on issues of conflict and women. She is the editor of *The Peripheral Centre: Voices from India's Northeast* as well as *Bearing Witness: A Report on the Impact of Conflict on Women in Nagaland and Assam.* Her writing has appeared in numerous journals and anthologies including *1984: In Memory and Imagination* (2016). Her documentary *Rambuai: Mizoram's 'Trouble' Years* (co-produced with Sanjoy Hazarika) was released in September 2016. She has also edited an anthology of murder stories by women, which will be published in December 2018.

She is the founder of Majha House, a literary and cultural space in Amritsar, as well as Café Kikli—a unique pop-up book café and library, which holds curated events every Saturday evening.

R.G. Lyngdoh is former Home and Education Minister of Meghalaya. He was subsequently the vice chancellor of the Martin Luther Christian University. Lyngdoh, a management graduate, was also a professional musician and authored a novel titled *Who the Cap Fits.*

Samrat, also known as Samrat X, co-editor of this anthology, is an author and journalist. A former editor of newspapers in the country's major metropolises, Delhi, Mumbai and

Bengaluru, he now divides his time between his hometown Shillong and his place of refuge, Kolkata. His writings have appeared in most major newspapers and news magazines in English published from India. He was also a columnist for the *Hindustan Times* and *DNA*, an OpEd writer for *The Dhaka Tribune* in Bangladesh, and a contributor for *The New York Times*. His first book, a novel, *The Urban Jungle*, was published in 2011. Some of his literary essays and short stories have appeared in translation in German, Spanish, Italian and Portuguese. He is the 2018 Asian Leadership Fellow from India at the International House of Japan in Tokyo.

Sanjoy Hazarika is the Director of the Commonwealth Human Rights Initiative. He was earlier honorary research professor at the Centre for Policy Research, and held the Dr Saifuddin Kitchlew Chair at Jamia Millia Islamia, New Delhi, where he also directed the Centre for North East Studies and Policy Research. He has been a member of various academic organisations and official committees, including the Justice Jeevan Reddy Committee to Review AFSPA, the Society of Indian Institute of Advanced Studies, Shimla, and the North East India Studies Programme at Jawaharlal Nehru University. He has also worked as a newspaper correspondent, columnist, and documentary filmmaker.

Sonal Jain was born in Shillong. She is an artist/filmmaker. In 2004 she co-founded Desire Machine Collective—a group that works with the intersection of film, art, ecology, technology and activism. Their practice spans film, video, photography, digital media, public intervention, curating and writing. She had been selected for the Three Rivers Residency in Italy in 2016.

Sonal is currently working on her first feature film project. She is also working on 'Periferry', an alternative, artist-led space and project.

Suhas Chakma is a human rights activist.

Thounoujam Brinda is a humanist who believes in the struggle for a classless society free from oppression, exploitation and injustice for a socio-political emancipation through an economic base that is independent and self-sustaining. She stands for the struggle of the people of Manipur against the onslaughts of imperialism and strives to achieve the dream of political self-determination of the natives of Manipur through a reoriented course of struggle. She served as Deputy Superintendent of Police in the Manipur Police Service, and left the job recently to freely work for the struggle of the people she believes in. She writes articles and essays that are analytical and critical of the system. She did the transliteration of Hijam Irabot's *Capitalism* into English. She is involved in various movements of the people of Manipur and is presently focussed on designing and implementing economic regeneration programmes from the grass-root level of various communities.